Barry Fantoni, novelist, broadcaster, jazz musician, reviewer, illustrator, film and TV actor, *The Times* diary cartoonist, was born on February 28th, 1940.

Also by Barry Fantoni in Sphere Books

BARRY FANTONI'S CHINESE HOROSCOPES: RAT
BARRY FANTONI'S CHINESE HOROSCOPES: BUFFALO
BARRY FANTONI'S CHINESE HOROSCOPES: TIGER
BARRY FANTONI'S CHINESE HOROSCOPES: CAT
BARRY FANTONI'S CHINESE HOROSCOPES: DRAGON
BARRY FANTONI'S CHINESE HOROSCOPES: SNAKE
BARRY FANTONI'S CHINESE HOROSCOPES: HORSE
BARRY FANTONI'S CHINESE HOROSCOPES: GOAT
BARRY FANTONI'S CHINESE HOROSCOPES: MONKEY
BARRY FANTONI'S CHINESE HOROSCOPES: ROOSTER
BARRY FANTONI'S CHINESE HOROSCOPES: DOG
BARRY FANTONI'S CHINESE HOROSCOPES: PIG
BARRY FANTONI'S CHINESE HOROSCOPES

BARRY FANTONI'S

CHINESE HOROSCOPES

A GUIDE TO LOVE, MARRIAGE AND FRIENDSHIP

SPHERE BOOKS LIMITED

To my family of Roosters

A *Sphere* Book

First published in Great Britain by Sphere Books Ltd 1989
1st reprint 1990

Printed and bound in Great Britain by
Cox & Wyman Ltd, Reading

ISBN 0 7474 0311 2

Sphere Books Ltd
A Division of
Macdonald & Co (Publishers) Ltd
Orbit House
1 New Fetter Lane
London EC4A 1AR
A member of Maxwell Macmillan Pergamon Publishing Corporation

CONTENTS

Acknowledgements   vi

Introduction   vii

Chinese Horoscopes and Compatibility   xi

Author's Note   1

The Chinese Animal Signs and Their Years   2

Rat: 1900 1912 1924 1936 1948 1960 1972 1984   4
Buffalo: 1901 1913 1925 1937 1949 1961 1973 1985   38
Tiger: 1902 1914 1926 1938 1950 1962 1974 1986   74
Cat: 1903 1915 1927 1939 1951 1963 1975 1987   108
Dragon: 1904 1916 1928 1940 1952 1964 1976 1988   142
Snake: 1905 1917 1929 1941 1953 1965 1977 1989   180
Horse: 1906 1918 1930 1942 1954 1966 1978 1990   214
Goat: 1907 1919 1931 1943 1955 1967 1979 1991   248
Monkey: 1908 1920 1932 1944 1956 1968 1980 1992   282
Rooster: 1909 1921 1933 1945 1957 1969 1981 1993   316
Dog: 1910 1922 1934 1946 1958 1970 1982 1994   350
Pig: 1911 1923 1935 1947 1959 1971 1983 1995   384

Reference Source   418

ACKNOWLEDGEMENTS

I should like to express my thanks to all those many friends, relatives and strangers who have both knowingly and otherwise helped with the compilation of this book. I should like to thank in particular Gillian Jason who researched the beautiful Chinese illustrations, The British Library for granting permission to reproduce them, and Dr Hin Hung Ho for the delightful calligraphy. But the bulk of my gratitude is reserved for my Rooster wife who ploughed on relentlessly with the list of celebrities whose names are scattered throughout, and without which this book could never have been written.

INTRODUCTION

It has now been half a decade and more since I wrote my first book on the Chinese Horoscopes. At that time, the Chinese New Year, with its week-long celebrations, was virtually unknown outside of those who lived or worked near a handful of streets south of Soho, which is now known as London's Chinatown. Certainly there was little or no information about the twelve animal signs and their annual influence. But an event that was once given a fifteen-second bulletin on the six o'clock news, at most, and a few lines in the national press has now mushroomed into a major celebration and a key tourist attraction. In 1988, the celebration of the Chinese Year of the Dragon doubled in number of people who thronged the narrow streets of Chinatown. In the preceding year, the Year of the Cat, 100,000 had joined the street parade, the fireworks and dancing. But in the Dragon Year, the most auspicious of all twelve signs, an estimated 200,000 cheered and danced as the ceremonial carnival Dragon, a creature created from paper and tinsel, was paraded beneath the brightly coloured lanterns of London's Chinese thoroughfares. And it is the same story in every city where the Chinese have settled in large numbers. How different to the time when the only interest in the influence of the stars, the sun, the moon and the planets revolved around Western astrology.

Today, everyone knows their zodiac sign and what it means to be born, for example, under Virgo or Pisces. Indeed, very often, when I first began studying Chinese Horoscopes, my question 'what year were you born?' would often elicit the person's zodiac sign. 'I am Cancer,' they might say, having failed to grasp that the Chinese Horoscopes are based on the *year*, not the month of birth. A more serious misunderstanding arises with those who call Chinese Horoscopes Chinese Astrology. In this case the Horoscopes – a word meaning roughly a place in time – have nothing to do with the study of stars (astrology), but with the phases of the moon. One way to avoid confusion is to subtitle Chinese Horoscopes, the science of lunology.

Whatever the term, Horoscope, Zodiac, Lunology, I find that today, more and more people know not only their Chinese sign but many implications generated by the animal's influence. A charming Rat person might easily be aware that he or she is best suited romantically to the impulsive Dragon, while a stubborn and complex Buffalo could foresee that the rebellious Tiger sign is the one to avoid. And those I refer to here are a large cross-section of our community, not just a handful of converts.

Much of the increase in public awareness has been due to the often chilling accuracy of the Chinese system of the twelve animal signs, a clear indication that what is on offer carries a full guarantee. Again and again people have told me how Western astrology would make predictions that failed, or offer personal insights that simply didn't hold water. True, in astrology – the study of the stars – a great deal of information is required by comparison with the basic date of birth used by those who compile a personal Chinese Horoscope. But to be fair to Western astrology, it is still a science in its infancy compared with the oriental system, and to be fairer still, it has attracted more than its share of fraudsters and charlatans.

For those who are unfamiliar with the essential ingredients of the Chinese Horoscope, or for those who might find a tiny refresher course helpful, the origins go back five hundred years before the birth of Christ. It has never been fully established exactly how the Chinese Horoscopes came into being but the legend does have a wonderful poetic charm which, if not true to the letter, I find irresistible. The story begins at the time of the first new moon of the very first lunar cycle, when Buddha invited all the animals in his Kingdom to celebrate Chinese New Year. For reasons no one can explain, only twelve animals turned up. They were, in order of arrival, the charming Rat, the tenacious Buffalo, the courageous Tiger, the virtuous Cat, the lucky Dragon, the wise Snake, the independent Horse, the artistic Goat, the fanciful Monkey, the candid Rooster, the idealistic Dog and, finally, the honest Pig. The legend has it that Buddha was so pleased to see the twelve that he decided to grant a year in each of their favours. The animal in question would exercise his influence over all born during that year and their particular traits and characteristics would dominate it. Pigs, for example, would be honest and hard-working, Dogs loyal but anxious, Snakes would be wise but bewitching, and so on.

In fifteen years of study, I still find myself occasionally wondering how the Chinese Horoscope works, how it can possibly affect us all. But each day invariably brings a news item or snippet of information, a personal encounter or a letter from a devotee which reinforces and enhances my understanding. The following letter is one I treasure. Not only does it sum up everything I hoped for in terms of the benefit Chinese Horoscopes would bring to others, but it serves as a constant source of encouragement.

Dear Mr Fantoni

I expect you have a lot of people who write to you about your book on Chinese Horoscopes. I am a Dragon (1928) and have been interested in astrology for many years. Your book is so true, I am actually writing to thank you sincerely for writing it.

I have two sons who have wives and families, and two ex-husbands. I live alone and have a hard job on my income. But I see everyone in a different light now and it's been very helpful to me. I have not made people 'fit' the book – it's all fallen into place in every detail. My first husband was a Cat and my second a Buffalo. Both marriages ended abruptly in divorce. I see my sons in a true light now, as I do their wives and grandchildren.

Many thanks to you and good wishes.

I am asked by many a sceptic still, 'Do you really believe that everyone born in the same year can be influenced by what are little more than the phases of the moon disguised as animal signs?' My answer is always the same: 'Is my own animal sign a true reflection of me? If the answer is "yes", then are the signs of those you know well true of them?' This way, we stop asking questions about the millions of people we don't know and never will, and deal with facts and not belief. As I said in the introduction to my first book, the peoples of the East enjoy games and mysteries. They use symbols for clarification, for signposts. The Chinese Horoscope is a wonderful game created for and played by adults, but none the less effective for being so. The animal signs, I repeat as often as I am able, cannot tell us our destiny and I am certain that if we are really honest few would really want it any other way. What the Chinese Horoscopes – the twelve animal signs and their respective influences – do is to put us in touch with our real selves, hold a mirror up to a part of our personality we have not yet glimpsed. In this book I not only outline our individual signs but provide a more comprehensive guide as to with whom we share our newly discovered personality.

CHINESE HOROSCOPES AND COMPATIBILITY

Unlike the Western zodiac, which has almost nothing to say about compatibility, the Chinese Horoscope was created almost exclusively to ensure that forming partnerhips became a less hit and miss affair. And if we are perfectly honest, many of our relationships are often less than rewarding experiences. Time after time, we dive into marriage, friendships and love affairs without the slightest idea who we are, or who the person is we are proposing to or swearing undying love to. For Westerners, love, marriage and pure friendship can exist without reference to each other. We may, and often do, love people without wanting to marry them. We have friends we don't love, lovers who are not friends. But until recently, the Chinese seldom if ever differentiated between the West's commonly accepted divisions of relationships. In China, right up to the present time it was unheard of for two people to marry as a result of falling in love. In virtually all cases marriages were arranged pretty well from the cradle. The signs of two likely candidates would have undergone the scrutiny of the Chinese Horoscope scale of compatibility and if they proved to be auspicious the marriage would be agreed. No one divorces in China, not even now. For the Chinese a marriage is a businesslike partnership first and foremost. Life is tough in remote villages, with the constant threat of famine and danger from the elements. In order to survive many Chinese couples must often fight hard. Love may come, as might friendship, but the nitty-gritty of everyday living needs the solid backbone provided by a relationship minus the emotional obstacles that frequently result from being 'in love'.

Clearly we in the West have an entirely different approach to marriage, love and friendship, but the rules that govern the compatibility of animal signs remains the same. But whatever your choice, whether you are a male Rat about to marry a female Rooster and find your chart gives you minus zero, or similarly, a female Tiger deciding to jump into bed with a male Buffalo, the scale of compatibility is only a guide. As useful and as accurate as they are, the compatibility charts, as I have said many times, are not the Ten Commandments. They are not cast in iron and there is no wrath of any deity if you should choose to go against them. If you love someone and do so in spite of a hundred reasons why you shouldn't, that's fine. If you wish to marry a person who you know will be a lifetime of trouble, it's up to you. But Tigers don't change their stripes and Dogs don't forget to bark. And there is help, at least for those who are sensible enough to seek it. By examining our relationships and the options open to us we can prepare ourselves for that chill moment when a friend, lover or marriage partner begins to act in a way we hadn't seen before. In this sense the animal signs and their scale of compatibility are a preparation for the future and guide as to how your partnership will develop. Those born under the Rat sign will in ninety-nine cases out at a hundred be better off with a Dragon; a Tiger should partner a Dog. And in my experience, our influencing animal always has the last word. By taking into account what the Chinese Horoscopes tell us about the right partner, we can also avoid them having the last laugh.

AUTHOR'S NOTE

THE YEAR OF THE CAT

Is it the year of the Cat, Rabbit or Hare? On the surface it is all a bit confusing, but there is a very simple explanation. The name you adopt depends very largely on which part of the world you come from. This is how is works.

Although it is true to say that the Chinese invented their wonderful horoscope, they are not the only ones who use it. During the 2,000 years it has been in existence the Chinese Horoscope has now travelled around the world. But if the horoscopes are new to us in the West, they have been with the nations close to China since the very start – well, almost. Not unnaturally each new country refined the twelve animal signs of the horoscope to suit themselves, to fit in with their particular culture. For instance, the people of Hong Kong name what the Chinese call the Rabbit, the Hare. In Vietnam, Cambodia and Korea, the Rabbit is called the Cat. The reason is simple. These people consider the word 'Rabbit' an insult. Likewise, many Chinese are offended at being termed a Cat.

My own researches show that the very first written word for the Cat/Rabbit/Hare year was, in Chinese, a 'creature with soft fur and a weak back'. Clearly it is a description which can easily fit all three animals.

Curiously the West did not learn about the Chinese Horoscopes from the Chinese, but from the Vietnamese who settled in France following the Indochinese war in the fifties. This is why so many Westerners call the years 1903, 1915, 1927, 1939, 1951, 1963, 1975 and 1987 the Year of the Cat.

But the most important point of all is to remember that all the experts agree that no matter what the word, Cat, Rabbit, or Hare, the influence is *exactly the same*!

Also, the Rooster is something called the Cock, the Buffalo the Ox, the Goat the Sheep and the Pig the Boar.

THE CHINESE ANIMAL SIGNS AND THEIR YEARS

The Chinese Horoscopes follow a lunar cycle which has twelve moons in a full year, and twelve years to a full cycle. But after the twelfth year, a curious event takes place in the heavens – a thirteenth moon appears. In the West, this is actually what we call a Blue Moon and it throws an unwelcome spanner in the works with regard to the Chinese New Year. As a result of the Blue Moon, Chinese New Year

RAT:	1900	1912	1924
BUFFALO:	1901	1913	1925
TIGER:	1902	1914	1926
CAT:	1903	1915	1927
DRAGON:	1904	1916	1928
SNAKE:	1905	1917	1929
HORSE:	1906	1918	1930
GOAT:	1907	1919	1931
MONKEY:	1908	1920	1932
ROOSTER:	1909	1921	1933
DOG:	1910	1922	1934
PIG:	1911	1923	1935

never falls on the same day in consecutive years. It falls, however, between January 20 and February 20, so beware if you have a birthday on or between these two dates. If you were, say, born on January 29th, 1960, you would first need to look up the year – the Rat in this case, and check out the change-over date. On that particular occasion, Chinese New Year fell on January 28th, so you will have been born a Rat, by just one day! The exact dates of each Chinese New Year are given at the beginning of their respective chapters. But obviously, if your birthday falls in any other time other than between January 20 and February 20, the list of animal years x–xi is all you'll need to discover your personal sign. Once you have found your sign, turn to the appropriate chapter and you will find the first ever complete lists of compatibility.

1936	1948	1960	1972	1984
1937	1949	1961	1973	1985
1938	1950	1962	1974	1986
1939	1951	1963	1975	1987
1940	1952	1964	1976	1988
1941	1953	1965	1977	1989
1942	1954	1966	1978	1990
1943	1955	1967	1979	1991
1944	1956	1968	1980	1992
1945	1957	1969	1981	1993
1946	1958	1970	1982	1994
1947	1959	1971	1983	1995

THE RAT

1900	January 31st to February 18th	1901
1912	February 18th to February 5th	1913
1924	February 5th to January 23rd	1925
1936	January 24th to February 10th	1937
1948	February 10th to January 28th	1949
1960	January 28th to February 14th	1961
1972	February 15th to February 2nd	1973
1984	February 2nd to February 19th	1985

'What a fellow you are for giving in,' said the Rat reproachfully. 'Why, only just now I saw a sardine opener on the kitchen dresser, quite distinctly; and everybody knows that means there are sardines about somewhere in the neighbourhood . . .'

The Wind in the Willows

THE YEAR OF THE RAT

Rats are born under the sign of charm. They are warm-hearted folk and their passionate personality is dominated by a sense of urgency. This means that Rats are greedy for life, looking to experience every moment to the full. Above all, the Rat is a supreme opportunist who lives for the moment and seldom plans for tomorrow. Rats are led by their highly developed senses which as a rule have little or no regard for the hands of the clock. But when they grow introverted, the free-wheeling Rat becomes obsessed by time-keeping and their open sense of humour vanishes completely.

When plans go badly or when they suffer a bad reversal, the normally outgoing Rat is the first to find fault. At times like these, the Rat's sometimes shallow outlook will get the better of them and they will grumble endlessly. All Rats have an undercurrent of aggression which frequently expresses itself in fretting over details and being ultra-concerned with trivialities. In extreme cases, Rats in distress may become preoccupied by making plans and sticking to them at all costs. Their charm and easy going manner is replaced by a tenacious stubbornness which nothing will overturn.

Rats seldom care much for possessions. If they have a full larder it doesn't often stay that way. Rats are not built for hard slog and when they make money it is usually as a result of their wits. As a general rule, Rats can deny themselves nothing. Quick witted, Rats have a sharp eye for detail, which provides them with a head start in business. In the story about Buddha's New Year Party and the twelve animals, legend has it that the Buffalo, being the most power-ful, was the first to arrive but the Rat pipped him to the post. Waiting until the last minute, the opportunist Rat ran up the Buffalo's tail, over his back and down his nose, to become the first at Buddha's door. It is said that the Buffalo has yet to forgive the Rat.

Those born under the sign of the Rat make uncritical friends who's advice is sound, well intentioned and always worth taking. In their family life Rats are devoted to their children, although the Rat parent tends to fret perhaps more than plan for their offspring's well being. The Rat home is usually comfortable rather than fashionable, with money going into the wine cellar as opposed to the wall-to-wall carpet. In work Rats prefer flexitime and avoid routine whenever possible. Rats are ideal critics, capable of clear, subjective judgement. Uncluttered by lofty principles, a Rat gets to the heart of the matter in a flash. In the East terms like 'rat race' and 'dirty rat' are unknown and Rats are rightly considered to be creatures of great intelligence.

The three phases of the Rat's life are marked by an easy childhood but a difficult middle period in which romance and financial problems frequently abound. In the middle stage, the Chinese warn that a Rat might meet a sudden and violent end. However, with their senses less demanding, old age is kinder to the restless and rootless Rat. Even Rats with no more than an old age pension are sure to find the bags of grain in the barn full, sweet and plentiful.

COMPATIBILITY OF MALE RATS IN LOVE

FEMALE RAT

Of all the twelve animal signs male Rats are without question the most passionate. His eager senses are ideal to cast him in the role of lover, which he adopts with ease. Provided he is an extrovert with everything going his way (a sudden reversal might throw him) the male Rat will tend to express the physical side of love, often to the neglect of the more subtle romantic niceties. When the partner is a female Rat it is unlikely there will be much room for holding hands in the cinema. Full-blooded, the Rat will expose the female Rat's equally passionate heart and nothing will stop them. Bed will be the main meeting place, followed by the wine bar and the Indian restaurant.

Star Rating: Five big ones every time.

FEMALE BUFFALO

Here's a strange relationship. Of all the twelve signs there are just one or two which produce a very high rating in the romance phase of a relationship but fall off the bottom of the graph when long term plans are put into operation. The male Rat is deeply attracted by the female Buffalo, but it is an attraction of sexual opposites. In most cases this kind of attraction rates poorly, but Rat and Buffalo get full marks. However, few animal signs have such little understanding of each other or respond to such different stimuli. And yet few other signs find each other so irresistible.

In my experience Rat and Buffalo is one of the most common pairings and has the highest chance of failing long term. The Prince of Wales is a Rat and the Princess of Wales is a Buffalo.

Star Rating: Four for the Big Bang on the first night. But beware of the decline, which might happen suddenly.

FEMALE TIGER

Tiger ladies are direct and up-front in love, as they are in everything else in life. They risk all they have for love and seldom question their actions until later. This naturally has an inspiring influence on the passionate male Rat and in the early days of a love affair, male Rat and female Tiger are unstoppable. But the Tiger is a strongly masculine sign, which tends to amplify the weaknesses of the feminine character. This means that when a lady Tiger cools down, she cools down for good. Not great at staying any course for long, both Rat and Tiger will part by mutual agreement and with fond memories.

Star Rating: Two, if only for the splendid opening.

FEMALE CAT

The male Rat's passion is only matched by their pronounced streak of opportunism. Given the chance to experience a new sensation they'll go for it and make excuses later. Female Cats respond warmly to the Rat's passionate attention but do not take kindly to his aggressive moods or his lame excuses on the nights he doesn't show. Lady Cats are subtle creatures who enjoy sensual stability and are too easily thrown off their delicate emotional balance by the Rat's last minute plans. There's plenty of open sexuality in the initial stages of a Rat/Cat affair, but it quickly fades.

Star Rating: One, with maybe an extra half-point for the early physical involvement.

FEMALE DRAGON

One of the all time great relationships, at any level. The Chinese Horoscopes are quite specific about the Rat and Dragon, placing them in the number one spot for sexual extravagance. The male Rat adores the Dragon's self assurance and in turn, the Dragon responds by satisfying all the Rat's sexual demands and the female Dragon is only faintly phased by the male Rat's aggressive outbursts. What is more, even the difficult, introverted Rat will find himself opening up in the face of the female Dragon's powerful identity. But if there is the slightest hint of a hitch in the smooth running of charming Rat and warm-hearted Dragon, it is in the fact that some lady Dragon's are endowed with a little too much self-esteem. They might, just might, scorch the Rat with their fire. Rat Marlon Brando's largely improvised handling of Dragon Maria Schneider in *The Last Tango in Paris* says something about Rat males and Dragon females on a sexual high.

Star Rating: Five, but the Rat must be careful not to get his tail scorched.

FEMALE SNAKE

On first meeting, Rat males view female Snakes not unlike the way they view Dragons, who are distant cousins of the snake family. The Snake lady appears to offer all the same sexual delights as the Dragon lady but there is a big difference. Snakes are not impulsive and they tend to bewitch from a far more passive standpoint. Because Rats are easily seduced by the female Snake, who's often mysterious sexuality promises so much, this sometimes means that the Rat will rush the relationship. But female Snakes take ages before putting their toes in the deep end and could be put off by the Rat's aggression, which is never far from the surface. Matters are not helped by the fact that once the female Snake has committed herself she might want to possess the Rat. Fatal! The Rat will be off in a flash.

Star Rating: Three, with a point lost or gained depending on the Rat's staying power.

FEMALE HORSE

This is not as bad as the one-star rating suggests, although it must be said that no great understanding exists between the two signs. The male Rat is undeniably attracted to the female Horse's wit, charm and elegance. But the lady Horse is a fiercely practical creature who is not greatly impressed by what she sees as the Rat's general lack of purpose. Because Horses in love tend to lose their way a wild romantic relationship can only leave both Rat and Horse emotionally adrift. Sex should be good but the lady Horse will quickly recover her composure and it will be adios Ratty.

Star Rating: One. Maybe another half-mark in some cases.

FEMALE GOAT

Here's a relationship which on the surface looks like a five-star special all the way. Rats make no secret of the fact they love life and sexuality is high on their list of priorities. Lady Goats are warm, sensuous and can't keep away from the

Good Life, in whatever shape or form it comes. And in keeping with the Rat's view, lady Goats see sex as something to be experienced in large long happy doses. But the problem is that Rat and Goat are too much alike, which means that they reflect the same image of each other. Great love affairs are often born out of genuine opposing qualities, and although many are doomed from the start, they do at least have a magnetic pull at the beginning. The very best affairs have that magnetism all the time. Sexual success is a question of putting together the right kind of opposites.

Star Rating: Zero, with a chance in a hundred it could be five-star-fantastic for a few hours!

FEMALE MONKEY

Lady Monkeys have few moral horizons and even fewer scruples when it comes to sexual intrigue. This is just too much for the Rat, who is bowled over by the Monkey's tricks. Both signs have a great deal in common when it comes to pleasure. They like plenty of it, often at the expense of other, more edifying activities. Give Monkey and Rat an open cheque and a week off and they will have a ball. But the lady Monkey is the cooler lover and both signs always have one eye open for the main chance. So, if something better comes along . . . goodbye romance. Prince Andrew is a Rat and his affair with Monkey Koo Stark probably tells us all we need to know about this particular partnership.

Star Rating: Four or five, depending on how long they stay interested in each other.

FEMALE ROOSTER

Some animals signs are attracted by sexual opposites but this pair isn't one of them. An all-time no-hoper, there is only the faintest chance that a Rat and the candid Rooster will survive the affair's first few moments. The high-minded lady Rooster has absolutely no understanding of the majority of Rats, in particular their eagerness to live life without planning or moral codes. The Rat's charm might keep the lady Rooster from being too critical for a while, but there's little chance of a long term relationship unless marriage is the outcome.

Star Rating: Zero, zero, zero.

FEMALE DOG

Rats and Dogs are not a pairing that is found very often in the Chinese Horoscope, as indeed they are not found often in nature. Cats and Dogs, yes. Dogs and Rats, er . . . not really. But Rats are attracted to the idealistic female Dog, who is frequently blessed with beautiful hair and eyes. And there is something else that attracts the Rat. Dog ladies are warm and forgiving, which they need to be when they fall in love with a Rat. Without intending to do so, a Rat might easily take their loyal Dog lover for granted. This in turn will tend to place a negative perspective on the relationship and lady Dog might become over anxious as a result. Turn off time for the Rat. Albert Finney lived with actress Dog Diane Quick for seven years.

Star Rating: Three, especially if the Rat is the introverted planner and stickler for detail.

FEMALE PIG

The Rat in love with a Pig has many advantages, one of the most notable being that it often leads to marriage. The combination of Rat and Pig is one of the most common in the Chinese Horoscopes and improves with marriage. But there is nothing at all wrong with Rat and Pig who wish to remain just good friends. The point is that since so much of their mutual interests are social and centred on good living it makes sense that they tie the knot and do it together forever. First class understanding sexually.

Star Rating: Three rising to four and even five in some cases.

COMPATIBILITY OF FEMALE RATS IN LOVE

MALE RAT

Few if any female Rats are introverted and most just can't wait to get on and enjoy life. It is a fact that Rats grumble endlessly when things go wrong and with a pair of Rats on a high, the corresponding lows might prove a regular occurrence. But given that there is plenty of money in the bank and time to spend it there won't be much for two Rats to grumble about. One word of caution: the aggression that lurks in the heart of all Rats must not be allowed too much room. Save it for the bedroom. Imagine Nastassja Kinski and Lee Marvin on a night out.

Star Rating: Five stars. No exceptions.

MALE BUFFALO

Of all the twelve signs there are just one or two which produce a very high rating in the romance phase of a relationship but fail dismally when long term plans are put into operation. The Rat is deeply attracted by the tenacious male Buffalo, but it is an attraction of sexual opposites. As sexual opposites go, this combination of signs produces very high points but is sadly doomed in the long term. The Rat sees great strength in the solid and dependable Buffalo. She is quick to spot his complex interior, which is seen as a challenge. Not as common as male Rat and female Buffalo, the lady Rat and male Buffalo is a frequent pairing and has one of the highest failure rates.

Star Rating: Four, sometimes three.

13

MALE TIGER

Tiger males are direct and up-front in love, as they are with everything else in life. They risk all for love and seldom question their actions until later. This naturally has an inspiring influence on the passionate female Rat and in the early days of a love affair, female Rat and vigorous male Tiger are unstoppable. They both give everything, and there's plenty to give! But there is no genuine understanding between the two signs and once it is clear that the whole deal has only been sexual, Rat and Tiger will part, often on good terms. The hit record 'Passing Strangers' was, appropriately, sung by a Rat and Tiger team – Sarah Vaughan and Billy Eckstine.

Star Rating: Two, but only for the mad, mad early days.

MALE CAT

The Tom looks like a good bet at the start. Nice manners, good taste in wines, thrifty and with a healthy bank account – it's hard to resist him! And male Cats respond quickly to the lady Rat's passion. There's plenty of open sexuality in the initial stages of a Rat/Cat affair, and lots of gentle humour, but it quickly fades. Rats want their passion in hard doses. The Cat, on the other hand, often places his sexuality alongside comfort and emotional security. It is said that Cats eat Rats. In China it is the other way round.

Star Rating: Two, or even three on rare occasions.

MALE DRAGON

One of the great, great relationships. The Chinese Horoscopes are quite specific about the Rat and the Dragon, placing them in the number-one spot for sexual extravagance. The female Rat adores the Dragon's self-assurance and in turn, the Dragon responds by satisfying all the Rat's sexual demands. Of the two Dragon/Rat relationships, the Rat lady and male Dragon is marginally the best. And if the Rat grumbles the Dragon is only faintly phased. What's more, even the difficult introverted Rat will find themselves opening up in the face of the male Dragon's powerful identity –

well, nearly always. The beautiful and very witty pop singer Lyndsey de Paul is a Rat, and her open affair with Dragon James Coburn is an example of how close these signs are.

Star Rating: Five.

MALE SNAKE

Rats are easily seduced by the Snake, who's natural sexuality promises so much excitement. This sometimes means the Rat will rush into the relationship, which might not always suit the Snake, who is never at his best when forced into making a decision in a hurry. But there is a great deal of sexual chemistry on hand for Rat and Snake if they can overcome their most pronounced animal influences – aggressiveness in the case of the Rat, over-possessiveness in the case of the Snake. Of the two Rat/Snake combinations, lady Rat and male Snake are the most auspicious coupling.

Star Rating: Three, with a point lost or gained depending on the Rat's staying power.

MALE HORSE

The female Rat is undeniably attracted by the male Horse's wit, charm and elegance. Although the Horse is a fiercely practical creature they become terribly weak when they fall in love. As a result they need a sexual partner who will not take advantage of this frequently occurring state. This partner is not the lady Rat, who will milk the affair dry. Following a sexually active start the Horse will quickly recover his composure and it will be a 'no calls situation' for the Rat. Olivia Newton-John is a Rat and John Travolta a Horse, and the relationship is very much a case of Saturday Night Fever.

Star Rating: Two minimum, with a few extra percentage points for what might have been.

MALE GOAT

Here's a relationship which on the surface, looks like a five-star special all the way. Rats make no secret of the fact they love life. Sexuality is high on their list of priorities and capricious Goats can't keep away from the Good Life, in whatever shape or form it comes. But the problem is that the Rat and Goat, no matter which sex, are too much alike and the image that they reflect of each other is identical. Great love affairs are usually born out of genuine opposing qualities and although many are doomed from the start, they do at least have a magnetic pull at the beginning. The most lasting affairs have that magnetism all the time. Sexual success is a question of putting together the right kind of opposites.

Star Rating: Zero, with a chance in a hundred it could be five-star fantastic for a few hours!

MALE MONKEY

Monkeys have few moral horizons and even fewer scruples when it comes to sexual intrigue. The lady Rat is vulnerable when gripped by a sexual affair and few can resist the Monkey's tricks. Both signs have a great deal in common when it comes to pleasure. They like plenty of it, often at the expense of other, more edifying activities. Give Monkey and Rat an open cheque and a week off and they will have a ball. But there are a few provisos. The Monkey is a cool lover and both signs always have one eye open for the main chance. So, if something better comes along . . . goodbye romance.

Star Rating: Five in some cases but usually four. It depends on how long they decide to stay interested in each other.

MALE ROOSTER

Some animal signs are attracted by sexual opposites but this pair isn't one of them. There is only the faintest chance that a Rat and Rooster will survive the first few moments. The high-minded and often boastful Rooster has absolutely no understanding of the majority of Rats, and although the lady Rat warms to most signs, she will not find the candid Rooster remotely interesting sexually. But there are some Rooster males she'll go for, in particular the introvert, who is sensitive and thoughtful. These, however, are in the minority and most Roosters are a mixture of deep conservative and bar-room braggart. Not for Rats.

Star Rating: One, drifting out to zero.

MALE DOG

Rats and Dogs are not a pairing that comes easily to mind, unlike cats and mice or cats and dogs. But female Rats are attracted to the idealistic male Dog, who is loyal and caring. These qualities are enough for the warm-hearted Rat to respond with open arms. And there is something else that attracts the Rat. Dogs are forgiving, which they need to be when they fall in love with a Rat. Without intending to do so, a Rat might easily take their Dog lover for granted. This in turn will tend to place a negative perspective on the relationship and the Dog might become over anxious as a result. Turn-off time for the Rat and much pessimistic barking from the Dog.

Star Rating: Three, especially if the Dog has not been too ill-treated as a puppy.

MALE PIG

The Rat in love with a Pig has many advantages, one of the most notable being that it often leads to marriage. The combination of Rat and Pig is one of the most common in the Chinese Horoscopes and improves when the banns are read. But there is nothing at all wrong with Rat and Pig who wish to remain just good friends. The point is that since so much of their mutual interests are social and centred on good living it makes sense that they tie the knot and do it together forever. First class understanding sexually. Both sexes have an equal chance of a wonderful relationship. The relationship between Rat Lauren Bacall and Pig Humphrey Bogart highlights how well the two signs make out.

Star Rating: Three rising to four and even five in some cases.

17

COMPATIBILITY OF MALE RATS IN MARRIAGE

FEMALE RAT

There is a problem here. Although two Rats enjoy huge pleasure from a purely sexual, no strings attached relationship, the prospect of marriage, with its inherent limits on personal freedoms, alters the whole picture. If a Rat couple can decide on their course of action and stick to it, if that is ever one hundred per cent possible for those born under the Rat's opportunist influence, it will work out. But marriage usually involves observing a book of strict rules. It is an often mundane existence, a bit like a business partnership, and few chances arise for either partner to enjoy their own life without leaving the other to hold the baby – quite literally in some cases. This is not an ideal state for the Rat to flourish in and only those Rats with a genuine mutual marital objective will survive.

Star Rating: Two. If one of the partners is a planner Rat, add a point.

FEMALE BUFFALO

A Rat falling in love with a Buffalo is not an uncommon event and receives a high star rating, but wedding bells are bad news. They do nothing but knock two stars off the relationship, and sometimes more. The male Rat is captivated by the female, if never truly feminine, Buffalo. As an attraction of sexual opposites they have few, if any, rivals. But marriage points to all sorts of hidden doors, which when opened, allow the more complete personality to emerge. This can produce no end of surprises, not all of them pleasant. The Buffalo is a world leader, no matter which sex, while the Rat uses his intelligence to quite different ends. The Buffalo lady will increasingly dominate the home and the Rat will be left feeling more and more impotent. In spite of the considerable warning signs, Rats tend to marry Buffaloes, and as a result, this pairing is one of the most common. It also has a high rating for divorce. Andrew Lloyd Webber is a Rat, and his second wife, Sarah Brightman, a Buffalo.

Star Rating: Two and that is being generous. Having children might help as it creates a mutual interest.

FEMALE TIGER

Both signs produce high-octane lovers, but marriage has the habit of putting more than a few specks of dust in the carburettor. The Tiger, in spite of her warmth and generosity, is a rebel at heart, and sees herself as the boss of any team. This might cause a serious rift, especially if the Rat is the introvert who insists on planning everything to the last detail. And when the Rat's life hits a bad spell there'll be another. Forced into a corner the Rat's aggressive streak will immediately dominate. He'll become pushy, his natural charm will go out of the window and he'll view his Tiger wife as an emotional threat. From then on it's downhill all the way. Captain Mark Phillips is a Rat and the Princess Royal is a Tiger. It is said they don't talk to each other much outside of horseriding.

Star Rating: Zero

FEMALE CAT

A modest romance turns into a less than satisfactory marriage. Rats and Cats are both creatures of comfort, but each has an entirely different approach to a full wine cellar and a well-stocked freezer. The female Cat enjoys a quiet, methodical life with the emphasis on routine whereas most

Rats rush around with seldom a thought for tomorrow. The Cat plans carefully and most Rats spend without thinking. The Rat eats everything in sight while the cautious Cat likes to know there is plenty put by for a rainy day. And so the differences go on.

Star Rating: Zero.

FEMALE DRAGON

Champagne time! Ring the bells and bring on the wedding cake. This is one of the all time great combinations. No matter how aggressive the male Rat becomes, the female Dragon won't even flinch, and she'll give as good as she gets. In between flare ups and shouting matches they will forge strong emotional bonds that will not be broken easily. Even the introverted, uptight and deeply critical Rat will find himself soothed by the inspiring female Dragon. For the normal extrovert Rat, bed continues to be a strong feature of married life, but Rat and Dragon will not neglect the many other fascinating areas that arise from a life spent in close harmony. Music, painting, the arts as a whole – all involve the senses and Rat and Dragon will spend much time exploring them. TV actor John Stride is a Rat and his wife, April, a former actress is a Dragon.

Star Rating: Five

FEMALE SNAKE

The early experiences in a Rat and Snake relationship largely determine how long it lasts. If the Rat can curb his opportunism and slow his delight in life to a pace that the subtle Snake can tolerate, then marriage is a reasonable idea. Both Rats and Snakes have a very strong sexual inner core, but it has to be remembered that marriages, however successful, tend to become more like business partnerships the longer they continue. It is here that the problems arise. A business requires an abundance of thrift, and although the subtle Snake can provide bundles of it, most Rats spend without thinking. There are difficulties at every level, even in the kitchen. Whereas the Rat is fond of his tummy, the Snake is seldom interested in food. Obviously, petty differences about cuisine are not enough to lead to a divorce, but they'll remain an ever-present reminder of what divides them.

Star Rating: Three

FEMALE HORSE

Born under the sign of charm, Rats achieve much of their success by a mixture of quick wits and warmth. Some signs fall easily under the spell of the exciting Rat, but the Horse is not one. Although they fall in love far too quickly, and too often for their own good, female Horses do not like to be charmed into action. It might be OK for one night, but in the long term a Horse wants reason and logic to rule the roost. The Rat will forever be cast in the role of spendthrift and his every action criticised for its opportunist horizons.

Star Rating: Zero

FEMALE GOAT

Although the Rat and Goat pairing has a very low standing in terms of a casual relationship, there is a massive improvement when the couple decide to cement their love in a marriage. Out of wedlock, Rat and Goat have a habit of keeping an eye open for the next best thing. Goats require much tethering to make the most of their talents whereas the Rat is generally a lacklustre administrator, preferring to let others decide for themselves. These influences are not the stuff from which marriages are made, at least not ones that run the course. But an agreement to marriage is a statement about wanting to make their relationship work. In a sense the nuptials provide both a framework in which the Rat can operate and a tethering post for the capricious Goat. A rich social life is on the cards, which creates the pleasurable backdrop against which most Rats and all Goats prefer to perform.

Star Rating: Four – almost.

FEMALE MONKEY

In the love category, male Rat and female Monkey are among the top handful of relationships. With no set limits, both animal signs are free to indulge their considerable appetites and a sexual affair is the perfect outcome. Marriage, on the other hand, demands a great many sacrifices, which neither sign is particularly inclined towards. As a rule, the astute Monkey will prevent the family finances from slipping into the red, although the Rat won't be too bothered either way. But with Mr and Mrs Chancer under the same roof for any lengthy period, the question must be asked, when will their true nature creep through the marriage-vow barrier? But both Rat and Monkey make splendid parents and should they wed, a family, the larger the better, will go a long way to keep them together.

Star Rating: Three. Sometimes a point less, sometimes a point more.

FEMALE ROOSTER

A big shift in gear in the unusual partnership of Rat and Rooster. In love, which is an equally rare relationship, there are zero marks for understanding and minus zero for compatibility. But as sometimes happens, matters greatly improve if signs of markedly different temperament can agree on the boundaries of married life, setting down at the outset what is to be expected of each other. From zero, Rat and Rooster stand a very good chance indeed of making a marriage blossom. Much depends on the type of Rooster. If she is the outgoing Rooster, with less than the normal dose of high moral fortitude that normally comes with her sign, there is a distinct possibility the marriage could survive. But it is never easy and there will be times when the Rat regrets sharing the perch in the hen house.

Star Rating: Two, which in this instance is really good.

FEMALE DOG

There is a marked decrease of understanding when a Rat and Dog get hitched. In a purely sexual/romantic relationship, the more negative aspects of each of these two animal signs are less obvious. But there is little of the Dog's strong sense of idealism in the Rat and setting the world to rights is not his priority. Dogs become more idealistic the older they get and the opportunism and aggressive streak which may often dominate the male Rat only succeeds in driving a wedge between them. This in turn causes the Dog to become increasingly anxious and critical. Should the Rat be introverted and keen on the minutiae of life, the marriage stands a marginally better chance. Actress Jane Asher is a Dog and her husband, self-promoting cartoonist Gerald Scarfe is a Rat. Another Rat/Dog pair are pop wizard Jean Michel Jarre and his wife, Charlotte Rampling.

Star Rating: One.

FEMALE PIG

There is not a great deal of point in a Rat and Pig simply living together when a fuller and more complete life is waiting for them with their marrying. That is not to say that being in love isn't without its complications, especially since the Rat always has his eye open for new experiences and the lady Pig is easily seduced. But marriage frequently creates the atmosphere in which a Rat and Pig can discover their most positive characteristics. Both are social and enjoy good living. Given their mutual interests, it makes sense to put their combined energy under one roof. And since most children flourish under a Rat and Pig's collective parental warmth, marriage is a natural step. Prince Andrew is a Rat and Fergie is a Pig.

Star Rating: Five.

COMPATIBILITY OF FEMALE RATS IN MARRIAGE

MALE RAT

There is a problem here. Although two Rats enjoy huge pleasure from a purely sexual, no strings attached relationship, the prospect of marriage with its inherent limits on personal freedoms alters the whole picture. If a Rat couple can decide on their course of action and stick to it, if that is ever one hundred per cent possible for those born under the Rat's opportunist influence, it will work out. But marriage usually involves observing a book of strict rules. It is an often mundane existence, a bit like a business partnership, and few chances arise for either partner to enjoy their own life without leaving the other to hold the baby – quite literally in some cases. This is not an ideal state for the Rat to flourish and only those Rats with a genuine mutual objective will survive.

Star Rating: Two. If one of the partners is a planner Rat, add a point.

MALE BUFFALO

A Rat falling in love with a Buffalo is not an uncommon event and receives a high-star rating, but wedding bells are bad news. They do nothing but knock two stars off the relationship. As an attraction of sexual opposites they have few if any rivals. But marriage opens up all sorts of hidden doors which, when opened, allow the more complete personality to emerge. This can sometimes produce no end of surprises, not all of them pleasant. The Buffalo is a world leader, no matter which sex, while the Rat uses her sharp mind to quite different ends. The Buffalo will dominate all aspects of the home and the Rat will be left feeling more and more a bystander, waiting for the sparks to fly once more. But she'll wait in vain. In spite of the considerable warning signs, Rats tend to marry Buffaloes, and as a result, this pairing is one of the most common. It also has a high rating for divorce. Of the two combinations, figures suggest more female Buffaloes marry male Rats than the other way round.

Star Rating: Two, although children might help to create a mutual interest.

MALE TIGER

Both signs produce the type of lover to act on impulse, and in some cases recklessly. But marriage has the habit of calming down even the most hot-blooded Romeo. The Tiger, in spite of his up-front generosity, is a rebel at heart, and quickly establishes himself as the boss of any team. This might cause a serious rift, especially if the Rat is the introvert who insists on planning everything to the last detail. And when the Rat's life hits a bad spell there'll be another. Forced into a corner the Rat's aggressive streak will immediately dominate. She'll become pushy, her natural charm, of which there is an abundance, will go out of the window and she'll view her Tiger husband as little more than an emotional threat. From then on it's downhill all the way.

Star Rating: Zero. Male Rat and female Tiger might manage a single star.

MALE CAT

A modest romance turns into a less than satisfactory marriage. Rats and Cats are both creatures of comfort, but each has an entirely different approach to a full wine cellar and a well-stocked freezer. The male Cat enjoys a quiet, methodical existence with the emphasis on routine whereas most female Rats rush at life with seldom a thought for tomorrow. Female Rats also have a habit of fretting when they have children, something that drives Tom up the wall. The Cat plans carefully and most Rats spend without thinking. The lady Rat stocks her larder, only to consume it at once, especially the sweet things, while the cautious Cat likes to know there is plenty put by for a rainy day. The relationship ends up a constant battle with Cat and Rat finding nothing in common at any level. Fifties film-star Doris Day is a Rat and her longest and perhaps most unhappy marriage was to a Cat, producer Martin Melcher. He apparently diddled her out of millions. Sorry folks.

Star Rating: Zero.

MALE DRAGON

Champagne time! Ring out the bells and bring on the wedding cake. This is one of the all time great combinations. In between flare-ups and shouting matches they will forge strong emotional bonds that will not be broken easily. Even the over-critical Rat will find themselves soothed by the inspiring male Dragon. For the normal extrovert Rat, bed continues to be a strong feature of married life, but Rat and Dragon will not neglect the many other fascinating areas that arise from a life spent in close harmony. Music, painting, the arts as a whole – all involve the senses and Rat and Dragon will spend much time exploring them. Princess Alexandra is a Rat and her husband, Angus Ogilvy, is a Dragon.

Star Rating: Five plus! OK – Six!

MALE SNAKE

The early experiences of a Rat and Snake relationship largely determine how long it lasts. If the Rat can curb her excitement and slow her delight in life to a pace that the subtle Snake can tolerate, then marriage is a reasonable idea. Both Rats and Snakes have a very strong sexual inner core, but it has to be remembered that marriages, however successful, tend to become more like business partnerships the longer they continue. It is here that the problems arise. A business requires an abundance of thrift, and although the Snake can provide bundles of it, most Rats spend without thinking. There are difficulties at every level and quarrels about trivial matters remain an ever-present symbol of that which divides them. But the Snake's deep reluctance to give up and the Rat's sharp wits will help keep the show on the road.

Star Rating: Three.

MALE HORSE

Born under the sign of charm, Rats achieve much of their success by a mixture of quick wits and warmth. Some signs fall easily under the spell of the exciting Rat, but the Horse is not one. Although they fall in love far too quickly, and too often for their own good, male Horses do not like to be charmed into action. It might be OK for one night, but in the long term a Horse wants reason and logic to rule the roost. The Rat will forever be cast in the role of spendthrift and her every action criticised.

Star Rating: Zero

MALE GOAT

Although the Rat and Goat pairing has a very low standing in terms of a casual relationship, there is a massive improvement when the couple decide to cement their love in a marriage. Out of wedlock, Rat and Goat have a habit of keeping an eye open for the next best thing. Goats require much tethering to make the most of their talents whereas the Rat, although giving sound advice, generally prefers to let others decide for themselves. These influences are not the stuff from which marriages are made, at least not ones that run the course. But an agreement to marriage is a statement about wanting to make their relationship work. In a sense the nuptials provide both a framework in which the Rat can operate and a tethering post for the capricious Goat. A rich social life is on the cards, which creates the pleasurable backdrop against which most Rats and all Goats prefer to perform.

Star Rating: Four – almost.

MALE MONKEY

In the love category, female Rat and male Monkey are among the top handful of relationships. With no set limits, both animal signs are free to indulge their considerable appetites and a sexual affair is the perfect outcome. Marriage, on the other hand demands a great many sacrifices which neither sign is particularly inclined towards. As a rule, the astute Monkey will prevent the family finances from slipping into the red, although the Rat won't be too bothered either way. But with Mr and Mrs Chancer under the same roof for any lengthy period, the question must be asked, when will their true nature creep through the marriage-vow barrier? But both Rat and Monkey make splendid parents and should they wed, a family, the larger the better, will go a long way to keep them together. Transport Minister, Peter Bottomley is a Monkey and his MP wife, Virginia, is a Rat.

Star Rating: Three. Sometimes a point less, sometimes a point more, but the male Rat/female Monkey partnership scores the highest points.

MALE ROOSTER

A big shift in gear in the unusual partnership of Rat and Rooster. In love, which is an equally rare relationship, there are zero marks for understanding and minus zero for compatibility. But as sometimes happens if signs of markedly different temperament can agree on the boundaries of married life, setting down at the outset what is to be expected of each other, matters greatly improve. From zero, Rat and Rooster stand a very good chance indeed of making a marriage blossom. Much depends on the type of Rooster. If he is the more tolerant Rooster, with less than the normal dose of high moral fortitude that normally comes with his sign, there is a distinct possibility the marriage could survive. But it is never easy and there will be times when the Rat regrets having such a candid creature around the place. Jill Ireland is a Rat, married to Rooster Charles Bronson. Former presidential candidate Michael Dukakis is another Rooster with a Rat wife, Kitty.

Star Rating: Three, which is a one star increase for the female Rat/male Rooster over the male Rat/female Rooster pairing.

MALE DOG

There is a marked decrease of understanding when a Rat and Dog get hitched. In a purely sexual/romantic relationship, the more negative aspects of each of these two animal signs are less obvious. But there is only a little of the Dog's strong sense of idealism in even the most idealistic lady Rat and setting the world to rights is not normally her priority. Dogs become more set in their ways the older they get and the openness and changeability which may often dominate the Rat's personality only succeeds in driving a wedge between them. This in turn causes the Dog to become increasingly anxious and critical. Should the Rat be introverted and keen on the minutiae of life, the marriage stands a marginally better chance.

Star Rating: One.

MALE PIG

There is not a great deal of point in a Rat and Pig simply living together when a fuller and more complete life is waiting for them with their marrying. That is not to say that being in love isn't without its complications, especially since the Rat always has her eye open for new experiences and the male Pig is easily seduced. But marriage frequently creates the atmosphere in which a Rat and Pig can discover their most positive characteristics. Both are social and enjoy good living. Given their mutual interests, it makes sense to put their combined energy under one roof. And since most children flourish under a Rat and Pig's collective parental warmth, marriage is a natural step.

Star Rating: Four and a bit. A female Pig/male Rat is a strong pair.

COMPATIBILITY OF MALE RATS IN FRIENDSHIP

MALE RAT

An unusual and, if formed, a not entirely fruitful relationship in which the similarity of the influencing sign is an obstruction to close understanding. Some pairings of the same sign provide a high rating but two Rats isn't one. There will be a modicum of respect but little else. Forming a business is out of the question as two Rats bring the same skills, and weaknesses.

Star Rating: Zero.

MALE BUFFALO

An interesting partnership which brings to play two signs with quite different approaches to life. When joined in friendship Rat and Buffalo have a great deal of respect for each other's abilities. Although there will be many difficult moments and lack of consideration from the complex Buffalo, the Rat will handle it without a fuss and they will nevertheless create a solid and lasting friendship. Richard Ingrams, former editor of *Private Eye*, is a Buffalo and his successor, chosen by him, Ian Hislop, is a Rat.

Star Rating: Four.

MALE TIGER

Not strong in marriage or love, friendship offers far fewer problems for the Rat and Tiger. The Tiger's energy is attractive to the Rat, especially where business is concerned. And the Rat brings much needed clarity of vision. A busy friendship and full of excitement. Although the Everlys, Don and Phil, are brothers they have been together so long that they could also be classed as friends. Don is the Rat.
    Star Rating: Three rising to four.

MALE CAT

Not the greatest idea in the world. The Rat's vitality and sharp wits only marginally engage the methodical Cat. In business, matters improve, especially if there is an artistic element. On the whole, a negative set up.
    Star Rating: Two-ish. Three for a business partnership.

MALE DRAGON

Few better relationships exist anywhere in the twelve animal signs. As married partners, as lovers and as friends, there can be no stronger pair. The Rat take the Dragon's raw thoughts and reshapes them. The Dragon, in turn, excites the Rat's bright and witty mind. There will be no reproaches and no bad feelings if things go wrong. The Rat will find himself with hardly anything to grumble over and the self-centered Dragon will be almost bearable.
    Star Rating: Six!

MALE SNAKE

Not much to recommend this friendship. In a romantic relationship there's a degree of mileage, but as friends pure and simple Rat and Snake do not enjoy much in common. Without the physical expression of their attraction they are two signs with directions pointing away from each other.
    Star Rating: One, at a pinch.

MALE HORSE

Of all the pairings open to the Rat, the one with the Horse presents the biggest obstacles. Neither fully understands the other's needs or departure points. The Horse works harder than most and it is often physical, whereas hard work for the Rat usually means using his wits. Graft is more what Horses do. A business partnership is out, and so is any other long term relationship.

Star Rating: Zero.

MALE GOAT

As long as there's a wine bar or pub nearby, Rat and Goat should make out pretty well. Both enjoy life and neither sign finds 'no thanks' easy to say in the face of a good time. There's much good humour, although the Rat might tire a little of the Goat's more capricious side. There again, the Rat is no stranger to a changed plan or two himself. Good vibes on the whole for two fun-lovers. Rolling Stone Bill Wyman is a Rat and both Mick Jagger and Keith Richards are Goats.

Star Rating: Between three and four. Seldom less.

MALE MONKEY

A very reasonable friendship, with the best coming at the beginning. Monkey's are wheeler-dealers to a man and the Rat loves in-fighting, especially in business, and so a commercial union is something to aim at. The only setback is that they will finally find themselves trying to outwit each other. Andrew Lloyd Webber is a Rat and Tim Rice a Monkey.

Star Rating: Four most days.

MALE ROOSTER

Astonishingly this is a friendship which can succeed, but there needs to be some very straight talking in order to establish what the boundaries are. Rooster, if they are the less moral type, and a Rat who has found his niche might well find they have formed a friendship, against all odds. A business partnership is no bad idea and the chances of success improve considerably if the pair are an introverted Rooster and an introverted Rat. Barry Hearne is a Rat and Steve Davis is a Rooster.

Star Rating: Three.

MALE DOG

A Rat might easily benefit from a friendship with a Dog, who brings a powerful sense of loyalty to any relationship. In turn, the Rat can offer his sharp wits and humour to help calm the Dog's more anxious moments. But there is no great understanding between them and it is not a common pairing. Perhaps that's why.

Star Rating: One, sometimes a point extra.

MALE PIG

One of the Rats better choices in friends. Plenty of late nights on the tiles will ensure that this couple of mates enjoy a long and good-humoured friendship. And if they have enough in common to start a business venture, they should go for it. The Pig's honesty and knack of making money will appeal greatly to the Rat. But the Pig will have to keep his eye on friend Rat's natural sense of opportunism. And he might keep the safe key on his key-ring. The way Pig sign Ronnie Reagan trusted and promoted Rat sign George Bush is typical of this animal relationship.

Star Rating: Four.

COMPATIBILITY OF FEMALE RATS IN FRIENDSHIP

FEMALE RAT

Lady Rats are keen observers of the human condition and have a bright intelligence which they can easily adapt to suit any company. But they also take reversals to heart and grumble, sometimes at length, at what they see as an intrusion into their lust for living. Another lady Rat will understand this low period and no doubt help with warmth and good advice. But there won't be a great deal else to share and a friendship between two female Rats is extremely uncommon. A day's shopping together or a night at a good restaurant is what they will probably enjoy most.

Star Rating: Zero through to four. One of the most difficult to judge.

FEMALE BUFFALO

There is no doubt that the Buffalo, both male and female, present themselves as strong and resolute friends. But there is not much leeway and the Buffalo insists on having the last word. They run the emotional side of any relationship and often make impossible demands on the loyalty of those they choose to befriend. Should they choose to, the Rat can cope easily with all but the most complex Buffalo, receiving a positive and fruitful role in a sound relationship for their efforts.

Star Rating: Four.

FEMALE TIGER

Not strong in marriage or love, friendship offers far fewer problems for the Rat and Tiger, but not two females. The Tiger's energy is attractive to the Rat, especially where business is concerned. And the Rat brings much needed clarity of vision. This should be a busy friendship and full of excitement, but there are times when the Tiger's uncertainty about her inner personality will tend to block out the warmth the Rat normally enjoys, and expects. Although the Rat may find the Tiger's low periods demanding, they will respond with good advice and understanding.

Star Rating: Two, sometimes one.

FEMALE CAT

Rat ladies appreciate the female Cat's calm and methodical approach to life. At the stage of motherhood, a Cat will be a useful aid, bringing a sense of order to the sometimes chaotic Rat's world. Cat ladies are seldom critical – not the catty people we are led to believe – and their care and attention to detail in a friendship will not go unnoticed.

Star Rating: Three, rising to four in some cases.

FEMALE DRAGON

All the signs point to a strong and harmonious friendship, and so it will be. The female Dragon, though, has a strong masculine streak to her influence, which in a woman creates a set of sexual and emotional contradictions. The Rat recognises this and will simply let the Dragon do her own thing, which often means simply helping the Dragon calm down and get life back into perspective. In return, the Dragon will inspire the Rat and ease away her more anxious moments.

Star Rating: Five.

FEMALE SNAKE

An unusual relationship in the female species of the sign. Both have deep sexual drives and unless they can find a way of channelling them into something that they can share, lady

Rat and lady Snake are not likely to find much in common. The Rat moves quickly and is seldom still, the Snake slides through life, acting on their intuition. In some senses, they are too much alike for real friendship, which often is most fruitful when there are two contrasting views.

Star Rating: One – just.

FEMALE HORSE

The independence and practicality which marks the Horse also marks a friendship with the Rat a no-no of the first order. Both are witty and good company in a crowd, yet as attractive as the relationship might first appear, the Horse has no understanding of the Rat's spontaneous behaviour, nor does she approve. In more areas than is helpful to real friendship, both signs cancel each other out. Rat's, though, are never ones to harbour grudges for long, finding them an obstruction to getting on with life. But they might make an exception in the case of the often vain, and as they might see it, over-critical Horse.

Star Rating: Zero

FEMALE GOAT

This pair of friends are good news. Their mutual interests in good food, fashion and the latest trends create a really positive attitude towards keeping the friendship buoyant. Both signs have a natural flair for all things new and they could easily make a success of any business venture should Rat and Goat choose that particular path to express themselves. Lots of fun and games. And talking of games, one of the greatest ever tennis double partnerships was a Rat and Goat – Rosie Casals and Billie-Jean King. They were extremely close both on and off the court. Rosie is the Rat.

Star Rating: Five most of the time.

FEMALE MONKEY

A first rate friendship with great intimacy. Neither signs are modest about their feelings and love to let their hair down. If gossip is the order of the day you can count on the Rat and Monkey making the most of it. Both signs enjoy emotional freedom and are not likely to make heavy demands on each other. A good intrigue is what this pair enjoy and if there isn't one in the offing, they'll be quick to create it.

Star Rating: Five.

FEMALE ROOSTER

If the Rat is the type to spend her money as she earns it, the extrovert Rat, and the Rooster is the kind to empty her bank account at a stroke, this pair can become good friends. Afternoons spending in the high street is the usual plan, followed by tea and a generous helping of cakes. But Roosters are moralists deep down and Rats tend not to be. There could be a few uneasy moments should the Rat let her comparative lack of moral fibre get the better of her. So it all depends on both signs being well-balanced outgoing types.

Star Rating: Four at best. Three as a rule.

FEMALE DOG

Of the two sexes, lady Dogs tend to be the most loyal and forgiving. They are not cynical as a rule and tend to look for the best in a friend. Rats on the other hand flow with the tide and, deep as their affections are, they can shift from one to another with ease. Of all the pairings, Dogs and Rats are one of the least common.

Star Rating: Two as an average. But anything goes.

FEMALE PIG

A right on friendship if ever there was one. Fast living, plenty of nights out and four hands grabbing all that's going is the way this team expresses their mutual affection. Obviously, as in all friendships, there will be moments of misunderstanding. This usually arises from the Pig's ability to get herself duped at the drop of a hat, landing the Rat in it with her. But there'll be no hard feelings and they'll soon be back in the swing.

Star Rating: Five.

THE BUFFALO

1901	February 19th	to	February 7th	**1902**
1913	February 6th	to	January 25th	**1914**
1925	January 24th	to	February 12th	**1926**
1937	February 11th	to	January 30th	**1938**
1949	January 29th	to	February 16th	**1950**
1961	February 15th	to	February 4th	**1962**
1973	February 3rd	to	January 22nd	**1974**
1985	February 20th	to	February 8th	**1986**

'This beast is but simple, though his aspect seems to be very grave.'

Topsell

THE YEAR OF THE BUFFALO

Buffaloes are born under the twin signs of equilibrium and endurance. They are the essense of reliability. Even so, stubborn in the extreme, they are not given to self criticism and have an incurable habit of blaming others for their own mistakes. Buffaloes are resolute and tireless in the pursuit of their ideals. Ruled by conviction, Buffaloes nevertheless suffer from a complex and sometimes uncontrollable heart. Unless a Buffalo can find expression for their deep-down feelings, they will direct their massive energy inwards. At this point the Buffalo personality may become extremely unpredictable and sometimes self-destructive. All attempts to get really close only force the Buffalo to retreat even further into themselves.

Incapable of sharing power, Buffaloes are strong, resolute and demand great loyalty from those around them. Returning loyalty, however, is quite a different matter. Buffaloes are born leaders and no one works harder to achieve their goal. With a single-mindedness that is sometimes astonishing, it is not surprising that few Buffaloes fall short of their objectives.

The Buffalo is essentially a masculine sign and female Buffaloes differ only very slightly. They love to garden and given the chance prefer to live in the countryside. Lady Buffaloes dress tidily and to suit themselves. But when they do dress up, watch out. They dress to kill. A stable family life is crucial to both male and female Buffaloes and both tend to make authoritative parents.

At heart, Buffaloes are solitary creatures who prefer honest toil to bright lights and high society. They are one-offs who have done more than any other sign to alter the world in which we live. Because they have such complex hearts, few Buffaloes risk falling in love on a regular besis and casual affairs are rare. A Buffalo might find conquering the world a piece of cake, but conquering their heart is a non-starter.

The three phases of a Buffalo's life are quite distinct. The Buffalo child is often isolated. Finding it difficult to form close friendships, Buffalo children tend to rely on themselves for amusement. For example, a boy Buffalo might collect stamps while girls will read a great deal. Middle life is equally unsure. Here marriages tend to go astray and work proves a problem. Buffaloes might easily marry more than once and start a second family. The third phase will be easier and in old age the Buffalo is discovered happily reliving the more memorable moments of their full life. But many unfulfilled Buffaloes quickly go to seed and face a miserable end. They spend their lonely days staring bleakly at the past, their hearts full of bitter regret.

COMPATIBILITY OF MALE BUFFALOES IN LOVE

FEMALE RAT

Here's a strange relationship. Of all twelve signs there are just one or two which produce a very high rating in the romance phase of a relationship but fall off the bottom of the graph when long term plans are put into operation. The male Buffalo is deeply attracted by the female Rat, but it is an attraction of sexual opposites. In most cases this kind of attraction rates poorly but Rat and Buffalo get full marks. However, few animal signs have such little understanding of each other or respond to such different stimuli. And yet few other signs find each other so irresistible. In my experience Rat and Buffalo is one of the most common pairings but has the highest chance of failing long term.

Star Rating: Four for the Big Bang on the first night. But beware of the decline, which might happen suddenly.

FEMALE BUFFALO

Some signs do well when they fall in love with the same sign. There is an attraction about seeing your own qualities mirrored by another close to you. But the Buffalo sign is not one. There is evidence that two Buffaloes might just hit if off for a short while, believing that their combined strength will increase the intensity of their deep feelings. And so it will for a time, but the problem is that one of the Buffaloes will be impelled to run things, especially the emotional side of the relationship. This will lead to endless fights and sulky silences. It will also end with a parting of the ways.

Star Rating: Two at best.

FEMALE TIGER

Most aspects of the Buffalo character are emphatic, and their relationships with other animal signs are no exception. Of all the signs, a match between male Buffalo and female Tiger rates the lowest. The Chinese Horoscopes write warnings against it in ten feet tall letters which say, DON'T! But the odd thing is that these two signs are powerfully attracted to each other and in my experience are frequently found trying to make a relationship work. The problem is, however, that the Buffalo tends to grind the Tiger down. His stubborn and intractable nature is in constant conflict with the fast moving but short paced Tiger. In love they have nothing in common. While the lady Tiger is full of generosity, taking any risk the affair demands, the Buffalo ponders and searches his complex heart for a way to control the situation. Do not be fooled by a sudden infatuation, Buffalo and Tiger should avoid each other like the plague.

Star Rating: Zero

FEMALE CAT

The male Buffalo in love frequently finds it difficult to express how he feels. One reason for this is they are never quite sure exactly what it is they are feeling. And love often makes them feel vulnerable. The Buffalo loves deeply but not without a struggle. Luckily the female Cat has great patience and understanding, and as long as the Buffalo is attentive and makes some attempt to hand out compliments on her hair, clothes and beautiful home there is hope. But the Cat must remember that although Buffaloes run the world, they can not run their hearts with the same conviction. The Buffalo is nevertheless an honest lover, something the female Cat will appreciate and repay in kind.

Star Rating: Three.

FEMALE DRAGON

There is nothing actually disastrous with a male Buffalo falling madly in love with a female Dragon. The problem is that it happens so rarely hardly any data exists to prove it one way or another. In principle it should be the same as a male Dragon and female Buffalo, which is common, but there are differences. Male Buffaloes dominate any partnership, no matter what the sign, while the female Dragon suffers from a pronounced sense of superiority which she inherits from her powerfully masculine sign. But as so often proves to be the case, there is an attraction of opposites which can be extremely exciting in the early stages of a love affair.

Star Rating: Two.

FEMALE SNAKE

Male Buffaloes are frequently seduced by the female Snake's highly bewitching personality. The lady Snake is humorous, artistic and wise. She has an endless well of sensuality which completely overwhelms the Buffalo. Using her subtle understanding of the senses, she winds her way into his most sheltered areas and cleverly soothes the male Buffalo's more complex emotions. The Buffalo's response is sometimes to be shocked by the depth of his own sensuality and at other times resistant. But he will give in fully at one stage to the Snake's bewitching charm. Of the two pairings, the male Buffalo and female Snake have by far the greater understanding and is the most common.

Star Rating: Three, sometimes four.

FEMALE HORSE

The female Horse holds many attractions for the male Buffalo. She is bright, witty and full of personality. But she isn't one to be pushed around by the male Buffalo's imperious temperament and there's something about the long silences that stem from his complex nature which alienates her. Both signs demand great independence in order to function properly, which is hardly the best of platforms to launch a loving union. Not exactly a no-no, this is not, however, a relationship which collects Oscars for long term understanding. David Bailey is a Buffalo and in the swinging sixties he spent a while with model Jean Shrimpton, a Horse. Of all Bailey's long term women (he's had four wives), 'The Shrimp' was the only one he didn't marry.

Star Rating: One.

FEMALE GOAT

Buffalo men seldom view women as mere sex objects and relationships tend to be formed with the long term in mind. However, lady Goats often have a coquettish side to their nature which can easily topple the straight-thinking Buffalo into more fun and games than he bargained for. But the affair offers the Buffalo more than the Goat, who strict to her sign's capricious influence is unlikely to stick around for long, especially when the Buffalo gets one of his moods. As with all the male Buffalo's partners, the lady Goat provides a stark contrast to his own highly individual personality and is therefore seen as a considerable temptation.

Star Rating: Zero as a rule, sometimes leaping to a surprising four.

FEMALE MONKEY

On the surface there doesn't seem much going for the fast-thinking Monkey lady, who lives off her wits, and the solid dependable Buffalo. But there is poetry in the heart of many a male Buffalo, even though they sometimes find it hard to express. The Monkey lady is a wizard at bringing out even the most repressed male, and she might well find the emotionally complex Buffalo something of a challenge. As far as a love affair goes, this is not at all bad. At best, however, the affair will be the on/off kind, with the Buffalo finding himself less in command than in other relationships.

    Star Rating: Three, sometimes four.

FEMALE ROOSTER

Jackpot time for the Buffalo male. Only two signs are completely compatible with the male Buffalo and the female Rooster is one. Neither is looking for a short term relationship and the love affair will soon establish itself as a winner and it won't be long before there's an announcement in the paper and a wedding list is on display at the local big store. Both animal signs are deeply conservative, usually with a big and small C, and neither cares to fool around once there's been a genuine commitment given. As a romance its short and sweet and quickly down the aisle.

    Star Rating: Five Big Ones.

FEMALE DOG

There is something in the idealism of the lady Dog that the strong-minded Buffalo finds both laudable and attractive. She is warm and open in her affection and the Buffalo responds to her attentiveness. In turn the female Dog feels herself protected by the male Buffalo's strength of character. So what's wrong? Dogs are apprehensive and tend to worry over details. They are anxious and uncertain at times whereas the Buffalo sets his path out before him and follows it come what may. There are times when lovers must by their very nature travel the same path, but Buffalo and Dog will eventually find their paths head in different directions.

Star Rating: Two, sometimes three.

FEMALE PIG

A big romance with all the frills for the male Buffalo and female Pig. The jovial Pig lady – full of fun and easy going – does wonders for the often romantically complex Buffalo. She laughs at his jokes, cooks him breakfast and makes him feel comfortable, the state most Pigs seek to obtain. There can be genuine understanding between a Buffalo and Pig, but there is a warning note which should be heeded. Pig ladies do not always enjoy life at the steady pace demanded by Buffalo males. What's more, the Chinese Horoscopes point out that Pigs care little for their reputation, which is another way of saying they are not over-interested in fidelity for its own sake. So Buffalo beware, do not take Miss Piggy for granted.

Star Rating: Four, with an occasional five.

COMPATIBILITY OF FEMALE BUFFALOES IN LOVE

MALE RAT

Here's a strange relationship. Of all twelve signs there are just one or two which produce a very high rating in the romance phase of a relationship but fall off the bottom of the graph when long term plans are put into operation. The female Buffalo is deeply attracted by the male Rat, but it is an attraction of sexual opposites. In most cases this kind of attraction rates poorly, but Rat and Buffalo get full marks. However, few animal signs have so little understanding of each other or respond to such different stimuli. And yet few other signs find each other so irresistible. In my experience Rat and Buffalo is one of the most common pairings and yet has the highest chance of failing long term.

Star Rating: Four for the Big Bang on the first night. But beware of the decline, which might happen suddenly.

MALE BUFFALO

Some signs do well when they fall in love with the same sign. There is an attraction about seeing your own qualities mirrored by another close to you. But the Buffalo sign is not one. There is evidence that two Buffaloes might just hit it off for a short while, believing that their combined strength will increase the intensity of their deep feelings. And so it will for a time, but the problem is that one of the Buffaloes will want to run things, especially the emotional side of the relationship. This will lead to endless fights and sulky sullen silences. It will also end with a parting of the ways.

Star Rating: Two at best.

MALE TIGER

Most aspects of the Buffalo are emphatic, and their relationships with other signs are no exceptions. Of all the signs, a match between female Buffalo and male Tiger rates the lowest. The Chinese Horoscopes write warnings against it in ten feet tall letters which say, DON'T! But the odd thing is that these two signs are powerfully attracted to each other and in my experience are frequently found trying to make a relationship work. The problem is, however, that the Buffalo tends to grind the Tiger down. Her stubborn and intractable nature is in constant conflict with the fast moving but short paced Tiger. In love they have nothing in common. While the male Tiger is full of generosity, taking any risk the affair demands, the lady Buffalo ponders and searches her complex heart for a way to control the situation. Do not be fooled by a

47

sudden infatuation, Buffalo and Tiger should avoid each other like the plague.

Star Rating: Zero, minus zero.

MALE CAT

The female Buffalo in love frequently finds it difficult to express how she feels, although she does a much better job than her male counterpart. One reason for this is that they are never quite sure exactly what it is they are feeling. And love often makes them feel vulnerable. The Buffalo loves deeply but not without a struggle. Luckily the male Cat has great patience and understanding. But the Cat must remember that although Buffaloes run the world, they can not run their hearts with the same conviction. The lady Buffalo is nevertheless a gentle, direct and faithful lover, something the majority of male Cats will appreciate and repay in kind. Twiggy is a Buffalo and her first important love affair was with a Cat, Justin de Villeneuve.

Star Rating: Three.

MALE DRAGON

When these two powerful signs meet there is an inevitable clash of personalities and the resulting sparks might easily set their large hearts aflame with passion. But both signs see each other as a challenge as opposed to a partnership. The male Dragon is surprised by the female Buffalo. Her sharp mind and rich, deep soul, so different on the surface at least, to the male of the species, are rare and exciting. The Buffalo's complexities are an attraction to begin with, something he hopes he might straighten out with the help of his abundant self-belief. But the affair turns sour when he finds the lady Buffalo wanting to take control of *him*. The lady Buffalo also underlines the somewhat shallow nature of the male Dragon's feelings, as it's sadly the case that he has a rather superficial view of romantic love. Luckily both signs are able to rectify mistakes quickly and their love affair will not drag painfully on.

Star Rating: Five slipping within a short while to two.

MALE SNAKE

Female Buffaloes are frequently intrigued by the male Snake's highly imaginative personality. The male Snake is humorous, artistic and wise. He has a form of sensuality which completely overwhelms the lady Buffalo. Using his subtle understanding of the senses, he winds his way into her most sheltered areas and cleverly soothes the female Buffalo's more complex emotions. The Buffalo's response is sometimes to be shocked by the depth of her own sensuality and at other times resistant. But she will give in fully at one stage to Snake's bewitching charm. Of the two pairings, the female Buffalo and male Snake have less understanding and is the least common.

Star Rating: Two, sometimes three.

MALE HORSE

The male Horse holds many attractions for the female Buffalo. He is a natural leader of any group, witty and full of personality. But he isn't one to be pushed around by the female Buffalo's often highly imperious temperament and there's something about the long moody silences that stem from her complex nature which alienates him. Both signs demand great independence in order to function properly, which is hardly the best of platforms to launch a loving union from. Not exactly a no-no, this is not, however, a relationship which collects Oscars for long term understanding.

Star Rating: One, and even two at a pinch.

MALE GOAT

Buffalo women seldom view men as mere objects of physical love and relationships tend to be formed with the long term in mind. However, male Goats often have a strongly sexual side to their nature which can easily topple the straight thinking female Buffalo into more fun and games than she bargained for. But the affair offers the Buffalo more than the Goat, who strict to his sign's capricious influence is unlikely to stick around for long, especially when the Buffalo gets one of her moods. As with all the female Buffalo's partners, the male Goat provides a stark contrast to her own highly individual personality and is therefore seen as a considerable temptation.

Star Rating: Zero as a rule, sometimes leaping to a surprising four.

MALE MONKEY

On the surface there doesn't seem much going for the fast thinking Monkey male, who lives off his wits and the more dependable, conversative Buffalo lady. But there is moving poetry in the heart of the female Buffalo, even though they sometimes find it hard to express. The Monkey male is a wizard at touching the sensual nerve of even the most reluctant female, and he might well find the emotionally complex Buffalo something of a challenge. As far as a love affair goes, this is not at all bad. At best, however, the affair will be the on/off kind, with the Buffalo finding herself less in command than in other relationships.

Star Rating: Three, sometimes four.

MALE ROOSTER

Jackpot time for the Buffalo female. Only two signs are completely compatible with the female Buffalo and the male Rooster is one. Neither is looking for a short term relationship and the love affair will soon establish itself as a winner and it won't be long before there's an announcement in the paper and a wedding list is on display at the local big store. Both animal signs are deeply conservative, usually with a big and small C, and neither cares to fool around when there's been a genuine commitment given. As a romance its short and sweet and then quickly down the aisle.

Star Rating: Five Big Ones

MALE DOG

There is something in the idealism of the gentleman Dog that the strong-minded Buffalo finds both laudable and attractive. He is warm and open in his affections and the Buffalo responds to his constant attentiveness. In turn the male Dog feels to a certain degree protected by the female Buffalo's strength of character. So what's wrong? Dogs are apprehensive and tend to worry over details. They are anxious and uncertain at times whereas the Buffalo sets her path out before her and follows it come what may. There are times when lovers must by their very nature travel the same path, but Buffalo and Dog will eventually find their paths head in different directions.

Star Rating: Two, sometimes three.

MALE PIG

A big romance with all the frills for the female Buffalo and male Pig. The jovial Pig male – full of fun and easy-going does wonders for the often romantically complex Buffalo. She laughs at his jokes, cooks him breakfast and makes him feel comfortable, the state most Pigs seek to obtain. In return, the Pig's honest and open brand of love-making creates an uncomplicated emotional state, something that Buffaloes seek to obtain. There can be a genuine understanding between a Buffalo and Pig, but there is a warning note which should be heeded. Pig fellows do not always enjoy life at the steady pace demanded by the Buffalo Ms. What's more, the Chinese Horoscopes point out that Pigs care little for their reputation, which is another way of saying they are not over interested in fidelity for its own sake. So Buffalo beware, do not take the big hearted Pig for granted.

Star Rating: Four, with an occasional five.

COMPATIBILITY OF MALE BUFFALOES IN MARRIAGE

FEMALE RAT

A Rat falling in love with a Buffalo is not an uncommon event and receives a high star rating, but wedding bells are bad news. They do nothing but knock two stars off the relationship. As an attraction of sexual opposites they have few if any rivals. But marriage opens up all sorts of hidden doors which, when opened, allow the more complete personality to emerge. This can sometimes produce no end of surprises, not all of them pleasant. The Buffalo is a world leader, no matter which sex, while the Rat uses her sharp mind to quite different ends. The Buffalo will dominate all aspects of the home and the Rat will be left feeling more and more a bystander waiting for the sparks to fly once more. But she'll wait in vain. In spite of the considerable warning signs, Rats tend to marry Buffaloes and as a result, this pairing is one of the most common. It also has a high rating for divorce. Of the two combinations, figures suggest more female Buffaloes marry male Rats than the other way round.

Star Rating: Two, although children might help to create a mutual interest.

FEMALE BUFFALO

Love is a fathomless sea of complexities for all Buffaloes and although there can be and often is great emotional involvement in a love affair, all the pointers show a path away from such a relationship. But marriage has some advantages that a short term affair doesn't. It creates a backbone, and conservative creatures like the Buffalo frequently flourish when the banns are read. The security of married life is one of the many constants they seek. But two Buffaloes! The best that a pair of these single minded, unique types can hope for is a life style that keeps them miles apart for long periods. Children will not help cement the marriage as they only underline the need for mother and father to stay close to each other. One Buffalo can not lead another, or share their natural powers of leadership. A big, big mistake. Playwright Tom Stoppard is a Buffalo, as is his TV doctor wife, Miriam. In their case it's so far, so good. But keep your eyes open for changes.

Star Rating: One at the very most. But usually minus zero.

FEMALE TIGER

In love, the male Buffalo and female Tiger have an unexpected attraction for each other. This they manage in spite of the fact they have absolutely nothing in common. After a few glorious hours when both animal signs experience the excitement of having their emotional extremes exposed, the flames die to a thick and choking smoke. Then there is nothing. Some animal signs who are dished out very low points for understanding *can* make it. But these signs are the exception and never the rule. A Buffalo and Tiger in marriage rate the lowest of the low and such comfort as they might give each other is wiped out by the horrendous differences which divide them.

Star Rating: Zero. The Pits.

FEMALE CAT

Of the two pairings the male Buffalo/female Cat is marginally less auspicious. But there is a great deal to be said for such a relationship. Curiously the affair rates no higher for turning into marriage and the understanding that exists between these two animal signs remain fairly constant no matter what the status. The female Cat adds a touch of refinement to the Buffalo's life, and her methodical approach to the home and family will suit him down to the ground. But the Cat is not given to great ideals and does not share the Buffalo's power seeking. This does form a gulf in their lives, but it is not serious.

Star Rating: Three.

FEMALE DRAGON

In a romance situation, male Buffalo and female Dragon might just about get themselves into a bed situation, but it won't be long before there's a parting of the ways. There really is nothing good to be said for this marriage and the fact that it is such a rarity is perhaps a vindication of the Chinese Horoscopes. The slightest ray of light appears when we are talking about a female Buffalo and male Dragon, but because these two powerful signs need to dominate even the smallest group, including the family, there can be no hope and nothing but enmity to fill their increasingly distant lives.

Star Rating: Zero.

FEMALE SNAKE

There's something about the female Snake which male Buffaloes find very difficult to resist. Not quite as openly warm as the Rat, a sign the Buffalo invariably falls for, the Snake has the power to bewitch, and to cling to those she adores. In marriage these two animal signs have a more than average chance of success, especially when the male is a Buffalo. He may well offer a unique view of life, which the female Snake, in her quiet wisdom will find absorbing. But she demands much understanding, especially during her moments of 'hibernation', those periods in which she is listening to her inner voice for direction. Here, alas, the male Buffalo will not be sympathetic.

Star Rating: Two, with a point up or down depending on the Buffalo's sensitivity.

FEMALE HORSE

The love affair which just about scraped home now blows up in a puff of wind. Independence is the key to the Horse's soul and you will always find that the lady Horse is her own boss regardless of who she chooses to walk life's path with. Male Buffaloes are incapable of genuinely sharing their position as head of the family, a fault which will drive the lady Horse to endless rages. Marriage has to be a shared partnership and here are two animal signs simply not capable of doing so, no matter what the circumstances. Peter Sellers was a Buffalo and once married Britt Eckland. Ms Eckland is a Horse and it was a very short marriage. On the other hand, a longer marriage for Buffalo Rod Steiger and Horse Claire Bloom.

Star Rating: Zero. But when a Buffalo's involved, anything is possible.

FEMALE GOAT

A better than average partner for the male Buffalo, and one which seems extremely popular by the number of female Goats who walk down the aisle with him. From a very low mark as lovers, the step into marriage seems the right one. With their mutual love of family life and the Goat's apparent acceptance of the tethering rope as a force for good in her life, it looks like full steam ahead. But the differences which divide them as romantic partners is ever present and there is always the likelihood that the lady Goat will wander, in the way that Goats do. And she must remember that although some animal signs are quick to overlook her indiscretions, the male Buffalo is not one. One of photographer David Bailey's four wives, Catherine, was born in a Goat year. It seemed an OK marriage while it lasted.

Star Rating: Three, maybe four, depending on the Goat's level of capriciousness.

FEMALE MONKEY

The female Monkey has few problems in any relationship, finding she can weave her clever spell, a mix of wit and flattery, on any animal sign. A love affair between female Monkey and male Buffalo rates high marks. She relaxes him and exposes his own highly individual personality. But marriage complicates the issue and the relationship has only a 50/50 chance of succeeding. Children are a good move in a Monkey and Buffalo marriage as they supply a focal point for both signs. Monkey ladies make first rate parents and the Buffalo male will always do his utmost, in a traditionalist kind of way, to insure his children's education is the best on offer. But the Monkey loves tricks and intrigue, and there is no room for either in the male Buffalo's home. Liz Taylor is a Monkey and her twice-married partner, the late Richard Burton a Buffalo. Nobody could say they didn't make a try of marriage or that they were closest when they weren't married.

Star Rating: Two.

FEMALE ROOSTER

A hundred per cent in love and now a hundred and one for marriage. Of all the choices open to the Buffalo and Rooster, this combination wins hands down. The conservative backbone of both animal signs is strengthened in partnership and their mutual support creates a solid and totally reliable unit. A family will help provide an even stronger base and should Buffalo husband and Rooster wife decide to go into business there will be few able to match them. A great natural relationship, it is none the less not as common a marriage as it should be, at least not first time round. One reason for this is that the Buffalo male is headstrong and his complex heart is too easily turned by signs that are not compatible, notably the Rat.

Star Rating: Five plus.

FEMALE DOG

Alas, a more than reasonable love affair does not improve with marriage. The Dog is an idealist and worries about the underprivileged at every level. Lady Dogs in particular care very strongly about injustices and are anxious to make this a better world. Buffalo males are not so caring. They are born to be leaders of men and often lack the kind of intimate sensitivity that the Dog seeks in a long term companion. A family might make a difference, offering some mutual interest outside their lack of shared ideals. But on the whole it is a marriage to avoid unless it is understood that ideals are not important. Wealth would help strengthen the bonds. Perhaps that's why Carlo Ponti, a Buffalo, and his beautiful Dog wife, Sophia Loren, have survived; not much idealism in Hollywood.

Star Rating: Zero rising to two at most.

FEMALE PIG

A fine romance but if it leads to marriage there'll be a few red faces and unhappy Pigs and Buffaloes. Things swing in a love affair, with the eager to please Piggy lady getting the most from the deeper sexuality found in the Buffalo chap. But the Buffalo male is a tough nut to crack in terms of long term relationships. He wants a lasting marriage, that is certain, but there is something in the Pig lady's character that falls short of his high handed demands. Perhaps it is her easy-going nature and her ability to flirt without feeling guilt that worry the complex Buffalo. It may be that the Pig wife wants more to life than the domestic role the Buffalo places her in. If the Pig lady lives up to her reputation as a home-maker, then the picture changes for the better. If, however, she is a Pig who is only interested in a good time, forget the wedding plans.

Star Rating: Two in most cases but with a point plus or minus depending on the Pig's ambitions.

COMPATIBILITY OF FEMALE BUFFALOES IN MARRIAGE

MALE RAT

A Rat falling in love with a Buffalo is not an uncommon event and receives a high star rating, but wedding bells are bad news. They do nothing but knock two stars off the relationship. As an attraction of sexual opposites they have few if any rivals. But marriage opens up all sorts of hidden doors which, when opened, allow the more complete personality to emerge. This can sometimes produce no end of surprises, not all of them pleasant. The Buffalo is a world leader, no matter which sex, while the Rat uses his sharp mind to quite different ends. The Buffalo will dominate all aspects of the home and the Rat will be left feeling more and more a bystander. In spite of the considerable warning signs, Rats tend to marry Buffaloes and, as a result, this pairing is one of the most common. It also has a high rating for divorce. Of the two combinations, figures suggest more female Buffaloes marry male Rats than the other way round. Prince Charles is a Rat and Princess Diana a Buffalo.

Star Rating: Two, although children might help to create a mutual interest.

MALE BUFFALO

Love is a fathomless sea of complexities for all Buffaloes and although there can be and often is great emotional involvement in a love affair, all the pointers show a path away from such a relationship. But marriage has some advantages that a short term affair doesn't. It creates backbone, and conservative creatures like the Buffalo frequently flourish when the banns are read. The security of married life is one of the many constants they seek. But two Buffaloes! The best that a pair of these single-minded, unique types can hope for is a life style that keeps them miles apart for long periods. Children will not help cement the marriage as they only underline the need for mother and father to stay close to each other. One Buffalo can not lead another, or share their natural powers of leadership. A big, big mistake. Playwright Tom Stoppard is a Buffalo, as is his TV-doctor wife, Miriam. In their case it's so far, so good. But keep your eyes open for changes.

Star Rating: One at the very most. But usually zero.

MALE TIGER

In love, the female Buffalo and the male Tiger have an unexpected attraction for each other. This they manage in spite of the fact they have absolutely nothing in common. After a few glorious hours when both animal signs experience the excitement of having their emotional extremes exposed, the flames die to a thick choking smoke. Then there is nothing. Some animal signs who are dished out very low points for understanding *can* make it. But these signs are the exception and never the rule. A Buffalo and Tiger in marriage rates the lowest of the low and such comfort as they might give each other is wiped out by the horrendous differences which divide them.

Star Rating: Zero. The Pits.

MALE CAT

Of the two pairings, the female Buffalo/male Cat is marginally less auspicious. But there is still a great deal to be said for such a relationship and the understanding that exists between these two animal signs remains fairly constant no matter what the status, married or not. The male Cat adds a touch of refinement to the Buffalo's life, and his methodical approach to the home, its finances and family will suit her down to the ground. But the Cat is not given to great ideals and does not share the Buffalo's power seeking. This does form a gulf in their lives, but it is not serious. Mrs Thatcher is a Buffalo and her husband, Denis, is a Cat.

Star Rating: Three.

MALE DRAGON

In a romance situation, female Buffalo and male Dragon might just about get themselves into a bed situation, but it won't be long before there's a parting of the ways. There really is nothing good to be said for this marriage and the fact that it is such a rarity is perhaps a vindication of the Chinese Horoscopes. The slightest ray of light appears when we are talking about a female Buffalo and male Dragon, but because these two powerful signs need to dominate even the smallest group, including the family, there can be no hope and nothing but enmity to fill their increasingly distant lives. Jane Fonda is a Buffalo and was once married to French director Roger Vadim, a Dragon. The marriage ended abruptly when he tried against her will to turn Jane into a sex goddess like Brigitte Bardot (Dog), whom he also married.

Star Rating:Zero

MALE SNAKE

There's something about the male Snake which female Buffaloes find very difficult to resist. Not quite as passionate as the Rat, whom the Buffalo invariably falls for, the Snake has great sexual power. In marriage these two animal signs have a more than average chance of success. The lady Buffalo may well offer a unique view of life, which the subtle male Snake will find absorbing. But the lady Buffalo must remember that Snakes demand much understanding, especially during moments of 'hibernation', those periods in which he is found inescapably listening to his ever present inner voice for direction. Here, alas, the active and often demanding female

Buffalo will not be as sympathetic as the situation requires. Mark Thatcher, a Snake, is married to a Buffalo, Diane – same sign as his mum. Sue Cook is a Buffalo, and *was* married to guitarist John Williams, a Snake.

Star Rating: Two, with a point up or down depending on the Buffalo's sensitivity.

MALE HORSE

The love affair which just about scraped home now blows up in a puff of wind. Independence is the key to the Horse's soul and you will always find that the Horse is his own boss regardless of whom he chooses to walk life's path with. Female Buffaloes are incapable of genuinely sharing their position as head of the family, a fault which will drive the male Horse into a sudden rage, another common trait of those born under their sign. Marriage has to be a shared partnership and here are two animal signs simply not capable of doing so, no matter what the circumstances.

Star Rating: Zero.

MALE GOAT

A better than average partner for the female Buffalo, and one which seems extremely popular by the number of male Goats who walk down the aisle with her. From a very low mark as lovers, the step into marriage seems the right one. With their mutual love of family life and the Goat's apparent acceptance of the tethering rope as a force for good in his life, it looks like full steam ahead. But the differences which divide them as romantic partners are ever present and there is always the likelihood that Billy Goat will wander, in the way that Goats do. And the Goat must remember that although some animal signs are quick to overlook his indiscretions, the female Buffalo is not one. Twiggy is a Buffalo lady and her latest husband, Leigh Lawson, is a Goat. They are said to be very happy.

Star Rating: Two, maybe three, depending on the Goat's level of capriciousness.

MALE MONKEY

The male Monkey has few problems in any relationship, finding he can weave his clever spell, a mix of wit, cunning and flattery on any animal sign. A love affair between male Monkey and female Buffalo rates higher than average marks. His cool style and humour relaxes her and exposes the Buffalo's own highly individual personality. But marriage complicates the issue and the relationship has only a 50/50 chance of succeeding. Children are a good move in a Monkey and Buffalo marriage as they supply a focal point for both signs. Monkey males make first-rate parents and the Buffalo female will always do her utmost, in a traditionalistic kind of way, to ensure her children's education is the best on offer. But the Monkey loves tricks and intrigue and there is no room for either in the female Buffalo's home.

Star Rating: Two.

MALE ROOSTER

A hundred per cent in love and now a hundred and one for marriage. Of all the choices open to the Buffalo and Rooster, this combination wins hands down. The conservative backbone of both animal signs is strengthened in partnership and their mutual support creates a solid and totally reliable unit. A family will help provide an even stronger base and should Buffalo wife and Rooster husband decide to go into business there will be few able to match them. A great natural relationship, it is none the less not as common a marriage as it should be, at least not first time round. One reason for this is that the Buffalo female is headstrong and her complex heart is too easily turned by signs that are not compatible, notably the Rat.

Star Rating: Five plus.

MALE DOG

Alas, a more than reasonable love affair does not improve with marriage. The Dog is an idealist and worries about the underprivileged at every level. Male Dogs care strongly about injustices and are anxious to make this a better world. Buffalo females are not so caring. They are born leaders of any group or relationship and often lack the kind of intimate sensitivity that the Dog frequently seeks in a long term companion. A family might make a difference, offering some mutual interest outside their lack of shared ideals. But on the whole it is a marriage to avoid unless it is understood that ideals are not important.

Star Rating: Zero rising to two at most.

MALE PIG

A fine romance but if it ends in marriage there'll be a few red faces and unhappy Pigs and Buffaloes. Things swing in a love affair, with the eager to please Piggy gentleman getting the most from the sexuality found in the Buffalo lady. But the Buffalo female presents difficulties in terms of long term relationships. She wants a lasting marriage, that is certain, but there is something in the male Pig that falls short of her high handed demands. Perhaps it is his easy-going nature and ability to flirt without feeling guilty that bother her. It may be that the Pig husband wants more to life than the domestic role the Buffalo unintentionally places him in. If the Buffalo lady lives up to the side of her influence which creates in her a home-maker, then the chances of success are greatly improved. If, however, she is a Buffalo who is only interested in domestic power struggles, forget the wedding plans. The marriage created by EastEnders Angie and Dirty Den is not untypical of Pig male and female Buffalo. Not surprisingly, in real life Anita Dobson is a Buffalo and Leslie Grantham a Pig.

Star Rating: Two in most cases but with a point plus or minus depending on the Buffalo's ambitions.

COMPATIBILITY OF MALE BUFFALOES IN FRIENDSHIP

MALE RAT

An interesting partnership which brings into play two signs with quite different approaches to life. When joined in friendship Rat and Buffalo have a great deal of respect for each other's abilities. Although there will be many difficult moments and lack of consideration from the complex Buffalo, the Rat will handle it without a fuss and they will nevertheless create a solid and lasting friendship. Richard Ingrams, former editor of *Private Eye* is a Buffalo and his successor, chosen by him, Ian Hislop, is a Rat.

Star Rating: Four.

MALE BUFFALO

Two Buffaloes in any kind of relationship is unusual. But as friends, and nothing more, there is every chance of a kind of friendship. There will be no quarter given, or taken, yet in spite of the outward lack of warmth there will be much inner admiration for each other's qualities and skills. Too individual ever to reach real understanding, mutual respect is what such a partnership produces. There are a number of Buffaloes in the left of British political life, Arthur Scargill, Tony Benn and Michael Foot among the leaders. But it could hardly be said that these men share much, inside or outside the political arena.

Star Rating: Two at a pinch. Never more than three and most cases much less.

MALE TIGER

Not much joy here for anything more than a passing friendship. There's plenty of room in any relationship for power, brains and bright wits joining hands, but this is not it. The Buffalo has the uncontrollable urge to dominate those close to him and the Tiger, usually brave and courageous, cannot find the extra reserve to meet the Buffalo's heavy demands. But there have been instances in which the Tiger was able to withstand the Buffalo's dominating personality, and together have created a partnership of lasting value. It is as if the very effort of keeping the relationship going forms the basis for the relationship itself. And it must be added that two such strong and imaginative creatures have much to give each other. Ernie Wise is a Buffalo and his long-time partner, Eric Morecambe, was a Tiger. However, I have heard that off-stage, the two comics had little in common.

Star Rating: Three at the most. Most times zero.

MALE CAT

A better than average friendship for the strong tough-minded Buffalo, who looks to the Cat for a second fiddle who is reliable and diplomatic in those areas of his life he finds a chore. This is to take nothing away from the Cat's thoughtful contribution to the partnership. It involves much self sacrifice to get really close to a Buffalo, and a great deal of understanding. And such loyalty will not always be rewarded. Even so, the Cat is aware of the Buffalo's temperament, and usually thinks the effort is worth it.

Star Rating: Three to four.

MALE DRAGON

One of the big off/on relationships, the Buffalo finds certain features of the Dragon infuriating but at the same time has enough intelligence to realise that they have more than a little to offer in the way of loyal friendship. Both signs dominate the world stage and as friends there is invariably a great deal of friction. But once they overcome their differences, however impermanently, many good things can grow from their collective strength. That said, it is not a common relationship and examples are few and far between.

Star Rating: Sometimes very low, sometimes just under five. A tough one to be specific about.

MALE SNAKE

It's commonly said that Buffaloes are solitary beasts who do not offer love or friendship easily. On the surface Snake people might be thought to be quite the opposite as many seem to possess an easy way with strangers and friends alike. But neither sign truly enjoys casual relationships and they are only really happy when they dig deep emotionally. The Snake clings to whomever or whatever he cares deeply about, sometimes strangling the object of his possessiveness in the process. The Buffalo, once their demand for loyalty is thwarted, is slow to forgive – if ever. The same is true of Snakes. So the problems of Snakes and Buffaloes in friendship are highlighted by the constant threat of high voltage temperaments clashing. Friendship is a case of giving and taking, two of these signs' weakest points. Van Gogh was a Buffalo and his faithful brother Theo, a Snake. Theo clung to Vincent and a year after the great artist committed suicide in 1890, Theo died of a broken heart.

Star Rating: Three is average. Seldom more, often less.

MALE HORSE

Every chance of a strong friendship here, with much mutual respect and understanding shown in the initial stages. But the Horse must have his freedom and must take important decisions on his own. The Buffalo's influence mirrors this aspect of the Horse's central trait. This means that working together ends up a fight for leadership, although if the boundaries can be clearly understood there is a chance that these two independent signs can form a friendship of lasting value. Goons Peter Sellers and Spike Milligan are a Buffalo and Horse respectively but it must be said that they have little in common outside of their wonderful working life together.

Star Rating: Three is usual, but with a point up for casual friends and two or more points down for business partners.

MALE GOAT

Although marriage between these two quite different signs stands a more than even chance of succeeding, in simple friendship the differences are exposed to a telling degree. The Buffalo is certainly able to tether the Goat's waywardness, but can he be bothered? Goats adore the good life and social intrigue whereas the Buffalo has little or no interest in what he usually sees as trivial pursuits. Not friends, not enemies, a non-starter if ever there was one and try as I might, I can find no examples of a successful partnership between Buffalo and Goat.

Star Rating: Zero.

MALE MONKEY

Not much to write home about, I am sorry to say. Most Buffaloes are straight talkers and straight dealers. They work to their positive strengths and succeed in all walks of life by using the full weight of their powerful personal conviction to reach whatever goal they decide. In relationships they use the same criteria, never shilly-shallying and demanding a one hundred per cent fidelity. This is not how the clever and sometimes artful Monkey runs their life. Tricks are what Monkeys are good at, and playing the field – even though you will never find a Monkey to admit it. In terms of a pure friendship, a Buffalo and Monkey is one for the birds. Imagine Alex Higgins (Buffalo) partnering Stephen Hendry (Monkey).

Star Rating: Zero.

MALE ROOSTER

So few relationships work out for a Buffalo that it is a delight to be able to say that the Rooster and Buffalo is a winner in practically every department. Both intensely private about their most personal feelings and conservative in their views, Buffalo and Rooster have an understanding which neither needs to openly admit. A long chat about the merits of courgette pollination is likely to be the centre of a conversation between Buffalo and Rooster. A strong and solid friendship without frills. Bobby Robson is a Rooster and Peter Shilton is a Buffalo. Robson's loyalty to Shilton has bordered, some have said, on the side of foolishness, playing him in an England side when the once-great keeper was past his international prime.

Star Rating: Five almost always.

MALE DOG

Faithful and idealistic the loyal dog demands little but affection and appreciation. Buffaloes in turn demand loyalty and lots of it. So why does this friendship rate so poorly? The truth is that in their hearts, Buffaloes are reactionaries, no matter what their political status and Dogs are left wing, determined radicals who will risk everything for what they believe. A clash of principles is inevitable. Martin Amis, the author and son of Kingsley, is a Buffalo. Mr Amis senior is a Dog. They have so little understanding that the two writers even refused to sit together to have their joint portrait painted for the National Portrait Gallery.

Star Rating: One, maybe two at most. Most times zero.

MALE PIG

A high number of Pigs and Buffaloes get on extremely well together and it is one of the better relationships. The Pig lacks a degree of initiative and the broad imagination of the Buffalo, his solid and dependable nature are all a bonus in forming the partnership and building confidence. Hard-working and honest, the Pig's influence is a highly compatible feature in the creation of a friendship. But the social life, which Pigs adore, is not something the Buffalo always places high on their list of priorities, so a business partnership is recommended. But even the most serious Buffalo is warmed by the open-hearted Pig. Charles Rolls was a Buffalo and his partner in building the world's finest automobile, Henry Royce, was a Pig.

Star Rating: Four tops, two bottom.

COMPATIBILITY OF FEMALE BUFFALOES IN FRIENDSHIP

FEMALE RAT

There is no doubt that the Buffalo, both male and female, present themselves as strong and resolute friends. But there is not much leeway and the Buffalo insists on having the last word. They run the emotional side of any relationship and often make impossible demands on the loyalty of those they choose to befriend. Should they choose to, the Rat can cope easily with all but the most complex Buffalo, receiving a positive and fruitful role in a sound relationship for their efforts.

Star Rating: Four.

FEMALE BUFFALO

This is not a relationship you will bump into every day of the week, month or even year. In fact, two female Buffaloes getting together as friends is almost unheard of. Having said that, in the unlikely event that these two solitary creatures are forced into understanding each other, a friendship *could* emerge. It might even be quite satisfying to both sides. The question is, could you imagine the Buffalo Mrs Thatcher forming a close relationship with someone like herself.

Star Rating: Zero minus 99 times out of 100.

FEMALE TIGER

This is an odd one. In nearly every instance the Chinese warn against Buffaloes and Tigers getting within ear shot of each other, and it must be stated that the Chinese are right – in most cases they are one hundred per cent correct. But the female Tiger and Buffalo are in a sense saved by their strong masculine influence. Both signs need to dominate, but in the female form of the Buffalo and Tiger, these powerful instincts cancel each other out. This leaves both vulnerable in areas where they might normally be strong and as a result opens them up to more than average interdependence.

Star Rating: Three, which is really high for this pairing, sometimes dropping to the usual zero.

FEMALE CAT

The Cat's gentle feline influences grace all lasting friendships, a fact the sometimes awkward Buffalo is not slow to appreciate. Normally speaking, Cats are not looking to run a relationship and they usually leave the running of even the most tenuous of friendships in the other's hands. Always thoughtful of what they say, Cats are generally happy to let the Buffalo dictate the friendship's path, dropping hints as to its future as opposed to making direct statements. A happy relationship as long as the Buffalo does not tread too often on the Cat's tail. Cats have very sharp claws. Famous tennis doubles stars of an earlier time Shirley Fry and Doris Hart were Cat and Buffalo respectively.

Star Rating: Three to four most times.

FEMALE DRAGON

Difficult. Another case of male influence on female shoulders, with the result that the female side of these strong personalities is subjected to an invasion of unnatural masculine impulses. But where the negative sides of these influences cancel each other out, there is hope. The influence creates two ladies who prefer their own company – not the most auspicious pointer to lasting friendship. And the advice from the Chinese is not, should it be on the cards, to go into business without firm ideas on who does what.

Star Rating: One, sometimes one and a half.

FEMALE SNAKE

Marriage and love offer Snake and Buffalo hope but not the mundane realm of day to day friendship. Passion is what binds these two animal signs and without it there is not a great deal left in common. The subtle Snake becomes increasingly difficult for the Buffalo, who likes her friendships cut and dried. Men are what Snake ladies understand best, and what Buffalo ladies understand least. The females of both species are better off without each other's company for more than a few hours at a time.

Star Rating: Zero. Maybe a teeny weeny one at a pinch.

FEMALE HORSE

Every chance of a strong friendship here, with much mutual respect and understanding shown in the initial stages. But the Horse must have her freedom and must take important decisions on her own. The Buffalo's influence mirrors this aspect of the Horse's central trait. This means that working together ends up as a fight for leadership, although if the boundaries can be clearly understood there is a chance that these two independent signs can form a friendship of lasting value.

Star Rating: Three is usual, but with a point up for casual friends and two or more points down for business partners.

FEMALE GOAT

Although marriage between these two quite different signs stands a more than even chance of succeeding, in simple friendship the differences are exposed to a telling degree. The Buffalo is certainly able to tether the Goat's waywardness, but can she be bothered? Goats adore the good life and social intrigue whereas the Buffalo has little or no interest in what she usually sees as trivial pursuits. Not friends, not enemies, a non-starter if ever there was one and try as I might, I can find no examples of a successful partnership between lady Buffalo and Goat.

Star Rating: Zero.

FEMALE MONKEY

Another non-starter. The Buffalo has little time for the easy going and over-flexible attitudes of the Monkey. As in many of the Buffalo's relationships, the reasons why they don't work out are often so deep and complex that no one, not even the Buffalo herself, can explain it. But nearly always, the Buffalo is capable of distant although quite sincere admiration for another's abilities. It is just tough for the Buffalo to pay lip service to them. Lady Monkeys are quick to make friends of almost anyone, but they will not find a great reward in their attempts to get close to the Buffalo.

Star Rating: An iddy-biddy one at most.

FEMALE ROOSTER

Hats off to one of the great relationships. Here, lady Rooster and lady Buffalo have no end of subjects in common. Both deeply conservative and careful not to let the other peer too deeply into their personal life, theirs is a friendship born from mutual trust and affection. Hours in the rose garden, chats over coffee, trips to the museum – there is no limit to the boundaries of friendship and understanding. Need I say more? The Chinese wouldn't.

Star Rating: Five plus!

FEMALE DOG

Dog ladies have fewer anxious moments than their male counterparts, or should I say that they allow anxiety to hold less sway. This may lead them to enjoy a relationship free of self-doubt and constant analysis: 'Have I done the right thing?'etc, etc. Friendships are the centre of a Dog's life and they often treat a relationship as carefully as a fragile flower. Buffaloes are not so friendship orientated. They ask loyalty and don't bother giving it in return. They make demands that the Dog is happy to go along with, at least in the early stages. For a picture of these two signs just bring to mind the attitude of Mrs Edwina Currie, a Dog, to that dear Buffalo Mrs T.

Star Rating: One or two. Three is the very top.

FEMALE PIG

A very good understanding exists between the Pig lady and her Buffalo friend. Pigs generally make pals with everyone, are extremely sociable and are capable of enjoying themselves without going over the top. With the Pig lady as a companion, the Buffalo is able to let herself go. Lacking a little initiative, Pigs are attracted to the Buffalo's sense of conviction. In turn, the Buffalo has a partner who does not attempt to try and direct the way the relationship should develop. Plenty for both to do and plenty to keep them together.

Star Rating: Four.

THE TIGER

1902	February 8th to January 28th	**1903**
1914	January 26th to February 13th	**1915**
1926	February 13th to February 1st	**1927**
1938	January 31st to February 18th	**1939**
1950	February 17th to February 5th	**1951**
1962	February 5th to January 24th	**1963**
1974	January 23rd to February 10th	**1975**
1986	February 9th to January 28th	**1987**

'Hold that Tiger, hold that Tiger, hold that
Tiger ...'

Tiger Rag

THE YEAR OF THE TIGER

Tigers are born under the sign of courage. In some Asian countries, the Tiger is a national symbol who, it is believed, acts as a protection against the Three Great Disasters: fire, theft and evil spirits. Tigers are both brave and powerful, with a strong sense of their personal identity. For those born under the Tiger's influence, to be *somebody* is paramount. But whoever the Tiger becomes, it must be of their own making. This said, Tigers will go to any lengths to prove themselves. But whoever they become, Tigers do not like being ignored.

Tigers are strong on ideas and seem to possess a never-ending stream. They are not types to go unnoticed and will frequently rise to a position of high command. Even so, Tigers seldom enjoy total responsibility, preferring to be captains rather than generals. They adapt easily to any role that gives them an opportunity to display their abundant courage and imagination.

Tigers are impetuous and born rebels. They love a good scrap and few other signs are better equipped to win. It is a great mistake to tangle with a Tiger or to try and push one around. But for all their power and strength, the Tiger has a serious flaw – they are short-paced creatures. First off the mark, a Tiger will quickly lead the field but the chances of them staying ahead over a long distance are remote. Emotionally stuck in the mud, a Tiger loses all sense of their identity. Depression quickly sets in and it takes a massive effort from all those around to get the Tiger up and running. But once back in the race, a Tiger soon forgets about yester-day, their concentration fixed firmly on the next exciting project.

Tigers are extremely generous and when a Tiger makes a

new friend they tend to give everything all at once. In love, Tigers are truly reckless and will often risk everything to obey their demanding heart. In fact, Tigers go through life taking risks, which is why the Chinese say that danger is a constant companion. Quick to praise, Tigers are also quick to criticise, and they do so openly. Nevertheless, the Tiger, helped by their fertile imagination, makes a first-class parent who teaches by example. Because their emotions tend to fizzle out, Tigers do not find lasting friendships easy.

The three phases of a Tiger's life will be unpredictable, a word which could easily sum up their character. During childhood, the Tiger is a constant source of worry to their parents. Young Tigers are full of vigour one second and go frighteningly silent the next. Tiger girls are usually tom boys, who will doubtless add a few extra lines to their parents' foreheads. The middle period, dotted with alternating self doubt and over confidence, is the most difficult. But once through the danger zone, a Tiger's old age is as peaceful as any Tiger is likely to want it to be.

COMPATIBILITY OF MALE TIGERS IN LOVE

FEMALE RAT

Tiger males are direct and up front in love as they are with everything else in life. They risk all they have for love and seldom question their actions until later. This naturally has an inspiring influence on the passionate female Rat and in the early days of a love affair female Rat and male Tiger are unstoppable. Not great at staying any course for long, both Rat and Tiger will soon part by mutual agreement and with fond memories. The hit record 'Passing Strangers' was, appropriately, sung by a Rat and Tiger team – Sarah Vaughan and Billy Eckstine.

Star Rating: Two, if only for the splendid opening.

FEMALE BUFFALO

Most aspects of the Buffalo character are emphatic, and their relationships with other animal signs are no exception. Of all the signs, a match between female Buffalo and male Tiger rates the lowest. The Chinese Horoscopes write warnings against it in ten feet tall letters which say, DON'T! But the odd thing is that these two signs are powerfully attracted to each other and in my experience are frequently found trying to make a relationship work. The problem is, however, that the Buffalo tends to grind the Tiger down. His stubborn and intractable nature is in constant conflict with the fast moving but short paced Tiger. In love they have nothing in common. While the Tiger is full of generosity, taking any risk the affair demands, the Buffalo ponders and searches his complex heart for a way to control the situation. Do not be fooled by the sudden infatuation, Buffalo and Tiger should avoid each other like the plague.

Star Rating: Zero minus zero.

FEMALE TIGER

This is a love affair which is over in a flash. Long term plans are not advised as the passion between these powerful and headstrong creatures will quickly die when one attempts to outdo the other in the love stakes. But the sparks might be worth the frustration at the end, when both parties are left down in the dumps asking themselves what all the fuss was about? And as always, no recriminations. Short and sweet.

Star Rating: Five for five minutes. Then a line of zeros.

FEMALE CAT

It is commonly believed that Cats and Tigers are part of the same family. Not so. Cats have always presented themselves as highly social creatures, whereas Tigers are happiest when carving out a more isolated life-style. Cat ladies are sensual and sometimes more private about their feelings than they care to admit. Tigers are up front, especially the males. They chase love hard when they so desire and do not like to be made to look foolish when they don't make it. Under certain kinds of emotional pressure, both signs tend to crack up – for different reasons, I must stress – and love is full of emotional pitfalls. But there is a chance, albeit slender, that the sensuous desires of the Cat will be attended to by the amorous if sometimes over demonstrative Tiger and vice versa.

Star Rating: One, sometimes two.

FEMALE DRAGON

One of the high scoring love affairs – a veritable top of the table relationship which allows both impulsive signs full rein. Headstrong and generous in any relationship, and usually at any stage, Tiger and Dragon find themselves totally gripped by love and both adore the romance of an affair. Of course, it will end, gloriously, either in marriage or as just friends; parting is such sweet sorrow. Of the two pairings, the male Dragon/female Tiger is the most complete but it is not worth splitting hairs over. Go for it, whatever the pairing and enjoy!

Star Rating: Five and more if there's room.

FEMALE SNAKE

Tigers are very often captivated by the bewitching charms of the female Snake. They behave in stark contrast to the Tiger's own volatile and often aggressive romantic antics. Cool in the first stages, and watchful of the predator's advances, Snakes must be truly certain of the man they choose to love before they let go. As so frequently happens in the case of the male Tiger, the female Snake is put off by the lack of subtlety and, in a sense, bites him out of fear. As you will have gathered, a pretty messy sort of relationship which promises more than is delivered by either side.

Star Rating: One at the very most.

FEMALE HORSE

This is a relationship worth pursuing. There is something in the influence of a Horse woman which brings out the more stable side to a Tiger's temperament. Horse ladies have a pronounced practical streak which bodes well for the long term problem of keeping the Tiger going through his bleaker moments. But she also enjoys a delightfully adoring heart, which in the first throes of a love affair excites all but the most stone-hearted. Ever amorous, the Tiger is warmed by his Horse lover and there are no limits to the relationship. But there is a tiny word of warning. Horses and Tigers both tire easily. Horses become bored for no reason and Tigers run out of puff.

Star Rating: Five with reservations. Three would be the lowest.

FEMALE GOAT

No one is more capricious than Miss Goat. Proclaiming love to one, she might easily be giving someone else the same story. Wayward and a tease, Goat ladies need a firm hand to lead them through even the most casual relationship. The Tiger is one such sign, and certainly not a creature to be stood up or passed over for another. They don't like being lied to, ignored, or indeed upstaged. So what's in it for these two? The answer is that Goats have great artistry and when they make love, tend to give themselves completely to who they happen to be with. This suits the Tiger fine.

Star Rating: A tough one. Three at a pinch. Occasionally four.

FEMALE MONKEY

This is a relationship very much created from a spirit of suck-it-and-see style optimism. Nothing can be said actually against it but however hard you look, it is not easy to find a lot to say in favour of Tiger male and Miss Monkey letting it all hang out. Monkeys have never been heard to say no to a new experience and the Tiger is no slouch when it comes to offering them. But there is something in the chemistry of both signs which does not sit comfortably when placed together. The Tiger is just a little too rebellious and active; the Monkey a teeny-weeny bit too open to other offers.

Star Rating: This is not a cop out, but this relationship is almost impossible to pin down. Two is average.

FEMALE ROOSTER

Private Rooster lady meets vigourous male Tiger and is usually left wondering what to do about it. However, there are compensations. The Tiger is intrigued by the Rooster lady's candour, and sees her openness as a quality sympathetic to his own rebellious instincts. But love affairs are not usually enhanced by the Tiger's sense of rebellion, or helped by the censorious wall the female Rooster places around her deepest feelings. But they do quite enjoy a mutual frankness, which gives these two animal signs a slight chance of making it. Overall, though, not much future.

Star Rating: One.

FEMALE DOG

In the early stages of romance, a Dog and Tiger discover they have more to share than just a physical relationship. There are few better partners for the Tiger and the Dog is quick to appreciate this happy state of affairs. Dogs tend to suffer from a constant niggling sense of anxiety, which the Tiger with his warm generosity and straight talk is more than capable of dispelling. In turn, the Tiger is fired by the Dog's strong will and care during his not infrequent periods of inner uncertainty. So good is the long term relationship that short term it merits fewer stars than expected.

Star Rating: Three, sometimes two.

FEMALE PIG

Another winner for the Tiger. Like the Dog, the Pig lady offers the energetic and powerful Tiger a splendidly solid emotional stage to perform on. Pig ladies build the Tiger's confidence. The Pig's influence is based on a mix of hard work and hard play, which offers the Tiger plenty of room to move around in. At no time will he feel caged – a fatal position for the Tiger, as you can doubtless imagine. Pigs get large doses of the Tiger's open heart and generous nature for their trouble, plus all the headaches when the Tiger is down in the dumps! But the honest Pigette is not one to shirk from a personal crisis and will be on hand to lift her Tiger's spirits.

Star Rating: Three minimum but often rising to five for the male Tiger/female Pig combination.

COMPATIBILITY OF FEMALE TIGERS IN LOVE

MALE RAT

Tiger females are direct and up front in love, as they are with everything else in life. They risk all for love and seldom question their actions until later. This naturally has an inspiring influence on the passionate male Rat and in the early days of a love affair, male Rat and vigorous female Tiger are unstoppable. They both give everything, and there's plenty to give! But there is no genuine understanding between the two signs and once it is clear that the whole deal has only been sexual, Rat and Tiger will part, often on good terms.

Star Rating: Two, if only for the mad, mad early days.

MALE BUFFALO

Most aspects of the Buffalo character are emphatic, and their relationships with other animal signs are no exception. Of all the signs, a match between male Buffalo and female Tiger rates the lowest. The Chinese Horoscopes write warnings against it in letters ten feet tall which say, DON'T! But the odd thing is that these two signs are powerfully attracted to each other and in my experience are frequently found trying to make a relationship work. The problem is, however, that the Buffalo tends to grind the Tiger down. His stubborn and intractable nature is in constant conflict with the fast moving but short paced Tiger. In love they have nothing in common. While the lady Tiger is full of generosity, taking any risk the affair demands, the Buffalo ponders and searches his complex heart for a way to control the situation. Do not be fooled by a sudden infatuation, Buffalo and Tiger should avoid each other like the plague.

Star rating: Zero

MALE TIGER

This is a love affair which is over in a flash. Long term plans are not advised as the passion between these powerful and headstrong creatures will quickly die when one attempts to outdo the other in the love stakes. But the sparks might be worth the frustration at the end, when both parties are left down in the dumps, asking themselves what all the fuss was about. And as always, no recriminations. Short and sweet.

Star Rating: Five for five minutes. Then a line of zeros.

MALE CAT

It is commonly believed that Cats and Tigers are part of the same family. Not so. Cats have always presented themselves as highly social creatures, whereas Tigers are happiest when carving out a more isolated lifestyle. Cat males are sensual and sometimes more private about their feelings than they care to admit. Tigers are up front, even the ladies. They love hard and deep and do not like to be made to look foolish as a result of love coming unstuck. Under certain kinds of emotional pressure, both signs tend to crack up – for different reasons, I must stress – and love is full of emotional pitfalls. But there is a chance, albeit slender, that the often sensuous desires of the Cat will be attended to by the amorous if sometimes over demonstrative Tiger and vice versa

Star Rating: Two. Lady Tiger and male Cat are the better coupling.

MALE DRAGON

One of the high-scoring love affairs – a veritable top of the table relationship which allows both impulsive signs full rein. Headstrong and generous in any relationship, and usually at any stage, Tiger and Dragon find themselves totally gripped by love and both adore the romance of an affair. Of course, it will end, gloriously, either in marriage or as just friends; parting is such sweet sorrow. Of the two pairings, the male Dragon/female Tiger is the most complete. Go for it and enjoy!

Star Rating: Five and more if there's room.

MALE SNAKE

Tigers are very often captivated by the charm, subtle humour and quiet sexuality of the male Snake. Tiger ladies are usually quite fearless in love and once they decide, they act without hesitation. But even the most forward male Snake, and there are many, acts on a different set of impulses. They still need time to feel right about their actions, however exciting the prospect. Whereas the female Tiger is dominated by a male sign, the Snake is essentially a female sign. As you will have gathered, a pretty messy sort of relationship which promises more than is delivered by either side.

Star Rating: One at the very most.

MALE HORSE

This is a relationship worth pursuing. There is something in the practical influence of a male Horse which balances the Tiger's often fluctuating temperament. Socially at ease, the Horse has an instinct for the Tigress's deepest passion. Ever amorous, the danger-loving side of the Tiger is excited by her elegant Horse lover and there are no limits to the relationship. But there is a tiny word of warning. Horses and Tigers both tire easily. Horses become bored for no reason and Tigers run out of puff.

Star Rating: Five with reservations. Three would be the lowest.

MALE GOAT

No one is more capricious than the Goat. Proclaiming his undying love to one, he might easily be giving someone else the same story. As a result, Goat males need a firm hand to lead them through even the most casual relationship. The lady Tiger is one such sign, and certainly not a creature to be stood up or passed over for another. They don't like being lied to, ignored, or indeed upstaged. So what's in it for these two? The answer is that Goats have a great artistry and when they make love, tend to give themselves completely to who they happen to be with. This suits the Tiger fine.

Star Rating; A tough one. Three at a pinch. Occasionally four.

MALE MONKEY

This is a relationship very much created from a spirit of suck-it-and-see-style optimism. Nothing can be said actually against it but however hard you look, it is not easy to find a lot to say in favour of the Tiger female and Mr Monkey letting it all hang out. Monkeys have never been heard to say no to a new experience and even the most feminine Tiger is no slouch when it comes to offering them. But there is something in the chemistry of both signs which does not sit comfortably when placed together. The Tiger is just a little too rebellious and active; the Monkey a tweeny-weeny bit too open to other offers.

Star Rating: This is not a cop out, but this relationship is almost impossible to pin down. Two is average.

MALE ROOSTER

Up front Rooster male meets exciting female Tiger and is usually left wondering what to do about it. It looks great on paper but the reality is not the five star that's promised. However, there are compensations. The Tiger is intrigued by the Rooster's candour, and sees his openness as a quality sympathetic to her own sometimes rebellious instincts. But love affairs are not usually enhanced by the Tiger's sense of rebellion, or helped by the often cocksure stance the male Rooster uses to protect his deepest feelings. But they do quite enjoy a mutual frankness, which gives these two animal signs a slight chance of making it. Overall, though, not much future.

Star Rating: One.

MALE DOG

In the early stages of romance, a Dog and Tiger discover they have more to share than just a physical relationship. There are few better partners for the Tiger and the Dog is quick to appreciate this happy state of affairs. Dogs, more the men than the women, tend to suffer from a constant niggling sense of anxiety, which the Tiger, with her warm generosity and straight talk, is more than capable of dispelling. In turn, the female Tiger is fired by the Dog's strong will and his thoughtfulness during her not infrequent periods of inner uncertainty. So good is the long term relationship that, short term, this pair merits fewer stars than expected.

Star Rating: Three, sometimes two.

MALE PIG

Another winner for Mistress Tiger. Like the Dog, the Pig male offers the energetic and powerful Tigress a splendidly solid emotional stage to perform on. Pig males build the Tiger's confidence. The Pig's influence is based on a mix of hard work and hard play, which offers the Tiger plenty of room to move around in. At no time will he feel caged – a fatal position for the Tiger, as you can doubtless imagine. Pigs get large doses of the Tiger's open heart and generous spirit for their trouble, plus a few headaches when the Tiger is down in the dumps! But the honest Pig is not one to shirk from a personal crisis and will be on hand to lift his wonderful Tiger's spirits.

Star Rating: Four.

COMPATIBILITY OF MALE TIGERS IN MARRIAGE

FEMALE RAT

Both signs produce the type of lover to act on impulse, and in some cases recklessly. But marriage has the habit of calming down even the most hot-blooded Romeo. The Tiger, in spite of his up-front generosity, is a rebel at heart, and quickly establishes himself as the boss of any team. This might cause a serious rift, especially if the Rat is the introvert who insists on planning everything to the last detail. And when the Rat's life hits a bad spell there'll be another. Forced into a corner the Rat's aggressive streak will immediately dominate. She'll become pushy, her natural charm, of which there is an abundance, will go out of the window and she'll view her Tiger husband as little more than an emotional threat. From then on it's downhill all the way.

Star Rating: Zero. Male Rat and female Tiger might just manage a single star.

FEMALE BUFFALO

In love, the female Buffalo and male Tiger have an unexpected attraction for each other. This they manage in spite of the fact that they have absolutely nothing in common. After a few glorious hours when both animal signs experience the excitement of having their emotional extremes exposed, the flames die to a thick and choking smoke. Then there is nothing. Some animal signs who are dished out very low points for understanding *can* make it. But these signs are the exception and never the rule. A Buffalo and Tiger in marriage rates the lowest of the low and such comfort as they might give each other is wiped out by the horrendous differences which divide them.

Star Rating: Zero. The Pits.

FEMALE TIGER

Two Tigers in the same cage! Well, to be honest, there isn't much to add. However, I do know two Tiger couples. One set have been married seventeen years. Both partners are extremely independently minded, as one might expect from the Tiger influence, and only really have their one daughter as a point of mutual understanding. The second set have only been married a matter of months. The lady Tiger has been married twice before, and the male Tiger once. This time, I am told by both and with typical Tiger optimism, it's for real. Hmm! To sum up, two Tigers in marriage *can* work, but the odds are really stacked firmly against it.

Star Rating: One, and that's being generous.

FEMALE CAT

A relationship that only just scrapes by as a romance does not get any better with marriage. In fact, there is a distinct possibility that matters will get worse. Cat ladies are easily thrown by the sudden emotional upheaval that Tigers frequently indulge in. Marriage is full of tiny moments of uncertainty, and a Cat's response is usually to shin up a tree when there's danger. Tigers sit tight, and fight it off. But Cats are good at listening and Tigers are full of ideas, which means a professional couple might make a go of it, especially where the positive influences of both signs can be utilised. Nanette Newman is a Cat and husband Bryan Forbes a Tiger.

Star Rating: Two.

FEMALE DRAGON

This is a marriage which promises a great deal and, provided neither party is made to feel over restricted by the other's highly personal needs, there is every chance it will succeed. Dragons and Tigers are hot-headed, explosive creatures with little or no time for the dim witted of this world. Together a Dragon and Tiger enjoy a high level of excitement and tend to treat marriage as an extended love affair. But with the female Dragon, there is always a tendency for them to want to run the show – something the male Tiger is never entirely happy about. A long talk prior to reading the banns about who does what is advisable. Weatherman Ian McCaskill is a Tiger and is married to a Dragon wife. He says they are best together when faced with adversity.

Star Rating: Four, with just a tiny reservation in respect of the long term viability.

FEMALE SNAKE

Lady Snakes, in the main, love deeply and usually focus their love on only one person at a time. The object of their desire will certainly know about it, often feeling possessed by his Snake partner. Bad news for the Tiger, who will feel caged.

However, there are female Snakes who are able, without quite knowing how and with apparent ease, to shift their affections from one to another. This kind of Snake is not what the male Tiger is looking for and heralds more bad news. But should the Snake restricted to a love for just one other happen on a less than ebullient Tiger, then there is a tiny, tiny chance that the marriage will last. However, the odds are that from the affair stage to the marriage something very serious will have got lost between female Snake and male Tiger, and in spite of the many attractions such a relationship continues to hold out, it will almost certainly end in disaster. The Chinese advise against it.

Star Rating: Zero.

FEMALE HORSE

Again we find two signs filled with mutual attraction. They both have great personalities and enjoy a full social life. The problem that continually faces the Tiger is his sudden loss of inner belief and when he is low he will need much in the way of gentle ego nursing. Lady Horses are witty, sociable and independent. They might fancy a spell at nursing, but there again, they might not. A marriage between a Tiger and a Horse working out depends entirely on how much give and take the Horse is prepared to offer. Horses, remember, fall in love at the drop of a hat, and Tiger males are easily seduced. Both, then, face difficulties in and out of their marriage.

Star Rating: Three.

FEMALE GOAT

The Chinese don't have a strong view either way about this relationship. Marriage between these two signs is a statistical rarity, which doesn't rule it out. Goat ladies do have a tendency to wander, but they have great social graces and are wonderful hostesses. Tigers are not slow to appreciate positive qualities in others, especially those close to them. And Goats adore being loved. If there is a problem, it is in the fact that Goats can't help wanting the limelight and Tigers do not enjoy being ignored. You pays your money and takes your choice. Comic film-maker Mel Brooks is a Tiger married to a Goat, the lovely actress Anne Bancroft.

Star Rating: Two? Difficult, but two is about right.

FEMALE MONKEY

A very middle of the road kind of marriage which promises bags of fun and ends up with both partners a touch confused as to why the bright lights went out. Strong on ideas, the Tiger is always quick to display his emotions whereas the Monkey is much more select in what they let on. Lovers of intrigue, the bright and witty Monkey prefers to play at love and their attitude to marriage is similarly affected. But children figure strongly in both signs and a family will certainly make all the difference to this couple's life.

Star Rating: Two.

FEMALE ROOSTER

Here's a rum couple. On the surface, the hot-headed Tiger and candid Rooster seem to have nothing in common but a long row about who's right and who's wrong. But from a poor romance grows a much better marriage. If the Tiger has a streak of controlled reason in his make-up, and there is nothing to suggest he hasn't, and the Rooster is not a spend-thrift, then the couple stand a fair chance of a fruitful and happy life together. Method and madness meet in the middle. With the Rooster in charge of the housekeeping and the Tiger firing on all cylinders (hopefully), these two can achieve a great deal together. But family life will not enhance their understanding of each other.

Star Rating; Three. Not more, not less.

FEMALE DOG

A short romance and a long and usually wonderfully productive marriage. From a few stars to the maximum for the Tiger and Dog, both of whom do not find long term relationships easy. Both signs demand a great deal from their partners and in this case they get everything and more. The idealist Dog has the perfect foil in the explosive and rebellious Tiger and few family units are better served or protected by these strong willed and often stubborn signs. The Tiger is the more inspiring parent, but the Dog is ever on hand to nurse, heal and love without reward. A top notch partnership in every single department and one helped by a large family.

Star Rating: Five plus.

FEMALE PIG

As discovered early in their romantic phase, marriage looks like a splendid idea, and it is. The homemaker-style Pig, which is the most usual variety, provides an ideal partner for the get-up-and-go Tiger. Offering plenty of support during his low periods, the Pig receives big helpings of Tiger generosity for her trouble – not that a Pig would ever think of it that way! This is a marriage full of mutual support, and there is little or nothing to prevent both partners enjoying a happy and eventful life together. Again, the Tiger is the more stimulating parent, and a family is advisable if these two signs are to retain their high star status. Male Tiger and female Pig get top marks.

Star Rating: Five.

COMPATIBILITY OF FEMALE TIGERS IN MARRIAGE

MALE RAT

Both signs produce high-octane lovers, but marriage has the habit of putting more than a few specks of dust in the carburettor. The Tiger, in spite of her warmth and generosity, is a rebel at heart, and sees herself as the boss of any team. This might cause a serious rift, especially if the Rat is the introvert who insists on planning everything to the last detail. And when the Rat's life hits a bad spell there'll be another. Forced into a corner, the Rat's aggressive streak will immediately dominate. He'll become pushy, his natural charm will go out of the window and he'll view his Tiger wife as an emotional threat. From then on it's downhill all the way. Captain Mark Phillips is a Rat and the Princess Royal a Tiger. It is said they don't talk to each other much out of horseriding.

Star Rating: Zero.

MALE BUFFALO

In love, the female Buffalo and male Tiger have an unexpected attraction for each other. This they manage in spite of the fact that they have absolutely nothing in common. After a few glorious hours when both animal signs experience the excitement of having their emotional extremes exposed, the flames die to a thick and choking smoke. Then there is nothing. Some animal signs who are dished out very low points for understanding *can* make it. But these signs are the exception and never the rule. A Buffalo and Tiger in marriage rates the lowest of the low and such comfort as they might give each other is wiped out by the horrendous differences which divide them.

Star Rating: Zero. The pits.

MALE TIGER

Two Tigers in the same cage! Well, to be honest, there isn't much to add. However, I do know two Tiger couples. One set have been married seventeen years. Both partners are extremely independently minded, as one might expect from the Tiger influence, and only really have their one daughter as a point of mutual understanding. The second set have only been married a matter of months. The lady Tiger has been married twice before, and the male Tiger once. This time, I am told by both and with typical Tiger optimism, it's for real. Hmm! To sum up, two Tigers in marriage *can* work, but the odds are really stacked firmly against it.

Star Rating: One, and that's being generous.

MALE CAT

A relationship that only just scrapes by as a romance does not get any better with marriage. In fact, there is a distinct possibility that matters will get worse. Cats of both sexes are easily thrown by the sudden emotional upheavals that Tigers frequently indulge in. A marriage is full of tiny moments of uncertainty, and a Cat's response is usually to shin up a tree when there's danger. Tigers sit tight, and fight it off. But Cats are good at listening and Tigers are full of ideas, which means a professional couple might make a go of it, especially where the positive influences of both signs can be utilised. Tiger Marilyn Monroe's happiest marriage was to Arthur Miller, a Cat.

Star Rating: Two.

MALE DRAGON

This is a marriage which promises a great deal and, provided neither party is made to feel over restricted by the other's highly personal needs, there is every chance it will succeed. Dragons and Tigers are hot-headed, explosive creatures with little or no time for the dim witted of this world. Together a Dragon and Tiger enjoy a high level of excitement and tend to treat marriage as an extended love affair. But the male Dragon always wants to run the show – something the female Tiger is never entirely happy about. Strong when faced with a crisis, a long talk prior to reading the banns about who does what is nevertheless advisable. The male Dragon/female Tiger pairing rates the better of the two.

Star Rating: Four to five, with just a tiny reservation in respect of the long term viability.

MALE SNAKE

Snakes, in the main, love deeply and usually focus their love on only one person at a time. The object of their desire will certainly know about it, often feeling possessed by his Snake partner. This is bad news for the Tiger, who feels such love as a form of being caged. And some male Snakes shift their affections, and are driven by sensual urges they have no control over. This heralds more bad news for the short-fused Tigress. The odds are that from the affair stage to the marriage something very serious will have got lost between male Snake and female Tiger, and in spite of the many attractions, if such a relationship continues to hold out, it will certainly end in disaster. The Chinese advise against it.

Star Rating: Zero.

MALE HORSE

Again we find two signs filled with mutual attraction. They both have great personalities and enjoy a full social life. The problem that continually faces the Tiger is her sudden loss of inner belief and when she is low she will need much in the way of gentle ego nursing. Male Horses are witty, sociable and independent. They might fancy a spell at nursing, but there again they might not. A marriage between a female Tiger and male Horse working out depends entirely on how much give and take the Horse is prepared to offer. Male Horses, remember fall in love at the drop of a hat, and Tiger females are seduced by danger. Both then face difficulties in and out of their marriage. Female Tiger and male Horse is the least auspicious pairing. Ali MacGraw married three times. Two were Horses – Steve McQueen and production boss Bob Evans.

Star Rating: Three, occasionally drifting lower.

MALE GOAT

The Chinese don't have a strong view either way about this relationship. Marriage between these two signs is a statistical rarity, which doesn't rule it out. Goat males do have a tendency to put themselves about a bit, even in marriage, but they are great company and warm and affectionate at heart. Tigers are not slow to appreciate positive qualities in others, especially those close to them. And Goats of both sexes adore being loved, to be the object of another's desire. If there is a problem, it is in the fact that male Goats can't help wanting the limelight and Tigers do not enjoy being ignored. On the other hand, the Tiger might be happy tethering the Goat. You pays your money and takes your choice. Ike and Tina Turner are a Goat and Tiger marriage – or they were.

Star Rating: Two? Difficult, but two is about right.

MALE MONKEY

A very middle of the road kind of marriage which promises bags of fun and ends up with both partners a touch confused as to why the bright lights went out. Strong on ideas, the female Tiger is always quick to display her emotions whereas the male Monkey is much more select in what they let on. Lovers of intrigue, the skilful Monkey is the master of his own heart and prefers to play at love. Their attitude to marriage

96

is similarly affected. But children figure strongly in both signs and a family will certainly make all the difference to this couple's life.

Star Rating: Two.

MALE ROOSTER

Here's a rum couple. On the surface, the hot-headed Tiger and candid Rooster seem to have nothing in common but a long row about who's right and who's wrong. But from a poor romance grows a much better marriage. If the Tiger has a streak of reason in her make-up, and there is nothing to suggest she hasn't, and the Rooster is not a spendthrift, then the couple stand a fair chance of a fruitful and happy life together. Method and madness meet in the middle. With the Rooster in charge of the housekeeping and the Tiger firing on all cylinders (hopefully), these two can achieve a great deal together. But family life will not enhance their understanding of each other. Male Rooster/female Tiger is the best combination, as in the relationship between HRH The Queen and Prince Philip.

Star Rating: Three. Not more, not less.

MALE DOG

A short romance and a long and usually wonderfully productive marriage. From a few stars to the maximum for the Tiger and Dog, both of whom do not find long term relationships easy. Both signs demand a great deal from their partners and in this case they get everything and more. The idealist Dog has the perfect foil in the explosive and rebellious Tiger and few family units are better served or protected by these strong willed and often stubborn signs. The Tiger is the more inspiring parent, but the Dog is ever on hand to add his own kind of devotional care without asking for any reward. A top notch partnership in every single department and one helped by a large family.

Star Rating: Five plus.

MALE PIG

As discovered early in their romantic phase, marriage looks like a splendid idea, and it is. The hard working, hard living, hard loving Pig provides an ideal partner for the get-up-and-go Tiger. Offering plenty of support during her low periods, the Pig receives big helpings of Tiger generosity for his trouble – not that a Pig would ever think of it that way! Lacking initiative, and better off when in a partnership, this is a marriage full of mutual support, and there is little or nothing to prevent both partners enjoying a happy and eventful life together. Again, the female Tiger is the more stimulating parent, and a family is advisable if these two signs are to retain their high star status. Male Tiger and female Pig get top marks.

Star Rating: Four lowest, five most times.

COMPATIBILITY OF MALE TIGERS IN FRIENDSHIP

MALE RAT

Not strong in marriage or love, male friendship offers far fewer problems for the Rat and Tiger. The Tiger's energy is attractive to the Rat, especially where business is concerned. And the Rat brings much needed clarity of vision. A busy friendship and full of excitement. Although the Everlys, Don and Phil, are brothers they have been together so long that they could also be classed as friends. Don is the Rat.

Star Rating: Three rising to four.

MALE BUFFALO

Not much joy here for anything more than a passing friendship. There's plenty of room in any relationship for power and bright wits joining hands, but this is not it. The Buffalo has the uncontrollable urge to dominate those close to him and the Tiger, usually brave and courageous, cannot find the extra reserve to meet the Buffalo's heavy demands. But there have been instances in which the Tiger is able to withstand the Buffalo's dominating personality, and together they have created a partnership of lasting value. It is as if the very effort of keeping the relationship going forms the basis for the relationship itself. And it must be added that two such strong and imaginative creatures have much to give each other. Ernie Wise is a Buffalo and his long-time partner, Eric Morecambe, was a Tiger. However, I have heard that off-stage, the two comics had little in common.

Star Rating: Three at the most. Most times zero.

MALE TIGER

Oh dear, what could be worse. Can you just picture the scene in the middle of the jungle, with two Tigers happily deciding which one is about to jump on and eat that luckless game hunter who has just run out of ammunition? No, no, a thousand times no to this relationship. When David Steel and David Owen had just formed their Alliance Party I was in the midst of doing an up-date version of my first Chinese Horoscope book. It was then the year of the Tiger and I warned the partnership would end in disaster. Indeed, I continued to write about these two Tigers as total non-starters right up until the final split.

Star Rating: The Pits.

MALE CAT

There's more to this friendship when there are no plans to be everlasting buddies. The Cat is methodical and refined, usually that is, and makes most signs an excellent companion.

The Tiger, by contrast, is vigorous and ever restless in his pursuit for inner awareness. Sometimes a little vain, Cats are not much interested in, nor do they suffer from, self-doubt. But they do cave in under pressure. This friendship will last just as long as the Tiger can cope with the Cat's more restrained life-style, and the Cat with the Tiger's attitude of changing everything at a moment's notice. Ex-Wham men George Michael and Andrew Ridgeley are a Tiger and Cat respectively. So were Laurel and Hardy.

Star Rating: Two, three if the Cat has a high Tiger tolerance. More if the Tiger doesn't run out of steam too soon.

MALE DRAGON

Because they are extremely strong willed and hot-headed in the face of authority, a Tiger's chum must reflect these characteristics. Yet at the same time he must do so without detracting from the Tiger's need to run things. Not an easy task, but one which the Dragon is more than able to cope with. Admittedly there are a few nettles to grasp in terms of who does what, if the friendship involves business, but once decided, each sign backs the other up to the hilt. Faced with a tough problem, a Tiger and Dragon are a force to be reckoned with and will not be taken for a ride. Both are generous to those around them and are always eager to help each other in the face of adversity.

Star Rating: Five.

MALE SNAKE

This is a real non-starter. The slow moving Snake, his deep intuition often disguised by a brash surface, has nothing in common with the fast thinking, ever changing Prince of the Jungle. Tigers charge about the place, emotionally, physically and just about every way there is. And they get results. Snakes sit and wait for the right moment to act – then they pounce and their bite is for keeps. It is the tortoise and the hare all over again.

Star Rating: Zero-0-0-0.

MALE HORSE

I have never quite understood why this relationship should be so strong. Tigers live in the jungle and fight alone. Horses are seldom wild, and in most cases helplessly domesticated. But perhaps that's the clue. In the wild, the Horse is more of a loner; certainly he enjoys a greater degree of independence. Tigers do need their friends to have guts and the ability to stick up two fingers at authority. The Horse is more than able to provide such back-up to the Tiger's anti-authoritarian traits. And the Horse has a slower fuse to his temperament, which creates a much needed balance. One of the best-selling author duos of the sixties consisted of a Tiger and Horse. Now better known as Home Secretary, Douglas Hurd, a Horse, and Andrew Osmond, a Tiger, wrote a string of best-sellers. *Smile on the Face of the Tiger* was the appropriate title of their most accomplished.

Star Rating: Four or five.

MALE GOAT

Tiger and Goats do not share much in common. However, it is sometimes the case that the Goat, ever in need of tethering, will respond to the Tiger's energetic nature. But there is always the difficulty that the capricious Goat will wander off just when the friendship demands he stick around. The composer Richard Rodgers was a Tiger, and worked with two brilliant lyricists, both Goats. Oscar Hammerstein and Lorenz Hart aided Rogers with his finest songs. The difficult genius, Lorenz Hart, could alter a lyric at a moment's notice, providing he could be kept away from the booze and his gay friends. Hammerstein preferred to write his lyrics in isolation, and found it a struggle even then.

Star Rating: Two minimum, four maximum.

MALE MONKEY

Tigers and Monkeys can only ever expect a middle to average understanding, no matter what sex or type of relationship they form. As in every other case, the Monkey carves his own lifestyle in stark contrast to that of the Tiger. Where these differences, or strengths, depending on your interpretation, can be welded together, there's an even chance of friendship. But I wouldn't place bets. Britain's most famous jazz singer, George Melly, is a Tiger and his long-standing trumpet playing side-kick, John Chiltern, is a Monkey. A more traditional musical relationship was that between light operetta masters Gilbert and Sullivan. Sir William Gilbert was the Monkey, and relied heavily on Tiger Sir Arthur Sullivan's clever music for his inspiration. So there is hope.

Star Rating: Two maximum.

MALE ROOSTER

Here's a pair of mates without a future. No matter that the Rooster is a saver or high spender or thrifty, and no matter how generous or overt the Tiger, these two have nothing in common. All Roosters are private at heart, and the Tiger is the most outgoing sign of all. When there's no hope, it's better to face up to it. That way, no one is left feeling bad about the consequences of a broken friendship. Try to imagine Jimmy White and Steve Davis having a night out together.

Star Rating: Zero.

MALE DOG

This is the odd couple out. In marriage and as lovers Dogs and Tigers rate among the best of all couples. The commitment, especially that made in a marriage, is central to a Dog and Tiger making the most of their respective influences. The less the commitment, the less will a Dog and Tiger find they have to offer each other. There's little doubt that as chums at the pub, or anywhere else, they will find more obstacles than bridges. On no account should they go into business.

Star Rating: Not easy to be accurate. Zero through to two.

MALE PIG

Nice one! Tigers and Pigs, especially the male variety, have a clear and precise understanding of each other and come to terms easily with their respective differences. Easy going Pigs go along with the Tiger's extremes and are not phased by the Tiger's hot-headed response to authority. In fact, the Pig enjoys most of what the Tiger offers. But Pigs are not rebels, and do not share the Tiger's constant need to change things – the only serious difference. Even so, with all the robust fun and bubbling energy these two create, there's plenty to keep them together. Elton John is a Pig. His influential lyricist, Bernie Taupin, is a Tiger and between them they enjoyed a highly successful, if on/off, relationship.

Star Rating: Three or four.

COMPATIBILITY OF FEMALE TIGERS IN FRIENDSHIP

FEMALE RAT

Not strong in marriage or love, friendship offers far less problems for the Rat and Tiger, but not two females. The Tiger's energy is attractive to the Rat, especially where business in concerned. And the Rat brings much needed clarity of vision. This should be a busy friendship and full of excitement, but the female version lacks an important ingredient which pushes it near the bottom. It might be the Rat's tendency to grumble or the Tiger's need to run things her way. My feeling is that the Tiger will tire of the Rat's open opportunism.

Star Rating: One.

FEMALE BUFFALO

This is an odd one. In nearly every instance the Chinese warn against Buffaloes and Tigers getting within ear shot of each other, and it must be stated that the Chinese are right – in most cases they are one hundred per cent correct. But the female Tiger and Buffalo are in a sense saved by their strong masculine influence. Both signs need to dominate, but in the female form of the Buffalo and Tiger, these powerful instincts cancel each other out. This leaves both vulnerable in areas where they might normally be strong and as a result opens them up to more than average interdependence.

Star Rating: Three, which is really high for this pairing, sometimes dropping to the usual zero.

FEMALE TIGER

Oh dear, what could be worse. Can you just picture the scene in the middle of the jungle, with two Tigers happily deciding which one is about to jump on and eat that luckless game hunter who has just run out of ammunition? Makes no difference whether or not they are Tiger ladies or Tiger gents. With both sides wanting to run the show, there can be no unity. No, no, a thousand times no to this relationship.

Star Rating: The pits.

FEMALE CAT

There's more to this friendship when there are no plans to make it everlasting. The Cat is methodical and refined, usually that is, and makes most signs an excellent companion. The Tiger, by contrast, is vigorous and ever restless in his pursuit for inner awareness. Sometimes a little vain, Cats are not much interested in, nor do they suffer from self-doubt. But they do cave in under pressure. This friendship will last just as long as the Tiger can cope with the Cat's more restrained lifestyle, and the Cat with the Tiger's attitude of changing everything at a moment's notice.

Star Rating: Two, three if the Cat has a high Tiger tolerance.

FEMALE DRAGON

Because they are extremely strong willed and hot-headed in the face of authority, a Tiger's chum must reflect these characteristics. Yet at the same time she must do so without detracting from the Tiger's need to run things. Not an easy task, but one which the Dragon is more than able to cope with. Admittedly there are a few nettles to grasp in terms of who does what, if the friendship involves business, but once decided, each sign backs the other up to the hilt. Faced with a tough problem, a Tiger and Dragon are a force to be reckoned with and will not be taken for a ride. Both are generous to those around them and are always eager to help each other in the face of adversity. The female version is less auspicious than the male.

Star Rating: Four.

FEMALE SNAKE

This is usually a real non-starter. The slow-moving Snake, with her deep intuition often disguised by a brash surface, has nothing in common with the fast thinking, ever changing Princess of the Jungle. Tigers charge about the place, emotionally, physically and just about every way there is. And they get results. Snakes sit and wait for the right moment to act – then they pounce and their bite is for keeps. It is the tortoise and the hare all over again. But with two females, since the Tiger is so masculine and the Snake so feminine, there is a tiny chance of a short relationship with just the hint of success. Julie Walters is a Tiger, and her erstwhile partner, Victoria Wood, a Snake.

Star Rating: Zero sometimes – most times, but one now and again.

FEMALE HORSE

I have never quite understood why this relationship should be so strong. Tigers live in the jungle and fight alone. Horses are seldom wild, and in most cases helplessly domesticated. But perhaps that's the clue. In the wild, the Horse is more of a loner; certainly he enjoys a greater degree of independence. Tigers do need their friends to have guts and the ability to stick up two fingers at authority. The Horse is more than able to provide such back-up to the Tiger's anti-authoritarian traits. And the Horse has a much slower fuse to her temperament, which creates a much-needed balance.

Star Rating; Four or five.

FEMALE GOAT

Tigers and Goats do not share much in common. However, it is sometimes the case that the Goat, ever in need of tethering, will respond to the Tiger's energetic nature. But there is always the difficulty that the capricious Goat will wander off when the friendship demands she stick around. Here again, the dominant influence of the Tiger's masculine sign might fit well with the extremely female Goat.

Star Rating; Two minimum, four maximum.

FEMALE MONKEY

Tigers and Monkeys can only ever expect a middle to average understanding, no matter what sex or type of relationship they form. As in every other case, the Monkey carves her own lifestyle in stark contrast to that of the Tiger. Where these differences, or strengths, depending on your interpretation, can be welded together, there's an even chance of friendship. But I wouldn't place bets. A Tiger, The Queen's relationship with the late Duchess of Windsor, Koo Stark and Princess Michael of Kent (who HRH calls Princess Pushy) gives the game away to this pair's true chances. On the other hand, one of Wimbledon's sharpest women's doubles teams in recent years was Pam Shriver (Tiger) and Martina Navratilova (Monkey).

Star Rating; Two maximum.

FEMALE ROOSTER

Here's a pair of females without a future. No matter that the Rooster is a saver or high spender or thrifty, and no matter how generous or overt the Tiger, these two have nothing in common. All Roosters are private at heart, and the Tiger is the most outgoing sign of all. When there's no hope, it's better to face up to it. That way, no one is left feeling bad about the consequences of a broken friendship. Try to imagine Princess Anne and Joan Collins forming a relationship.

Star Rating; Just about Zero.

FEMALE DOG

This is the odd couple out. In marriage and as lovers Dogs and Tigers rate among the best of all couples. The commitment, especially that made in a marriage, is central to a Dog and Tiger making the most of their respective influences. The less the commitment, the less will a Dog and Tiger find they have to offer each other. There's little doubt that as companions they will find more obstacles than bridges. On no account should they go into business. As in a number of cases, ladies have a better chance of a friendship working out than males.

Star Rating; Not easy to be accurate. One, two or three.

FEMALE PIG

Nice one! Tigers and Pigs usually have a clear and precise understanding of each other and come to terms easily with their respective differences. Easy going Pigs go along with the Tiger's extremes and are not phased by the Tiger's hot-headed response to authority. In fact, the Pig enjoys most of what the Tiger offers. But Pigs are not rebels, and do not share the Tiger's constant need to change things – the only serious difference. Even so, with all the robust fun and bubbling energy these two create, there's plenty to keep them together.

Star Rating; Three or four.

THE CAT

貓

1903	January 29th to February 15th	1904
1915	February 14th to February 2nd	1916
1927	February 2nd to January 22nd	1928
1939	February 19th to February 7th	1940
1951	February 6th to February 26th	1952
1963	January 25th to February 12th	1964
1975	February 11th to January 30th	1976
1987	January 29th to February 16th	1988

*Before the Cat will condescend
To treat you as a friend,
Some little token of esteem
Is needed, like a dish of cream.*

T. S. Eliot

THE YEAR OF THE CAT

Cats are born under the sign of virtue. In Chinese terms this means that they inherit both the social and artistic graces. Although a feminine sign, males and females born in Year of the Cat are highly refined and seem to possess an inner mystery. In some Eastern countries, the Cat is also known as the Rabbit or the Hare. This often leads to a slight confusion in the initial stages, but regardless which of the names is chosen, the influence of all three is exactly the same. The Cat, the name I prefer, is sensitive and circumspect in their day to day dealings.

People born in a Cat year love beauty in all its forms and place a great emphasis on establishing a beautiful home. They also have a fine nose for a bargain which often leads them to be collectors – usually of antiques and paintings. Cats dress elegantly, normally with an eye for high fashion, and lady Cats in particular are said to have wonderful hair.

Cats of both sexes respond poorly to pressure and emotional stress and the Chinese Horoscopes point out that female felines have a tendency to cry easily. What's more, a Cat may sometimes abuse their position if given power beyond their capability. In general, Cats do not worry too much about international disasters as they have an aversion to suffering. But should a Cat take on the world and its problems, the Chinese warn that they quickly cave in. Cats place their home, its comforts and family life above all else.

Because Cats listen well, their judgement, particularly on financial matters, is extremely sound. But since Cats do not deal easily with emotional upsets, their advice on such matters is usually less profound. However, a Cat will always listen carefully when spoken to, and their readiness to sit quietly while others talk frequently casts them in the role of the diplomat – a job in which they excel.

As creatures of habit Cats seldom act impulsively. Routine

is paramount to a Cat's well being and they are seldom found making sudden changes to their lifestyle. Methodical and cautious, the Cat's ordered approach to life had its uses. In business, they keep their word and don't generally make promises they can't fulfil. Cats are blessed with a quick wit and an often gossipy sense of humour. They adore good food and fine wines, and enjoy gossip even more. But there is something of the snob in every Cat which sometimes forces friendships to exist on a somewhat superficial level. Given a choice, a Cat will choose an evening in the company of fashionable people to one spent on their own. But the Chinese say that Cat ladies often prefer to live alone, keeping their secrets well protected.

The three phases of Cats life are not distinct. All are marked by the Cat's love of beautiful objects, a well ordered though sometimes fastidious routine and preference for agreeable and informed conversation. But there is a bonus in the shape of the third stage. In the West, Cats are thought to have nine lives, while the Chinese believe the Cat is blessed with longevity. Same thing.

COMPATIBILITY OF MALE CATS IN LOVE

FEMALE RAT

Male Cats respond quickly to the lady Rat's passion. And from the lady Rat's point of view the Tom looks a good bet at the start. Nice manners, good taste in wines, thrifty and with a healthy bank account – it's hard to resist him! There's plenty of open sexuality in the initial stages of a Rat/Cat affair and lots of gentle humour, but they quickly fade. Rats want their passion in hard doses. The Cat, on the other hand, often places his sexuality alongside comfort and emotional security. It is said that Cats eat Rats. In China it is the other way around.

Star Rating: Two, or even three on rare occasions.

FEMALE BUFFALO

The Cat who falls for a female Buffalo will discover that when in love she frequently finds it difficult to express how she feels. One reason for this is that she is never quite sure exactly what it is she is actually feeling. Above all, love often makes them feel vulnerable. The Buffalo loves deeply but not without a struggle. Luckily the male Cat has great patience and understanding. But the Cat must remember that although Buffaloes run the world, they cannot run their hearts with the same conviction. The lady Buffalo is nevertheless a gentle, direct and faithful lover, something the majority of male Cats will appreciate and repay in kind. Twiggy is a Buffalo and her first important love affair was with a Cat, Justin de Villeneuve.

Star Rating: Three.

FEMALE TIGER

It is commonly believed that Cats and Tigers are part of the same family. Not so. Cats have always presented themselves as highly social creatures, whereas Tigers are happiest when carving out a more isolated lifestyle. Cat males are sensual and sometimes more private about their feelings than they care to admit. Tigers are up-front, even the ladies. They love hard and deep and do not like to be made to look foolish as a result of love coming unstuck. Under certain kinds of emotional pressure, both signs tend to crack up – for different reasons, I must stress – and love is full of emotional pitfalls. But there is a chance, albeit slender, that the often sensuous desires of the Cat will be attended to by the amorous if sometimes over demonstrative Tiger and vice versa. Lady Tiger and male Cat are the better coupling.

Star Rating: Two.

FEMALE CAT

Two cats in love rate really high marks and there are few better relationships to be found, especially when it comes to sharing a sensuous and highly refined lifestyle. There is only one stage better for Cats in love and that is Cats in marriage. Stability and method is essential to Cats if they wish to remain close. Hard knocks, most of all those which arise from the inevitable difficulties that surround unstructured romance, do nothing to help poor pussy. Cats easily cave in, so the advice is clear: get hitched!

Star Rating: Four.

FEMALE DRAGON

Bundles of goodies going for this affair of hot-headed and emotional Dragon lady and sensuous, witty, tender male Cat. It promises much sexual pleasure and not many problems, so the indications are clear: go for it! Dragon ladies have a sign which is masculine in the extreme, and the male Cat enjoys, well I hope he does, a strongly feminine influence. With this mixture of role reversals anything is possible, but it is in the sexual stakes that these two will run out winners. Esther Rantzen is a Dragon and was responsible for her then lover, TV man Desmond Wilcox, a Cat, leaving his wife. Esther, as we all know, then married Des and saved the world from child abusers.

Star Rating: Five.

FEMALE SNAKE

The Cat has a soft nature, usually, and has a highly tuned sense of what makes life worth living. They expect their partners to share their love of good food and fine wines, and the female Snake is quick to respond. She can match his sexual expression and although the lady Snake might easily become possessive and make demands the Cat is not always able to meet, he will nevertheless make plenty of hay while the sun shines, as it promises to do regularly during this affair. Much

113

laughter, much love. But the possessive nature of the Snake does pose a bit of a problem in the long run.

Star Rating: Three, sometimes four. Sometimes even five! (but only for a very short romance).

FEMALE HORSE

Plenty to keep the Cat and Horse happy. Both have a pronounced sense of humour, an essential ingredient for any romantic affair and strong sexual personalities. And there'll be hours spent wandering around designer clothes shops as an alternative to the bedroom. Both signs are skilful at human relationships and enjoy many different types of people, each for their own individual personalities. The Horse in particular is not stable in love, and of the two, will probably be the first to move out of the relationship – one which marriage will neither help nor hinder. It will or it won't happen. TV Cat David Frost, whose fling with actress Lynne Frederick, a Horse, was more like a long affair than a short marriage, proves the point.

Star Rating: Four big ones.

FEMALE GOAT

The Cat is a lucky fellow – even though luck is the Dragon's sign. Cats have the pick of the field to chose their partners from and apart from one (the Rooster), they hit it off with just about everyone. It is true they find some easier going than others, but the Goat is no problem. Together they share much of life's more agreeable aspects, especially when it includes la dolce vita. Faithfully inclined, in spite of their Tom cat reputation, the Cat will not be over the moon when his lady Goat starts showing off to the other guys at the party. But as long as the Cat puts his foot (paw?) down, Miss Goat will not cause too many upsets.

Star Rating: Four. It depends on the Goat's capricious heart.

FEMALE MONKEY

Cats do not usually meet Monkeys in nature. One is domestic and the other a very intelligent creature of the wild. And to a certain extent, this is true of the relationship between these two Chinese animal signs. Cats like life cut and dried if they are to get the most from it, and this is also how they view romance. They like their lovers to arrive on time and when it is suggested they meet on Friday, they are not crazy about last minute cancellations. Monkeys are prone to living life to suit themselves and both sexes are emotional wheeler-dealers. However, there are a few points they have in common – wit and an appreciation of life's more subtle sides being high on the list.

Star Rating: Three tops.

FEMALE ROOSTER

Oh dear, a big hiccup for the Cat. All the other signs love Tom, but not the Rooster, at least not usually. The problem arises from the fact that Roosters do not like casual affairs – ever. They are deeply personal, private, conservative ladies and the idea of a bit of randy Tom-style slap and tickle is not normally for them. Of course, not all Cats behave that way, in fact, very few do. But the point is that these two signs fare slightly better when married, should this event ever take place. Some Cats, though, can be too well mannered and sexy for the prudish Rooster to resist. The Chinese give this pair no marks, but I must say that I have found one or two couples who have made surprisingly good friends. Rooster female/male Cat rates the better pair.

Star Rating: Zero. But sometimes one or two.

FEMALE DOG

Cats and Dogs are supposed to fight, but in my experience this is not the case. The Chinese agree and explain that the loyal and idealistic Dog looks to the Cat for support. Dog ladies generally are not so shy as their male counterparts and less prone to the anxiety which dogs all Dog people. The Cat is a thoughtful and considerate lover, if at times a little too easily defeated by the inevitable emotional stress that comes from being in love. But there is plenty of warmth in a love created and shared by both Cat and Dog, the male Cat/female Dog pair having the slightest of edges.

Star Rating: Three is about right.

FEMALE PIG

Another middle of the road relationship which can easily catch fire. Honesty is a strong feature of Pigs, as is their love of a good time. A Cat chap responds quickly to the Pig lady's fun loving antics and approves of their single minded attitude to romance. But in spite of their honesty, some Piggy people are easily duped or, in the case of romance, seduced. This is not what the male Cat is looking for and unless he has an easy going temperament with plenty of understanding, this affair will not last.

Star Rating: Three is average, but it can go higher or lower depending on the level of fidelity.

COMPATIBILITY OF FEMALE CATS IN LOVE

MALE RAT

The male Rat's passion is only matched by their pronounced streak of opportunism. Given the chance to experience a new sensation they'll go for it and make excuses later. Female Cats respond warmly to the Rat's passionate attention but do not take kindly to his aggressive moods or his lame excuses on the nights he doesn't show. Lady Cats are subtle creatures who enjoy sensual stability and are too easily thrown off their delicate emotional balance by the Rat's last minute plans. There's plenty of open sexuality in the initial stages of a Rat/Cat affair, but it quickly fades.

Star Rating: One, with maybe an extra half point for the early physical involvement.

MALE BUFFALO

The female Buffalo in love frequently finds it difficult to express how she feels, although she does a much better job than her male counterpart. One reason for this is that they are never quite sure exactly what it is they are feeling. And love often makes them feel vulnerable. The Buffalo loves deeply but not without a struggle. Luckily the male Cat has great patience and understanding. But the Cat must remember that although Buffaloes run the world, they cannot run their hearts with the same conviction. The lady Buffalo is nevertheless a gentle, direct and faithful lover, something the majority of male Cats will appreciate and repay in kind. Twiggy is a Buffalo and her first important love affair was with a Cat, Justin de Villeneuve.

Star Rating: Three.

MALE TIGER

It is commonly believed that Cats and Tigers are part of the same family. Not so. Cats have always presented themselves as highly social creatures, whereas Tigers are happiest when carving out a more isolated lifestyle. Cat ladies are sensual and sometimes more private about their feelings than they care to admit. Tigers are up front, especially the males. They chase love hard when they so desire and do not like to be made to look foolish when they don't make it. Under certain kinds of emotional pressure, both signs tend to crack up – for different reasons, I must stress – and love is full of emotional pitfalls. But there is a chance, albeit slender, that the sensuous desires of the Cat will be attended to by the amorous if sometimes over demonstrative Tiger and vice versa.

Star Rating: One, sometimes two.

MALE CAT

Two Cats in love rates really high marks and there are few better relationships to be found, especially when it comes to sharing a sensuous and highly refined lifestyle. There is only one stage better for Cats in love and that is Cats in marriage. Stability and method is essential to Cats if they wish to remain close. Hard knocks, most of all those which arise from the inevitable difficulties that surround unstructured romance, do nothing to help poor pussy. Cats easily cave in, so the advice is clear: get hitched!

Star Rating: Four.

MALE DRAGON

Bundles of goodies going for this affair of hot-headed and highly emotional Dragon male and sensuous, witty, tender female Cat. It promises much sexual pleasure and not many problems, so the indications are clear: go for it! But just the tiniest word of warning for the female partner. Dragons are only tolerant up to a point. Too many moodies from Ms Cat – there'll be one or two when the Dragon doesn't show on time – and Mr Dragon will be on his merry way, not over sad that it has not altogether worked out as a long term relationship. Anyway, both signs have plenty of other fish – so to speak – to fry.

Star Rating: Five.

MALE SNAKE

The female Cat has a soft nature, usually, and a highly tuned sense of what makes life worth living. They expect their partner to share their love of good food and fine wines, and the male Snake is quick to respond. The lady Cat can match his sexual expression and although the male Snake might easily become possessive and make demands the Cat is not always able to meet, she will nevertheless make plenty of hay while the sun shines, as it promises to do regularly during this affair. Much laughter, much love. But the possessive nature of the Snake does pose a bit of a problem in the long run.

Star Rating: Three, sometimes four. Sometimes even five! (but only for a very short romance).

MALE HORSE

Plenty to keep the Cat and Horse happy. Both have a pronounced sense of humour, an essential ingredient for any romantic affair and strong sexual personalities. And there'll be hours spent wandering around designer clothes shops as an alternative to the bedroom. Both signs are skilful at human relationships and enjoy many different types of people, each for their own individual personalities. The Horse in particular is not stable in love, and of the two, will probably be the first to move out of the relationship – one which marriage will neither help nor hinder. It will or it won't happen.
Star Rating: Four big ones.

MALE GOAT

The Cat is a lucky lady even though luck is the Dragon's sign. Cats have the pick of the field to chose their partners from and apart from one (the Rooster), they hit it off with just about everyone. It is true they find some easier going than others, but the Goat is no problem. Together they share much of life's more agreeable aspects, especially when it includes la dolce vita. Faithfully inclined, in spite of their tom-cat reputation, the Cat will not be over the moon when her Goat starts showing off to the other girls at the party. But as long as the Cat puts her foot (paw?) down, Master Goat will not cause too many upsets.
Star Rating: Four. It depends on the Goat's capricious heart.

MALE MONKEY

Cats do not usually meet Monkeys in nature. One is domestic and the other a very intelligent creature of the wild. And to a certain extent, this is true of the relationship between these two Chinese animal signs. Cats like life cut and dried if they are to get the most from it, and this is also how they view romance. They like their lovers to arrive on time and when it is suggested they meet on Friday, they are not crazy about last-minute cancellations. Monkeys are prone to living life to suit themselves and both sexes are emotional wheeler-dealers. However, there are a few points they have in common – wit and an appreciation of life's more subtle sides being high on the list. Lady Cat/male Monkey are the more likely to make it work.

Star Rating: Three tops.

MALE ROOSTER

Oh dear, a big hiccup for the Cat. All the other signs love Pussy, but not the Rooster, at least not usually. The problem arises from the fact that Roosters do not usually go in for casual affairs, although there is the odd one who behaves more in keeping with his Cock reputation. Most Rooster males are deeply personal, private, conservative men and even if the idea of a bit of stray sex with a beautiful Cat lady comes up, they will not be as quick as some to react. The point is that these two signs fare slightly better when married, should this event ever take place. The Chinese give this pair no marks, but I must say that I have found one or two couples who have made surprisingly good friends.

Star Rating: Zero. But sometimes one or two.

MALE DOG

Cats and Dogs are supposed to fight, but in my experience this is not the case. The Chinese agree and explain that the loyal and idealistic Dog looks to the Cat for support. The Cat is a thoughtful and considerate lover, if at times a little too easily defeated by the inevitable emotional stress that comes from being in love. But there is plenty of warmth in a love created and shared by both Cat and Dog. The lady Cat, it must be said, does a great job calming the ever anxious Dog, who in turn is not slow to show his gratitude.

Star Rating: Three is about right.

MALE PIG

Another middle of the road relationship which can easily catch fire. Honesty is a strong feature of Pigs, as is their love of a good time. A Cat lady responds quickly to the Pig chap's fun loving antics and approves of their single minded attitude to romance. But in spite of their honesty, some Piggy people are easily duped, or, in the case of romance, seduced. This is not what the female Cat is looking for and unless she has an easy going temperament with plenty of understanding, this affair will not last.

Star Rating: Three is average, but it can go higher or lower depending on the level of fidelity.

COMPATIBILITY OF MALE CATS IN MARRIAGE

FEMALE RAT

A modest romance turns into a less than satisfactory marriage. Rats and Cats are both creatures of comfort, but each has an entirely different approach to a full wine cellar and a well stocked freezer. The male Cat enjoys a quiet, methodical existence with the emphasis on routine whereas most female Rats rush at life with seldom a thought for tomorrow. Female Rats also have a habit of fretting when they have children, something that drives Tom up the wall. The Cat plans carefully and most Rats spend without thinking. The lady Rat stocks her larder, only to consume it at once, especially the sweet things, while the cautious Cat likes to know there is plenty put by for a rainy day. The relationship ends up as a constant battle, with Cat and Rat finding nothing in common at any level. Fifties film star Doris Day is a Rat and her longest and perhaps most unhappy marriage was to a Cat, producer Martin Melcher. He apparently diddled her out of millions. Sorry folks.

Star Rating: Zero.

FEMALE BUFFALO

Of the two pairings, the female Buffalo/male Cat is marginally less auspicious. But there is still a great deal to be said for such a relationship and the understanding that exists between these two animal signs remains fairly constant no matter what the status, married or not. The male Cat adds a touch of refinement to the Buffalo's life, and his methodical approach to the home, its finances and family will suit her down to the ground. But the Cat is not given to great ideals and does not share the Buffalo's power seeking. This does form a gap in their lives, but it is not serious. Mrs Thatcher is a Buffalo and her husband, Denis, is a Cat.

Star Rating: Three.

FEMALE TIGER

A relationship that only just scrapes by as a romance does not get any better with marriage. In fact, there is a distinct possibility that matters will get worse. Cats of both sexes are easily thrown by the sudden emotional upheavals that Tigers frequently indulge in. Marriage is full of tiny moments of uncertainty, and a Cat's response is usually to shin up a tree when there's danger. Tigers sit tight and fight it off. But Cats are good at listening and Tigers are full of ideas, which means a professional couple might make a go of it, especially where the positive influences of both signs can be utilised. Tiger Marilyn Monroe's happiest marriage was to Arthur Miller, a Cat. More Hollywood: Cary Grant's last wife, actress Dyan Cannon, said she was born in a Tiger year.

Star Rating: Two.

FEMALE CAT

Ring out the bells for one of the all time great marriage partnerships. The Cats of both sexes are blessed with any number of partners with whom to form long and enduring marriages, but two Cats has to be one of the best. Financially and artistically, two Cats are perfectly matched and as a couple they will seldom if ever come to grief when putting their ideas forward for mutual benefit. They will share all the best life has to offer, but it must always be remembered that neither will be a great help to each other should disaster befall one or both. A low threshold of suffering means that a bad spell will cast serious gloom over them. Queen Victoria and her Prince Consort, Albert, were a Cat couple, and a better illustration of two Cats would be impossible to find, although Cats Johnny Dankworth and Cleo Laine might do.

Star Rating: Five of the best!

FEMALE DRAGON

Another five star relationship in marriage and love and all points north and west. The sensuous Cat knows just how to make the deeply passionate Dragon let go – not that any male or female Dragon worth their salt needs much prompting – and in marriage a strong sexual element will continue to dominate matters. The Cat must also keep a mental note that his wife has a mega-masculine influencing sign, which means a headstrong and sometimes not entirely feminine response to life. He will, for example, discover a powerful lady at his side who will tend to take the upper hand. After their affair, Dragon Esther Rantzen did actually marry her Cat lover, Desmond Wilcox.

Star Rating: Five, as long as the Cat doesn't mind sometimes playing second fiddle.

FEMALE SNAKE

The third of four in a row of five star relationships for the Cat male. Ever diplomatic, often mysterious and given the ability to surprise his noisiest critics with his sharp wit, the Cat finds a long term partnership with the equally subtle, humorous and deeply sensuous Snake irresistible. The Chinese place a high premium on the female Snake, saying she will make the rice grow fat. Her sexuality will, I am certain, do much to keep her Tom in trim, and the Cat will enjoy every second. A business might easily grow from such a marriage, especially since both are generally good with money. Plenty of support for each other in the bleaker moments points to a perfect duo. Sir Michael Levey, former director of London's National Gallery, is married to a Snake, the authoress Brigid Brophy.

Star Rating: Five and more.

FEMALE HORSE

Four five star marriage years in a row for the refined, cultured and ever-willing-to-listen Cat; and perhaps that is why he fares so well. Ever keen to let others have their say, by listening carefully the Cat builds up a strong picture of those he can trust and those he can't. Cats love the order and routine that married life offers, but there are moments in all marriages when he feels the need to explore his private sensual interior. Here, the willing and witty Horse provides a marvellous foil. Although not much given to introspection, Cats are warm and gentle in their approach to family life and enjoy children. Horse ladies can please themselves *vis à vis* kids. Good in the bedroom, good in the garden, good in the dining room.

Star Rating: Five.

FEMALE GOAT

This is the best of the two pairings and in some cases, most, in fact, reaches top marks. The only cloud on the horizon is that neither Cats nor Goats suffer adversity well, and in many a marriage there are times when either the money gets low or the emotional well runs a bit dry. Then the Goat will tend to find her stimulation elsewhere, much to the Cats sadness and even anger. But if there's money in the bank, plus time to enjoy it, Goat and Cat will find themselves with few if any rifts growing between them. The good life is what both tend to crave and a beautiful, well cared for home, well stocked with goodies, is what they'll produce.

Star Rating: Four to five.

FEMALE MONKEY

Monkey ladies always live life the way they want it, although they have an uncanny knack of making you think you are in charge. Never one hundred per cent honest about their true feelings, Monkey women are nevertheless extremely perceptive. Cats are particularly fragile in terms of their temperament, especially when compared with the easy adaptability and emotional self control of the Monkey. Male Cats like refinement, method and routine, and are frequently saved from being a victim of life's duller side by a sharp and sometimes snobbish sense of humour. The more acerbic the Cat, the more the sharp-as-a-knife Monkey lady will want to stick around and make this marriage last. Kids will make a big difference in its favour. Actor Michael Denison was born in a Cat year, and his actress wife, Dulcie Gray, in the year of the Monkey.

Star Rating: Two, maybe three. Seldom more.

FEMALE ROOSTER

Only two marriage partners are truly unsuitable for the Cat – the Rooster and the Rat. Roosters, although illustrating a tendency towards poor understanding with a Cat in love, do make a slightly better impression when marriage is involved. One of the many areas of poor mutual understanding lies in the Rooster's open, frank response, which contrasts badly with the Cat's quieter, more reserved approach. Married life is full of tense moments, and it is during these times that Cat and Rooster fail to see eye to eye. Children will not make it easier, and nor will a healthy bank balance, something most spendthrift Roosters have never known.

Star Rating: Normally Zero, but there are two on offer for real triers.

FEMALE DOG

A good middle of the road marriage for the Cat and Dog – the male Cat/female Dog being the best of the two pairings. There is much understanding from the Cat for his Dog wife's more trivial anxieties, a common problem facing all Dogs, and plenty of Dog devotion in return. Dog ladies, more than Dog men, do create the most wonderful homes, and male Cats are not slow to introduce their own highly accomplished sense of refinement and decorative skills. A lovely home with gentle people and varied friendships is the result of a Dog and Cat going down the aisle. Not a great place for untidy kids perhaps.

Star Rating: Three.

FEMALE PIG

Another very good marriage, without going over the top on points. Pig ladies are usually splendid cooks and the very best Pigettes do create the most wonderfully warm and generous homes. Cats adore creature comforts with plenty of fresh cream and quiet snoozes by the fire in winter. Routine is essential to a Cat marriage as it is in all things. However, there's a certain type of Pig lady who hates being pinned down and lives only for the minute. Unfortunately she is usually the most attractive to Cats. This Pig lady works hard and plays hard and her social life is every bit as rich as any domestic environment she establishes. This Pig is also a victim of emotional greed and it is here that the trouble might start – the Cat wanting more mental and physical support than the Pig lady is prepared to give, or is capable of giving. But because both signs are good with money there's usually enough in the bank to cheer up even the most dismal rainy day. Famous TV stars of the fifties Lucille Ball (Pig) and Dezi Arnez (Cat) enjoyed a long and happy marriage – for Hollywood.

Star Rating: Three.

COMPATIBILITY OF FEMALE CATS IN MARRIAGE

MALE RAT

A modest romance turns into a less than satisfactory marriage. Rats and Cats are both creatures of comfort, but each has an entirely different approach to a full wine cellar and a well stocked freezer. The female Cat enjoys a quiet, methodical life with the emphasis on routine whereas most Rats rush around with seldom a thought for tomorrow. The Cat plans carefully and most Rats spend without thinking. The Rat eats everything in sight while the cautious Cat likes to know there is plenty put by for a rainy day. And so the differences go on.
Star Rating: Zero.

MALE BUFFALO

Of the two pairings the male Buffalo/female Cat is marginally less auspicious. But there is a great deal to be said for such a relationship. Curiously the affair rates no higher for turning into marriage and the understanding that exists between these two animal signs remains fairly constant no matter what the status. The female Cat adds a touch of refinement to the Buffalo's life, and her methodical approach to the home and family will suit him down to the ground. But the Cat is not given to great ideas and does not share the Buffalo's power seeking. This does form a gap in their lives, but it is not serious.
Star Rating: Three.

MALE TIGER

A relationship that only just scrapes by as a romance does not get any better with marriage. In fact, there is a distinct possibility that matters will get worse. Cat ladies are easily thrown by the sudden emotional upheavals that Tigers frequently indulge in. A marriage is full of tiny moments of uncertainty, and a Cat's response is usually to shin up a tree when there's danger. Tigers sit tight and fight it off. But Cats are good at listening and Tigers are full of ideas, which means a professional couple might make a go of it, especially where the positive influences of both signs can be utilised. Nanette Newman is a Cat and husband Bryan Forbes a Tiger.

Star Rating: Two.

MALE CAT

Ring out the bells for one of the all time great marriage partnerships. The Cats of both sexes are blessed with any number of partners with whom to form long and enduring marriages, but two Cats has to be one of the best. Financially and artistically, two Cats are perfectly matched and as a couple they will seldom if ever come to grief when putting their ideas forward for mutual benefit. They will share all the best life has to offer, but it must always be remembered that neither will be of great help to each other should disaster befall one or both. A low threshold of suffering means that a bad spell will cast serious gloom over them. Queen Victoria and her Prince Consort, Albert, were a Cat couple, and a better illustration of two Cats would be impossible to find, although Cats Johnny Dankworth and Cleo Laine might do.

Star Rating: Five of the best!

MALE DRAGON

Another five star relationship in marriage and love and all points north and west. The sensuous Cat knows just how to make the deeply passionate Dragon let go – not that any male or female Dragon worth their salt needs much prompting and in marriage a strong sexual element will continue to dominate matters. The Cat must also keep a mental note that her husband has a mega-masculine influencing sign which means a headstrong and entirely unbending response to life. She will, for example, discover a powerful figure at her side who will tend to take the upper hand and demand perfection in all things. But both enjoy routine and rituals.

Star Rating: Five, as long as the Cat doesn't mind sometimes playing second fiddle.

MALE SNAKE

The third of four in a row of five star relationships for the Cat female. Ever graceful and often mysterious the Cat finds a long term partnership with the equally humorous and sensuous Snake irresistible. Male Snakes are generally gentle husbands, and the Cat lady will adore his inner strengths and appreciative nature. A business might easily grow from such a marriage, especially since both are generally good with money. Plenty of support for each other in the bleaker moments points to a perfect duo. Humorist Miles Kington, famous for his *Let's Parlais Franglais*, is married to a Cat, Caroline.

Star Rating: Five and more.

MALE HORSE

Four five star marriage years in a row for the refined, cultured and ever willing to listen Cat; and perhaps that's why she fares do well. Ever keen to let others have their say, by listening carefully the Cat eventually holds all the cards and can play them any way she wants. She loves the order and routine that married life offers, but there are moments in all marriages when she feels the need to explore her private sensual interior. Here, the willing and witty Horse provides a marvellous foil. Although not given much to introspection, Cats are warm and gentle in their approach to family life and enjoy children. Horse gentlemen can please themselves *vis à vis* kids. Good in the bedroom, good in the garden, good in the dining room. A home of happiness.

Star Rating: Five.

MALE GOAT

This is the best of the two pairings and in some cases, most, in fact, reaches top marks. The only cloud on the horizon is that neither Cats or Goats suffer adversity well, and in many a marriage there are times when either the money gets low or the emotional well runs a bit dry. Then the Goat will tend to find her stimulation elsewhere, much to the Cat's sadness and even anger. But if there's money in the bank, plus time to enjoy it, Goat and Cat will find themselves with few if any rifts growing between them. The good life is what both tend to crave and a beautiful, well cared for home, well stocked with goodies, is what they'll produce.

Star Rating: Four to five.

MALE MONKEY

Monkeys always live life the way they want it, although they have an uncanny knack of making you think you are in charge. Never one hundred per cent honest about their true feelings, Monkey men are nevertheless extremely perceptive. Female Cats are particularly fragile in terms of temperament, especially when compared with the easy adaptability and emotional self control of the Monkey. This difference might well create problems. In her favour, Ms Cat adores refinement, method and routine, and is frequently saved from being a victim of life's duller side by a sharp and sometimes snobbish sense of humour. The more acerbic the lady Cat, the more the bright Monkey male will want to make this marriage last. Kids will make a big difference in the couple's favour.

Star Rating: Two, maybe three. Seldom more.

MALE ROOSTER

Only two marriage partners are truly unsuitable for the Cat –
the Rooster and the Rat. Roosters, although illustrating a
tendency towards poor understanding with a Cat in love, do
make a slightly better impression when marriage is involved.
One of the many areas of poor mutual understanding lies in
the Rooster's open, frank response, which contrasts badly
with the Cat's quieter, more reserved approach. Married life
is full of tense moments, and it is during these times that Cat
and Rooster fail to see eye to eye. Children will not make it
easier, and nor will a healthy bank balance, something most
spendthrift Roosters have never known.

Star Rating: Normally Zero, but there are two on offer for
real triers.

MALE DOG

A good middle of the road marriage for the Cat and Dog
although the male Cat/female Dog is the better of the two
pairings. There is much understanding from the Cat for her
Dog husband's more trivial anxieties, a common problem
facing all Dogs, and plenty of Dog devotion in return. Dog
men look to homes that provide both elegance and safety – a
bit like a well appointed kennel, I suppose – and female Cats
are not slow to introduce their own highly accomplished
sense of refinement and decorative skills. A lovely home with
gentle people and varied friendships is the result of a Dog
and Cat going down the aisle. Not a great place for untidy
kids perhaps, or too much stress.

Star Rating: Three.

MALE PIG

Another very good marriage, without going over the top on
points. Pig blokes are usually great socialisers and love nothing more after a tough day at the office than to greet a
bunch of fun lovers with the mutual purpose of enjoying a
tough night out somewhere. Cats adore being made a fuss of

and respond well to the providers of creature comforts. If there is plenty of fresh cream and quiet snoozes by the fire in winter, so much the better. Routine is essential to a Cat in marriage as it is in all things. But there's a certain type of Pig who hates being pinned down and lives only for the minute, and he is the type usually the most attractive to Cats. This Pig is rather too full of himself and it is here that the trouble might start – the Cat wanting more mental and physical support than the Pig is prepared to give, or is capable of giving. But there'll always be money in the bank for the rainy day. TV host and hostess Michael Parkinson and his wife, Mary, are Pig and Cat respectively. They seem OK; plenty of spondulicks.

Star Rating: Three.

COMPATIBILITY OF MALE CATS IN FRIENDSHIP

MALE RAT

Not the greatest idea in the world. The Rat's vitality and sharp wits only marginally engage the methodical Cat. In business, matters improve, especially if there is an artistic element. On the whole, a negative set-up.

Star Rating: Two-ish. Three for a business partnership.

MALE BUFFALO

A better than average friendship for the strong, tough minded Buffalo, who looks to the Cat for a second fiddle who is reliable and diplomatic in those areas of his life he finds a chore. This is to take nothing away from the Cat's thoughtful contribution to the partnership. It involves much self sacrifice to get really close to a Buffalo, and a great deal of understanding. And such loyalty will not always be rewarded. Even so, the Cat is aware of the Buffalo's temperament, and usually thinks the effort is worth it.

Star Rating: Three to four.

MALE TIGER

There's more to this friendship when there are no plans to be everlasting buddies. The Cat is methodical and refined, usually that is, and makes most signs an excellent companion. The Tiger, by contrast, is vigorous and even restless in his pursuit for inner awareness. Sometimes a little vain, Cats are not much interested in, nor do they suffer from, self doubt. But they do cave in under pressure. This friendship will last just as long as the Tiger can cope with the Cat's more restrained lifestyle, and the Cat with the Tiger's attitude of changing everything at a moment's notice. Ex-Wham men George Michael and Andrew Ridgeley are a Tiger and Cat respectively. So were Laurel and Hardy.

Star Rating: Two. Three if the Cat has a high Tiger tolerance. More if the Tiger doesn't run out of steam.

MALE CAT

Another top hole relationship for the Cat, who scores maximum in every department when joining forces with a fellow feline. As long as there are not too many external pressures, any number of male Cats will get on brilliantly. I once spent time in an office where there were no less than three Cats happily working together. When one left, they got yet another to fill his place. It is not surprising that playwright Cat Alan Ayckbourn has constantly cast Cat actor Michael Gambon as his male lead.

Star Rating: Five big ones.

MALE DRAGON

Here's a couple of swells with a long future. The diplomatic Cat acts like blotting paper when the hot-headed Dragon blows his top – even if it is with the Cat. Both are two sides of the same coin, a perfect balancing act with one providing the other what he most lacks. No problems in sight here, as long as the Dragon remembers to say sorry once in a while. The great 'Road' movie stars, Bob Hope and Bing Crosby, were a Cat and Dragon team. Bob's first movie hit, curiously enough, was *The Cat and the Canary*. Cute? And top newsreaders Sir Alistair Burnet and Sandy Gall seem the most comfortable pair on *News at Ten*. They are a Dragon and Cat team – Sandy is the Cat.

Star Rating: Five all the way.

MALE SNAKE

Cats and Snakes are just fine. In a friendship which includes some sort of business deal there would be few better partnerships. Both are cautious with money as a rule, and both Cat and Snake have a terrific sense of what is beautiful, and what is not. Supportive and understanding of each other's need for inner peace, there is not a lot that can go wrong with this pairing. Ken Tynan was a Cat, and apart from being the first person to say f**k on TV, was one of the most influential theatre critics of the fifties. It was he who became the central figure in promoting the name of the 'angry young man' playwright, John Osborne, a Snake. Tynan said once, 'I doubt if I could love anyone who did not wish to see *Look Back in Anger*.'

Star Rating: Five at least.

MALE HORSE

No big setbacks here. Cats find the Horse an extremely sympathetic partner, and the feeling is mutual. As in all good friendships, it is essential that both bring different, but harmonious qualities to bear. The Horse brings powerful leadership and the Cat, diplomacy and good taste. Lenin was a Horse, and his thoughtful revolutionary chum Trotsky, a Cat. Stalin was also a Cat and had Trotsky assassinated, which, going back to the five star rating of two Cats, raises a doubt. It can only be explained, I think, by the fact that Stalin had everyone bumped off who threatened him, and even those who didn't. A more positive partnership existed between the creator of our most enduring children's character, Pooh Bear, and his illustrator. Writer A A Milne was a Horse and illustrator E H Shepard a Cat.

Star Rating: Four of five. Seldom less.

MALE GOAT

Another solid friendship for the Cat, who finds that life at a social level is much enhanced by the fun loving and lively minded Goat. These two signs share a genuine love of the arts at all levels and with the Cat's diplomacy acting as a gentle tether for the Goat's more wayward moments, there is every possibility this relationship could last a lifetime. Good fun and a deep understanding make this a winner. It has been noted that two of the Monty Python team, Eric Idle (Goat) and John Cleese (Cat), always get on really well.

Star Rating: Four to five.

MALE MONKEY

This is not a good idea. The Cat looks for all kinds of stability in his relationships, or perhaps consistency would be a better word. The Monkey is a law unto himself, and although he may promise great friendship to one and all, he will always end up by suiting himself. And this might mean a good chum, in this case the Cat, will be left hanging around.

Star Rating: One at the most.

MALE ROOSTER

The male Cat has an easy way with even the most tricky people, and he is an expert at concealing his true feelings. That's why the Chinese consider the Cat to be such a fine diplomat. And the Cat will need all his qualities of diplomacy and human understanding to deal with the male Rooster, especially if he is the extrovert. Never one for hiding from others what he thinks, the Rooster speaks his mind and does so often. But he is honest and usually incorruptible, something the Cat applauds. Not the greatest of pairings, but better than would at first appear. Richard Briers, a Rooster, has long been one of the favourite leads of playwright and Cat, Alan Ayckbourn.

Star Rating: Two, and that's good here.

MALE DOG

It is said that Cats and Dogs fight, but that is not true of the animal signs of the Chinese Horoscope. Here the relationship is reasonably strong, one in which the thoughtful and considerate Cat does much to quell the Dog's frequently anxious nature. The Dog pays back the Cat's concern with large helpings of loyal protection, especially in those periods when the Cat, under pressure, tends to find life too much.

Star Rating: Three.

MALE PIG

A very strong bond can exist between male Cats and Pigs. The good natured and honest Pig has almost as many choices as the Cat when choosing a chum, and making a life long friend is no problem. Since both animal signs look for the best in others and tend, on the whole, not to be over-zealous in their criticism of each other's weaker points, these two signs are a splendid match. But the Cat has not got the robust energy of a Pig, who must remember to live at the Cat's more even pace. The greatest jazz composer partnership of all times was between a Pig and a Cat, Duke Ellington and Billy Strayhorn.

Star Rating: Four and five.

COMPATIBILITY OF FEMALE CATS IN FRIENDSHIP

FEMALE RAT

Rat ladies appreciate the female Cat's calm and methodical approach to life. At the stage of motherhood, a Cat will be a useful aid, bringing a sense of order to the Rat's sometimes chaotic world. Cat ladies are seldom critical – not the catty people we are led to believe – and their care and attention to detail in a friendship will not go unnoticed.

Star Rating: Three, rising to four in some cases.

FEMALE BUFFALO

The Cat's gentle feline influences grace all lasting friendships, a fact the sometimes awkward Buffalo is not slow to appreciate. Normally speaking, Cats are not looking to run a relationship and they usually leave the running of even the most tenuous of friendships in the other's hands. Always thoughtful of what they say, Cats are generally happy to let the Buffalo dictate the friendship's path, dropping hints as to its future as opposed to making direct statements. A happy relationship as long as the Buffalo does not tread too often on the Cat's tail. Cats have very sharp claws. Famous tennis doubles stars of an earlier time Shirley Fry and Doris Hart were Cat and Buffalo respectively.

Star Rating: Three to four most times.

FEMALE CAT

Another top hole relationship for the Cat, who scores maximum in every department when joining forces with a fellow feline. As long as there are not too many external pressures, any number of female Cats will get on brilliantly. The mutual love of all things beautiful and the pleasures they get from hours of endless gossip ensures the basis for a long and lasting relationship. But there is always a slight danger of cattyness if one should prove too successful, although the bond of affection is often too strong to break.

Star Rating: Five Big Ones.

FEMALE TIGER

There's more to this friendship when there are no plans to make it everlasting. The Cat is methodical and refined, usually that is, and makes most signs an excellent companion. The Tiger, by contrast, is vigorous and ever restless in his pursuit for inner awareness. Sometimes a little vain, Cats are not much interested in, nor do they suffer from, self doubt. But they do cave in under pressure. This friendship will last just as long as the Tiger can cope with the Cat's more restrained lifestyle, and the Cat with the Tiger's attitude of changing everything at a moment's notice.

Star Rating: Two, three if the Cat has a high Tiger tolerance.

FEMALE DRAGON

Here's a couple of girls with a long future. The diplomatic Cat acts like blotting paper when the hot-headed Dragon blows her fuse, even if it is with the Cat. Both are two sides of

the same coin, a perfect balancing act with one providing the other what she most lacks. No problems in sight here, as long as the Dragon remembers to say sorry once in a while.
Star Rating: Five all the way.

FEMALE SNAKE

Cats and Snakes are just fine. In a friendship which includes some sort of business deal there would be few better partnerships. Both are cautious with money as a rule, and both Cat and Snake have a terrific sense of what is beautiful, and what is not. Supportive and understanding of each other's need for inner peace, there is not a lot that can go wrong with this pairing.
Star Rating: Five at least.

FEMALE HORSE

The Horse is a powerful leader, endowed with much independence. The influence of the Cat is less so, making its presence felt more in the quieter and less demanding moments. As in all good friendships, it is essential that both bring different but harmonious qualities to bear. The Horse brings thoughtful direction and the Cat, diplomacy and good taste.
Star Rating: Four of five. Seldom less.

FEMALE GOAT

Another solid friendship for the Cat, who finds that life at a social level is much enhanced by the fun loving and lively minded Goat. These two signs share a genuine love of the arts at all levels and with the Cat's diplomacy acting as a gentle tether for the Goat's more wayward moments, there is every possibility this relationship could last a lifetime. Good fun and a deep understanding makes this a winner.
Star Rating: Four to five.

FEMALE MONKEY

This is not a good idea. The Cat looks for all kinds of stability in her relationships, or perhaps consistency would be a better word. The Monkey is a law unto herself, and although she may promise great friendships to one and all, she will always end up by suiting herself. And this might mean a good companion, in this case the Cat, will be left hanging around.

Star Rating: One at the most.

FEMALE ROOSTER

The female Cat has an easy way with even the most tricky people, and she is an expert at concealing her true feelings. That's why the Chinese consider the Cat to be such a fine diplomat. And the Cat will need all her qualities of diplomacy and human understanding to deal with the female Rooster, especially if this bird is the extrovert. Never one for hiding from others what she thinks, the Rooster speaks her mind and does so often. But she is honest and usually incorruptible, something the Cat applauds. Not the greatest of pairings, but better than would at first appear.

Star Rating: Two, and that's good here.

FEMALE DOG

It is said that Cats and Dogs fight, but that is not true of the animal signs of the Chinese Horoscope. Here the relationship is reasonably strong, one in which the thoughtful and considerate Cat does much to quell the Dog's frequently anxious nature. The Dog pays back the Cat's concern with large helpings of loyal protection, especially in those periods when the Cat, under pressure, tends to find life too much.

Star Rating: Three.

FEMALE PIG

A very strong bond can exist between a female Cat and Pig. The good natured and honest Pig has almost as many choices as the Cat when choosing a companion, and making a life long friend is no problem. Since both animal signs look for the best in others and tend, on the whole, not to be over-zealous in their criticism of each other's weaker points, these two signs are a splendid match. But the Cat has not got the robust energy of a Pig, who must remember to live at the Cat's more even pace.

Star Rating: Four and five.

THE DRAGON

龍

1904	February 16th	to	February 3rd	1905
1916	February 3rd	to	January 22nd	1917
1928	January 23rd	to	February 9th	1929
1940	February 8th	to	January 26th	1941
1952	February 27th	to	February 13th	1953
1964	February 13th	to	February 1st	1965
1976	January 31st	to	February 17th	1977
1988	February 17th	to	February 5th	1989

'The Dragon's eyes are precious stones, and
bright as fire, in which there is affirmed to be
much virtue against many diseases.'

Topsell

THE YEAR OF THE DRAGON

Dragons are born under the sign of luck. In the West, the legend of Saint George has done much to damage our understanding of the Dragon's personality, which is usually regarded as evil. However, in China the Dragon is the national emblem and considered the harbinger of the Four Great Blessings; long life, virtue, harmony and wealth. Created from fable, the Dragon leads the famous Chinese New Year carnival, which provides a perfect clue to the Dragon's larger than life personality.

Dragons are usually showmen, characters who are both boastful and precocious. They are hot heads who let their hearts rule their heads. Dragon people love to stimulate those around them. This they do by virtue of their extraordinary self belief; the more they believe in themselves, the more they pass belief on to others. Put another way, the carnival king is a mixture of cheerleader and magician, which explains much of the Dragon's influence. And history shows that those born in the Dragon year are unusually blessed.

An important ingredient in the Dragon make-up is their desire for perfection. Once they set their minds on a task, they will see it through to the bitter end, regardless of any merit involved. As a result, they are double quick to find fault with anyone who doesn't give 101 per cent twenty-five hours a day, eight days a week. Curiously, a Dragon is most critical of those he loves most dearly and tends to create an embarrassing scene over the most trivial incident. And no one holds a grudge longer. It goes without saying that Dragons are the world's worst diplomats and even poorer gossips – always getting their facts wrong.

For all their abundant wealth of self belief and inner certainty, the Dragon cannot stand routine of any kind.

Should a Dragon feel imprisoned – either spiritually or physi-cally – they will almost certainly go mad. Once in decline, a Dragon tends to become lazy, fat and bitter. Impetuous and arrogant, Dragons are easily infatuated and chase endlessly after lost causes. Consequently, Dragons are often found making fools of themselves. But for all their outward brash-ness and apparent lack of sensitivity, the Dragon has a romantic and generous heart.

Because the Dragon is a deeply masculine sign, women born under its influence do not find life quite the same bowl of cherries as their male counterparts. Relationships are more difficult for female Dragons, who tend to want to run the whole works and accept little or no advice. Male Dragons, on the other hand, step into relationships with the ease of a duck taking to water. But Dragons, it must be added, do not make natural parents or nurses.

The three phases of a Dragon's life will be varied, marked by a difficult childhood. Here the baby Dragon will be misunderstood by parents and classmates; a tough time in which some Dragons will fall, never to rise. In the middle phase, the Dragon is expected to make as many friends as enemies. But fame and wealth usually come easily. In old age, a Dragon will find a life without regret. Always ready to lead one more carnival, Dragons are very much what we make them.

COMPATIBILITY OF MALE DRAGONS IN LOVE

FEMALE RAT

One of the great, great relationships. The Chinese Horoscopes are quite specific about the Rat and Dragon, placing them in the number one spot for sexual extravagance. The female Rat adores the Dragon's self assurance and in turn, the Dragon responds by satisfying all the Rat's sexual demands. Of the two Dragon/Rat relationships, the Rat lady and male Dragon is marginally the best. And if the Rat grumbles the Dragon is only faintly phased. What's more, even the difficult introverted Rat will find themselves opening up in the face of the male Dragon's powerful identity – well, nearly always. The beautiful and very witty pop singer Lyndsey de Paul is a Rat, and her open affair with Dragon James Coburn is an example of how close these signs are.

Star Rating: Five.

FEMALE BUFFALO

When these two powerful signs meet there is an inevitable clash of personalities and the resulting sparks might easily set their large hearts aflame with passion. But both signs see each other as a challenge as opposed to a partnership. The male Dragon is surprised by the female Buffalo. Her sharp mind and rich, deep soul, so different, on the surface at least, to the male of the species, are rare and exciting. The

146

Buffalo's complexities are an attraction to begin with, something he hopes he might straighten out with the help of his abundant self belief. But the affair turns sour when he finds the lady Buffalo wanting to take control of *him*. The lady Buffalo also underlines the somewhat shallow nature of the male Dragon's feelings, as it's sadly the case that he has a rather superficial view of romantic love. Luckily both signs are able to rectify mistakes quickly and their love affair will not drag painfully on.

Star Rating: Five slipping within a short while to two.

FEMALE TIGER

One of the high scoring love affairs – a veritable top of the table relationship which allows both impulsive signs full rein. Headstrong and generous in any relationship, and usually at any stage, Tiger and Dragon find themselves totally gripped by love and both adore the romance of an affair. Of course, it will end, gloriously, either in marriage or as just friends; parting is such sweet sorrow. Of the two pairings, the male Dragon/female Tiger is the most complete. Go for it, and enjoy!

Star Rating: Five and more if there's room.

FEMALE CAT

Bundles of goodies going for this affair of hot-headed and highly emotional Dragon male and sensuous, witty, tender female Cat. It promises much sexual pleasure and not many problems, so the indications are clear: go for it! But just the tiniest word of warning for the female partner. Dragons are only tolerant up to a point. Too many moodies from Ms Cat – there'll be one or two when the Dragon doesn't show on time – and Mr Dragon will be on his merry way, not over sad that it has not altogether worked out as a long term relationship. Anyway, both signs have plenty of other fish – so to speak – to fry.

Star Rating: Five.

FEMALE DRAGON

This is another love affair that holds all the promise in the world, with the sparks flying in it like no other. But the Chinese warn it is very much a hit and run affair with both sides doing their best to outdo the other in strength of passion. No prisoners are taken, no quarter is given in this do or die affair and, as ever when Dragons are involved, there will not be too many recriminations at the end. There will even be attempts at another fling as the flames die – Dragons are the supreme optimists!

Star Rating: Five for five minutes.

FEMALE SNAKE

One of the really great sexual partnerships. The Chinese are quite emphatic about the male Dragon and female Snake relationship, which, they say, has the hallmarks of developing into a life-long affair. The Dragon is, in fact, the distant cousin of the Snake, both of whom are members of the serpent family. Serpents are deeply connected with sex in our unconscious and with good reason. They are creatures who live in a world dominated by sexual instincts, and, it has to be said, few others. Added to this, the Chinese explain that in practically all circumstances, the Dragon can't help himself adoring the female Snake. Given this background, it is not surprising to find they score maximum points. Self satisfied Dragon and ex-editor of *The Times* and the *Sunday Times*, Harold Evans, left his wife for a Snake. She is the editor and journalist Tina Brown.

Star Rating: Five plus!

FEMALE HORSE

The fourth animal sign in a row of six which produces one hundred per cent love relationships for the sexually energetic and boastful Dragon. Full of self-confidence, the Dragon forms better partnerships when his lovers are not put off by his bragging. In fact, the signs the Dragon has strongest links with are, in the main, a touch on the vain side themselves. This means the Dragon and Horse look at each other as mirror images. They love each other's best points and in a short affair, overlook the weakest. A little helpless in love, should the Horse commit her wonderful self to a love affair with a Dragon, it will really go with a bang – in every sense. However, Ms Horse will eventually grow tired of her fiery lover, bored even, as they do with everyone. But while it lasts – oh boy! And again, the Dragon will not be too downcast in the parting.

Star Rating: Five all the way.

FEMALE GOAT

Here's an intense love affair that's doomed from the start, but then, most such love affairs usually are. So what's in it for the Dragon and Goat? The answer is found in the Goat, who with her fickle heart and wayward nature, has such a strong sense of the mischievous – a quality the Dragon can't resist. This adds up to the easily seduced Dragon being taken for a bit of a ride, which in the opening stages is delightful. Goats are sensuous and giving in sexual matters, but they wander, ever aware that it is possible the grass is greener somewhere else. Poor old Dragon, he might be having fun but he'll pay the price of a wayward mistress. And sure as eggs are eggs he'll not be the only one enjoying Mistress Goat's favours.

Star Rating: Four.

FEMALE MONKEY

The last of the five star love relationships on the Dragon's list of six. And it is unlike the others because although, as in all love affairs, there is plenty of physical contact, there is also much meeting of the mind. Both sides are more than capable of taking themselves not at all seriously, and although the Dragon is prone to over heating, he tends to be more relaxed with the Monkey than with any other. She is a great reader of the Dragon's inner strengths, and weaknesses, and will manipulate her colourful lover almost any way she wants. And the

Dragon won't mind one bit. In turn, he will push for the Monkey to act even more irresponsibly in matters of passion, and there will be no stopping these two positive signs. During his stay at Number Ten, it was often noted how close Premier Harold Wilson, a Dragon, worked with Marcia Williams, his Monkey secretary.

Star Rating: Five alive.

FEMALE ROOSTER

This is a case of putting the cart before the horse, or should it be the Dragon before the Rooster, or even sex before marriage? The point is that Roosters and Dragons are the best marriage partners of all the sign combinations, but the lady Rooster is not given to wild romances. She is a deeply conservative creature who is not inspired to open demonstrations of her innermost feelings. She builds romantic castles in the air, but that, for the Dragon, is no place for a castle, as appreciative as he might well be of the effort. The course of action here is for both male Dragon and female Rooster is to get themselves hitched pronto.

Star Rating: Two, seldom more, seldom less.

FEMALE DOG

The Dog and Dragon are a long term disaster area, more so if both signs, especially the Dragon, live up fully and honestly to their animal influences. Dog ladies do have great warmth and their openness utterly beguiles the impulsive Dragon, but the troublespot is that the Dragon has no real heart. The carnival leader is paper and paste, easily seduced and just a bit too fond of himself. The lady Dog will forgive his indiscretions, but she is a genuine and loyal lover who can be hurt. The chances are neither side will ever truly understand the other, and although the lady Dog/male Dragon is by far the better of the two combinations, it is still a difficult affair.

Star Rating: One at most.

FEMALE PIG

This is a jolly good tumble in the hay. The robust and easy-going Pig (how difficult it is not to call her a bit of a push-over) is a perfect foil for the positive and self assured Dragon. But the Chinese Horoscopes do not rate this love match very highly, suggesting that the over amorous Pig lady does not 'read' the Dragon's moods and that she has a tendency to be demanding at the wrong moments. But my experience is that most Western Dragons are pleased for the uncomplicated attention a Pig lady might easily give. She will certainly not spare herself in trying to please – a bit unsubtle at times, but a real raver. Male Dragon and female Pig are the hottest of the two pairs.

Star Rating: The Chinese say two. I say four.

COMPATIBILITY OF FEMALE DRAGONS IN LOVE

MALE RAT

One of the all time great relationships, at any level. The Chinese Horoscopes are quite specific about the Rat and Dragon, placing them in the number one spot for sexual extravagance. The male Rat adores the Dragon's self assurance and in turn, the Dragon responds by satisfying all the Rat's sexual demands, and the female Dragon is only faintly phased by the male Rat's aggressive outbursts. What is more, even the difficult introverted Rat will find himself opening up in the face of the female Dragon's powerful identity. But if there is the slightest hint of a hitch in the smooth running of charming Rat and warm hearted Dragon, it is in the fact that some lady Dragons are endowed with a little too much self esteem. They might, just might, scorch the Rat with their fire. Rat Marlon Brando's largely improvised handling of Dragon Maria Schneider in *The Last Tango in Paris* says something about Rat males and Dragon females on a sexual high.

Star Rating: Five, but the Rat must be careful not to get his tail scorched.

MALE BUFFALO

There is nothing actually disastrous with a male Buffalo falling madly in love with a female Dragon; the problem is that it happens so rarely hardly any data exists to prove it one way or another. In principle it should be the same as a male Dragon and female Buffalo, which is common, but there are differences. Male Buffaloes dominate any partnership, no matter what the sign, while the female Dragon suffers from a pronounced superiority which she inherits from her powerfully masculine sign. But as so often proves to be the case, there is an attraction of opposites which can be extremely exciting in the early stages of a love affair.

Star Rating: Two.

MALE TIGER

One of the high scoring love affairs – a veritable top of the table relationship which allows both impulsive signs full rein. Headstrong and generous in any relationship, and usually at any stage, Tiger and Dragon find themselves totally gripped by love and both adore the romance of an affair. Of course, it will end, gloriously, either in marriage or as just friends; parting is such sweet sorrow. Of the two pairings, the male Dragon/female Tiger is the most complete, but it is not worth splitting hairs over. Go for it, whatever the pairing, and enjoy it!

Star Rating: Five and more if there's room.

MALE CAT

Bundles of goodies going for this affair of hot-headed and emotional Dragon lady and sensuous, witty, tender male Cat. It promises much sexual pleasure and not many problems, so the indications are clear: go for it! Dragon ladies have a sign which is masculine in the extreme, and the male Cat enjoys – well, I hope he does – a strongly feminine influence. With this mixture of role reversals anything is possible, but it is in the sexual stakes that these two will run out winners. Esther Rantzen is a Dragon and was responsible for her then lover, TV man Desmond Wilcox, a Cat, leaving his wife. Esther, as we know, then married Des, got rich and saved the world from child abusers.

Star Rating: Five.

MALE DRAGON

This is another love affair that holds all the promise in the world, with the sparks flying in it like no other. But the Chinese warn it is very much a hit and run affair, with both sides doing their best to outdo the other in strength of passion. No prisoners are taken, no quarter is given, in this do or die affair and, as ever when Dragons are involved, there will not be too many recriminations at the end. There will even be attempts at another fling as the flames die – Dragons are the supreme optimists!

Star Rating: Five for five minutes.

MALE SNAKE

One of the really great sexual partnerships. The Chinese are quite emphatic about the female Dragon and male Snake relationship, which, they say, has the hallmarks of developing into a life long affair. The Dragon is, in fact, the distant cousin of the Snake, both of whom are members of the serpent family. Serpents are deeply connected with sex in our unconscious and with good reason. They are creatures who live in a world dominated by sexual instincts, and, it has to be said, few others. Added to this, the Chinese explain that in practically all circumstances, the Dragon can't help herself adoring the male Snake. Given this background, it is not surprising to find they score maximum points.

Star Rating: Five plus!

MALE HORSE

The fourth animal sign in a row of six which produce one hundred per cent love relationships for the sexually energetic and forceful Dragon. Full of self confidence, the Dragon has better partnerships when her lovers are not put off by her sometimes rather masculine character. In fact, the signs the Dragon has strongest links with, are in the main, a touch on the vain side themselves. This means the Dragon and Horse look at each other as mirror images. They love each other's best points and, in a short affair, overlook the weakest. A little helpless in love, should the Horse commit himself to a love affair with a Dragon, it will really go with a bang – in every sense. However, the Horse will eventually grow tired of his fiery lover, bored even, as they do with everyone. But while it lasts – oh boy! And again, the Dragon will not be too downcast at the parting.

Star Rating: Five all the way.

MALE GOAT

Here's a love affair that's doomed from the start, but then, most love affairs usually are. So what's in it for the Dragon and the Goat? The answer is found in the Goat, who, with his capricious heart and wayward nature, has a strong sense of the sexually mischievous – a quality the Dragon lady can't resist. This adds up to the easily seduced Dragon being taken for a bit of a ride, which in the opening stages is delightful. Goats are sensuous and giving in sexual matters, but they wander, always aware that it is possible the grass is greener somewhere else. Poor Dragon, she might be having fun but she'll pay the price of a wayward lover. And for sure she'll not be the only one enjoying the Goat's good time favours.

154

And pity the poor Goat when the Dragon lady finds out!
Star Rating: Four and dropping . . .

MALE MONKEY

The last of the five star love relationships on the Dragon's list
of six. And it is unlike the others because although, as in all
love affairs, there is plenty of physical contact, there is also
much meeting of the mind. Both sides are more than capable
of taking themselves not at all seriously, and although the
Dragon is prone to over heating, she tends to be more
relaxed with the Monkey than with any other. He is a great
reader of the Dragon's inner strengths, and weaknesses, and
will manipulate his colourful lover almost any way he wants.
And the Dragon won't mind one bit. In turn, she will push
for the Monkey to act even more irresponsibly in matters of
passion, and there will be no stopping these two positive
signs. Many have commented on the praise Monkey Tim
Rice has so often heaped on his Dragon star, Elaine Paige.
Star Rating: Five alive.

MALE ROOSTER

This is a case of putting the cart before the horse, or should it
be the Dragon before the Rooster, or even sex before
marriage? The point is that Roosters and Dragons are the
best marriage partners of all the sign combinations, but the
male Rooster, in spite of his boasts to the contrary, is not
given to wild romances. He is a deeply conservative creature
who is not inspired to open demonstrations of his innermost
feelings. He builds romantic castles in the air, but that, for
the Dragon, is no place for a castle, as appreciative as she
might well be for the effort. The course of action here is for
both female Dragon and male Rooster is to get themselves
hitched pronto.
Star Rating: Two, seldom more, seldom less.

MALE DOG

The Dog and Dragon are a long term disaster area, more so if both signs, especially the Dragon live up fully and honestly to their animal influences. Dog ladies do have great warmth and their openness utterly beguiles the impulsive Dragon, but the troublespot is that the Dragon has no real heart. The carnival leader is paper and paste, easily seduced and just a bit too overpowering. The male Dog will struggle with the lady Dragon's self assurance and forgive her determination to act as she wishes, but he is a genuine and loyal lover who can be easily hurt. The chances are neither side will ever truly understand the other.

Star Rating: One at the most.

MALE PIG

This is a jolly good tumble in the hay. The robust and easy-going Pig (how difficult it is not to call him a bit of a push-over) is a perfect foil for the positive and self assured Dragon. But the Chinese Horoscopes do not rate this love match very highly, suggesting that the over amorous Pig male does not 'read' the Dragon's moods and that he has a tendency to be demanding at the wrong moments. But my experience is that most Western Dragons are pleased for the uncomplicated attentions a Pig male might easily give. He will certainly not spare himself in trying to please – a bit unsubtle, but a real raver.

Star Rating: The Chinese say two. I say four.

COMPATIBILITY OF MALE DRAGONS IN MARRIAGE

FEMALE RAT

Champagne time! Ring the bells and bring on the wedding cake. This is one of the all time great combinations. In between flare ups and shouting matches they will forge strong emotional bonds that will not be broken easily. Even the rare over critical Rat will find themselves soothed by the inspiring male Dragon. For the normal extrovert Rat, bed continues to be a strong feature of married life, but Rat and Dragon will not neglect the many other fascinating areas that arise from a life spent in close harmony. Music, painting, the arts as a whole – all involve the senses, and Rat and Dragon will spend much time exploring them. Princess Alexandra is a Rat and her husband, Angus Ogilvy, is a Dragon.

Star Rating: Five plus! OK – Six!

FEMALE BUFFALO

In a romantic situation, female Buffalo and male Dragon might just about get themselves into a bed situation, but it won't be long before there's a parting of the ways. There really is nothing good to be said for this marriage and the fact that it is such a rarity is perhaps a vindication of the Chinese Horoscopes. The slightest ray of light appears when we are talking about a female Buffalo and male Dragon, but because these two powerful signs need to dominate even the smallest group, including the family, there can be no hope and nothing but enmity to fill their increasingly distant lives. Jane Fonda is a Buffalo and was once married to French director Roger Vadim, a Dragon. The marriage ended abruptly when he tried against her will to turn Jane into a sex goddess like Brigitte Bardot (Dog), whom he also married.

Star Rating: Zero.

FEMALE TIGER

This is a marriage which promises a great deal and, provided neither party is made to feel over restricted by the other's highly personal needs, there is every chance it will succeed. Dragons and Tigers are hot-headed, explosive creatures with little or no time for the dim witted of this world. Together a Dragon and Tiger enjoy a high level of excitement and tend to treat marriage as an extended love affair. But the male Dragon always wants to run the show – something the female Tiger is never entirely happy about. Strong when faced with a crisis, a long talk prior to reading the banns about who does what is nevertheless advisable. The male Dragon/female Tiger pairing rates the better of the two.

Star Rating: Four to five, with just a tiny reservation in respect of long term viability.

FEMALE CAT

Another five star relationship in marriage and love and all points north and west. The sensuous Cat knows just how to make the deeply passionate Dragon let go – not that any Dragon worth their salt (male or female) needs much prompting – and in marriage a strong sexual element will continue to dominate matters. The Cat must also keep a mental note that her husband has a mega-masculine influencing sign, which means a headstrong and entirely unbending response to life. She will, for example, discover a powerful figure at her side who will tend to take the upper hand and demand perfection in all things. But both enjoy routine and rituals.

Star Rating: Five, as long as the Cat doesn't mind sometimes playing second fiddle.

FEMALE DRAGON

The Chinese give a marriage between two Dragons a short term success, which really isn't a success at all – marriages are, or should be, a life long commitment. But perhaps a few years before the trip to a divorce court is all some Dragons want, in which case go for it. But for those who want a long term marriage, a male and female Dragon does not bode well. Sharp tongued, spiky and hard to please, Dragon marrieds find life increasingly difficult. What a Dragon really needs is a partner to deflect their negativity, not highlight it. But there are cases in which two Dragons have lasted, although I am told there's never a shortage of sparks. TV stars John Alderton and Pauline Collins are both Dragons, and maybe it is significant that when I invited them on my Radio Four programme on Chinese Horoscopes they agreed, but only if they did not appear together.

Star Rating: Could be anything from zero to five. Usually zero.

FEMALE SNAKE

Dragon men are bewitched by female Snakes and it does not take a great leap of the imagination to see that a marriage of some substance might easily develop. But there is a tiny word of warning. Snake ladies fall into two camps: those who cling possessively to the man in their life, who are the greater in number, and those who can't resist any man who hoves into view. Providing Mrs Snake is a one man girl, little can go wrong, apart from the Dragon feeling a bit hemmed in – another red alert, by the way. The great literary couple, Virginia Woolf and her husband Leonard were a Snake and Dragon. Pakistan's beautiful Bhenazir Bhutto is also a Snake and, I am reliably informed, has happily married a Dragon.

Star Rating: Four or five.

FEMALE HORSE

A love affair between these two amorous signs, being so strong, implies that a wedding looks a good bet. And if they are as headstrong as the two signs usually are, male Dragon and female Horse won't stop to think. But once married, there is a problem. Horse ladies are easily seduced and no matter how strong and appealing their Dragon partner might be, they tend to give in. And sadly, Dragons are a push over for any bright little thing in a short skirt. So, it is the old curse of fidelity, or the lack of it, which acts as the fly in this particular ointment. However, should both Dragon and Horse agree that the odd extra-marital fling is not serious enough to damage the marriage, it will work surprisingly well, and emerge as a very practical outfit. For instance, kids won't be a problem and, if anything, might help bond the union.

Star Rating: Two through to five.

FEMALE GOAT

The female goat is prone to an extremely fickle heart and, loves the good life and all the many sensual experiences that good living brings. Mistress Goat, for ever thinking that the grass is greener somewhere else, finds it difficult to say no to any new offer of excitement. For the Dragon, her changing moods are impossible to understand, let alone live with. All in all, not the kind of thing to appeal to a Dragon, who is only really interested in leading life's carnival and not being led up the garden path. Capricious Goats have their moments and some Dragons might even enjoy tethering them but most won't bother. Marriage is not a good idea.

Star Rating: One, creeping up to two.

FEMALE MONKEY

One of the best of all marriages, especially if there is a hint of professional or business interest involved. The Monkey lady has a great skill when it comes to organisation and, coupled with the Dragon's drive and imagination, the sky's the limit. Both Dragons and Monkeys do have the potential to experiment, and it is said the Monkey finds it hard to turn down the offer of a new experience. This could mean the marriage is threatened by the Monkey suddenly deciding she wants to change her lifestyle. But there is usually so much mutual respect between Monkey wife and Dragon husband that whatever fate brings, they see it through together. And this is another marriage in which a review of the marriage vows, highlighting the one to be faithful, might not be a bad idea once in a while. Fifties singing star Dragon Eddie Fisher married two Monkeys to prove the point – Debbie Reynolds and Elizabeth Taylor.

Star Rating: Five. Top whack.

FEMALE ROOSTER

Another terrific marriage for the lucky Dragon, who does seem to have more than his fair share of options when it comes to stepping down the aisle with the right goods. Unlike the Monkey wife, who tends to over indulge the Dragon's weakest points, the morally incorruptible Rooster makes it clear there will be no hanky-panky while she's around. Sometimes both Dragon and Rooster are over critical of each other, and here I speak from personal experience (Mrs Fantoni/mum and Mrs Fantoni/wife are both Roosters). But when Rooster wife and Dragon husband are faced with a genuine threat, especially one which contains an abuse of power, there is no couple more able to cope. No pair is better capable of putting up a fight, or starting one! Jeffrey Archer is a Dragon and his wife, Mary, is a Rooster. Remember the way they saw off the blackmailing callgirl and a dubious Fleet Street?

Star Rating: Five all the way.

FEMALE DOG

Not recommended. The Chinese Horoscopes go to great lengths to point out that Dogs and Dragons have little or no understanding. In my experience I have found this to be mainly the case, but I must say that I have met a number of very successful Dog and Dragon marriages – if not love affairs. The act of marriage does give the Dog the security she craves at heart, and in turn the male Dragon's often self-important existence is given a broader horizon by being in constant contact with the Dog lady's sense of idealism. But it must be remembered that the Dog's anxiety to do the right thing may be misunderstood as merely fretting over details, and that the Dragon might, as a result of his own self importance, overlook the Dog's efforts to please. Ringo Starr is a Dragon and his second wife, Barbara Bach, is a Dog, which might just have something to do with his drinking habits. For an up-date watch this space!

Star Rating: Zero, but there might be two or even three in the right circumstances.

FEMALE PIG

On paper, this looks like a first class marriage, and it might well turn out that way. The Pig lady is in the main a home-maker and eager to display her domestic skills. But the problem is that some Pig ladies, the introverts, care nothing for their home and live in a tip. It is this particular brand of Pigette that the Dragon should avoid. Perfectionists, Dragons like tidy homes and they place a great deal of importance on rituals, in which tidiness often plays a part. It is odd, but marriages frequently fail because one partner is a slob and can't handle the simple routines marriage creates.

Star Rating: One, two or three.

COMPATIBILITY OF FEMALE DRAGONS IN MARRIAGE

MALE RAT

Champagne time! Ring the bells and bring on the wedding cake. This is one of the all time great combinations. No matter how aggressive the male Rat becomes, the female Dragon won't even flinch, and she'll give as good as she gets. In between flare-ups and shouting matches they will forge strong emotional bonds that will not be broken easily. Even the introverted, uptight and deeply critical Rat will find himself soothed by the inspiring female Dragon. For the normally extrovert Rat, bed continues to be a strong feature of married life, but Rat and Dragon will not neglect the many other fascinating areas that arise from a life spent in close harmony. Music, painting, the arts as a whole – all involve the senses, and Rat and Dragon will spend much time exploring them. TV actor John Stride is a Rat and his wife, April, a former actress, is a Dragon.

Star Rating: Five.

MALE BUFFALO

In a romantic situation, male Buffalo and female Dragon might just about get themselves into a bed situation, but it won't be long before there's a parting of ways. There really is nothing good to be said for this marriage and the fact that it is such a rarity is perhaps a vindication of the Chinese Horoscopes. The slightest ray of light appears when we are talking about a female Buffalo and male Dragon, but because these two powerful signs need to dominate even the smallest group, including the family, there can be no hope and nothing but enmity to fill their increasingly distant lives.

Star Rating: Zero.

MALE TIGER

This is a marriage which promises a great deal and, provided neither party is made to feel over restricted by the other's highly personal needs, there is every chance it will succeed. Dragons and Tigers are hot-headed, explosive creatures with little or no time for the dim witted of this world. Together a Dragon and Tiger enjoy a high level of excitement and tend to treat marriage as an extended love affair. But with the female Dragon, there is always a tendency for them to want to run the show – something the male Tiger is never entirely happy about. A long talk prior to reading the banns about who does what is advisable. Weatherman Ian McCaskill is a Tiger and is married to a Dragon wife. He says they are best together when faced with adversity.

Star Rating: Four, with just a tiny reservation in respect of the long term viability.

MALE CAT

Another five star relationship in marriage and love and all points north and west. The sensuous Cat knows just how to make the deeply passionate Dragon let go – not that any Dragon worth their salt (male or female) needs much prompting – and in marriage a strong sexual element will continue to dominate matters. The Cat must also keep a mental note that his wife has a mega-masculine influencing sign, which means a headstrong and sometimes not entirely feminine response to life. He will, for example, discover a powerful lady at his side who will tend to take the upper hand. After their affair, Dragon Esther Rantzen did actually marry her Cat lover, Desmond Wilcox.

Star Rating: Five, as long as the Cat doesn't mind sometimes playing second fiddle.

MALE DRAGON

The Chinese give marriage between two Dragons a short term success, which really isn't a success at all – marriages are, or should be, a life long commitment. But perhaps a few years before the trip to a divorce court is all some Dragons want, in which case go for it. But for those who want a long term marriage, a male and female Dragon marriage does not bode well. Sharp-tongued, spiky and hard to please, Dragon marrieds find life increasingly difficult. What a Dragon really needs is a partner to deflect their negativity, not highlight it. But there are cases in which two Dragons have lasted, although I am told there's never a shortage of sparks. TV stars John Alderton and Pauline Collins are both Dragons, and maybe it is significant that when I invited them on my Radio Four programme on Chinese Horoscopes they agreed, but only if they did not appear together.

Star Rating: Could be anything from zero to five. Usually zero.

MALE SNAKE

Dragon ladies are often bewitched by male Snakes and it does not take a great leap of the imagination to see that a marriage of some substance might easily develop. But there is a tiny word of warning. Snake males fall into two camps: those who cling possessively to the woman in their life, who are the greater in number, and those who can't resist any woman who hoves into view. Providing Mr Snake is a one girl man, little can go wrong, apart from the Dragon feeling a bit hemmed in – another red alert, by the way.

Star Rating: Four or five.

MALE HORSE

A love affair between these two amorous signs, being so strong, implies that a wedding looks a good bet. And if they are as headstrong as the two signs usually are, female Dragon and male Horse won't stop to think. But once married, there

165

is a problem. Horse males are weakest when smitten by romance, and no matter how strong and appealing their Dragon partner might be, they tend to give in. And sadly, Dragon ladies can fall pretty heavily when given the opportunity. So, it is the old curse of fidelity, or the lack of it, which acts as the fly in this particular ointment. However, should both Dragon and Horse agree that the odd extra-marital fling is not serious enough to damage the marriage, it will work surprisingly well, and they will emerge as a very practical outfit.

Star Rating: Two through to five.

MALE GOAT

The male Goat is prone to an extremely fickle heart, and loves the good life and all the many sensual experiences that good living brings. The Goat, for ever thinking that the grass is greener somewhere else, finds it difficult to say no to any new offer of excitement. For the female Dragon, his changing moods are impossible to understand, let alone live with. All in all, not the kind of thing to appeal to a Dragon, who is only really interested in leading life's carnival and not being led up the garden path. Capricious Goats have their moments and some Dragons might even enjoy tethering them, but most won't bother. Marriage is not a good idea.

Star Rating: One, creeping up to two.

MALE MONKEY

One of the best of all marriages, especially if there is a hint of professional or business interest involved. The Monkey has great skills when it comes to organisation and adaptability, and coupled with the Dragon's self confidence and imagination the sky's the limit. Both Dragons and Monkeys do have the potential to experiment, and it is said that the Monkey finds it hard to turn down the offer of a new experience. This could mean the marriage is threatened by the Monkey suddenly deciding he wants to change his lifestyle. But there is usually so much mutual respect between Monkey husband

and Dragon wife that whatever fate brings, they see it through together. And this is another marriage in which a review of the marriage vows, highlighting the one to be faithful, might not be a bad idea once in a while. The male Monkey/female Dragon is not the strongest of the pairs, as Dragon Shirley Temple found when marrying her first husband, actor Monkey John Agar.

Star Rating: Five (most times).

MALE ROOSTER

Another terrific marriage for the lucky Dragon, who does seem to have more than her fair share of options when it comes to stepping down the aisle with the right goods. Unlike the Monkey husband, who is prone to over indulge the Dragon's weakest points, the morally incorruptible Rooster makes it clear there will be no hanky-panky while he's around. Sometimes both Dragon and Rooster are over critical of each other. In the negative, this could prove disastrous, and sometimes is. But when Rooster husband and Dragon wife are faced with a genuine threat, especially one which contains an abuse of power, there is no couple more able to cope. No pair is better capable of putting up a fight, or starting one!

Star Rating: Five all the way.

MALE DOG

Not recommended. The Chinese Horoscopes go to great lengths to point out that Dogs and Dragons have little or no understanding. In my experience I have found this to be mainly the case, but I must say that I have met a number of very successful Dog and Dragon marriages – if not love affairs. The act of marriage does give the Dog the security he craves at heart, and in turn the female Dragon's often self centred existence is given broader horizons by being in constant contact with the Dog's sense of idealism. But it must be remembered that the Dog's anxiety to do the right thing may be misunderstood as merely fretting over details, and that the Dragon might, as a result of her own self esteem, overlook the Dog's efforts to please. Dog males/female Dragons are the best of the two pairs.

Star Rating: Zero, but there might be two or even three in the right circumstances.

MALE PIG

On paper, this looks like a first class marriage, and it might well turn out that way. But the problem is that the Pig males have a somewhat high opinion of their considerable home making talents, which the Dragon lady admires but prefers not to have too openly displayed – she's the boss, or thinks she is! Pig chaps are honest souls at heart and easily duped as a result, something the Dragon is constantly irritated by. And it must be said that some male Pigs treat their home a little too casually – mess everywhere and friends staying till the early hours. Marriages frequently fail because one partner is a slob and can't handle the simple routines marriage creates. Billionaire Saudi businessman Adnan Khashoggi is a Pig and his former wife, socialite Saraya, a Dragon. A typical female Dragon, she demanded $1 billion as a divorce settlement. But for once the Pig was not duped and she ended up with a lot less out of court.

Star Rating: One, two or three.

COMPATIBILITY OF MALE DRAGONS IN FRIENDSHIP

MALE RAT

Few better relationships exist anywhere in the twelve signs. As married partners, as lovers and as friends, there can be no stronger pair. The Rat takes the Dragon's raw thoughts and reshapes them. The Dragon in turn excites the Rat's bright and witty mind. There will be no reproaches and no bad feelings if things go wrong. The Rat will find himself with hardly anything to grumble over and the self-centred Dragon will be almost bearable.
Star Rating: Six!

MALE BUFFALO

One of the big off/on relationships, the Buffalo finds certain features of the Dragon infuriating but at the same time has enough intelligence to realise that they have more than a little to offer in the way of loyal friendship. Both signs dominate the world stage and as friends there is invariably a great deal of friction. But once they overcome their differences, however impermanently, many good things can grow from their collective strength. That said, it is not a common relationship and examples are few and far between.
Star Rating: Sometimes very low, sometimes just under five. A tough one to be specific about.

MALE TIGER

Because Tigers are extremely strong willed and hot-headed in the face of authority, their chums must reflect these characteristics. Yet at the same time they must do so without detracting from the Tiger's need to run things. Not an easy task, but one which the Dragon is more than able to cope with. Admittedly there are a few nettles to grasp in terms of who does what, if the friendship involves business, but once decided, each sign backs the other up to the hilt. Faced with a tough problem, a Tiger and Dragon are a force to be reckoned with and will not be taken for a ride. Both are generous to those around them and are always eager to help each other in the face of adversity.

Star Rating: Five.

MALE CAT

Here's a couple of swells with a long future. The diplomatic Cat acts like blotting paper when the hot-headed Dragon blows his top – even if it is with the Cat. Both are two sides of the same coin, a perfect balancing act with one providing the other with what he most lacks. No problems in sight here, as long as the Dragon remembers to say sorry once in a while. The great 'Road' movie stars, Bob Hope and Bing Crosby, were a Cat and Dragon team. Bob's first movie hit, curiously enough, was *The Cat and the Canary.* Cute? And top news-readers Sir Alistair Burnet and Sandy Gall seem the most comfortable pair on *News at Ten.* They are a Dragon and Cat team – Sandy is the Cat.

Star Rating: Five all the way.

MALE DRAGON

This is the most promising of all the Dragon relationships – it certainly has the most legs (or should it be wings?) Dragon males are up-front and they hate pussyfooting around. They will certainly enjoy a sense of mutual respect, and it is a good idea to play to each other's strengths, not compete. If a couple of Dragons are going to last the course, they must also always remember to air their differences sooner rather than later, and try not to be too surprised when the other Dragon demands the same attention from those around. But even if the partnership is to succeed, no matter whether it is business or pure friendship, the best is to be had at the beginning. One of the *greatest ever* pop records and an instant smash hit was entirely the result of the Dragon's influence. 'You've Lost that Loving Feeling' was recorded by the Righteous Brothers, and produced and co-written by Phil Spector, a producer who, many claim, changed the face of pop music from teenage mush into an art form. Both the Brothers and Phil are Dragons and the record was made in 1964, the year of the Dragon. Near as they came, neither artists or producer were to repeat their initial colossal success.

Star Rating: One or five, seldom much in between.

MALE SNAKE

Given the good news in terms of marriage and love, this ought to be a stronger pairing. But there is a point in a Snake's life which leads him to become ineffective and incapable of making decisions. This is during their periodic spells of 'hibernation', a time when they have no direct control over their actions. Where a Snake lady is concerned, a Dragon male might easily bide his time, but when it's a mate or worse, a business friend, then the lack of input will drive the Dragon up the wall. But during the positive spells, there is much in common and a great deal of subtle understanding takes place. One of the great musical partnerships of all time existed between Sir Edward Elgar, a Snake, and the boy Dragon genius, Sir Yehudi Menuhin. Their recording of the composer's violin concerto, recorded when Menuhin was only sixteen, is considered among the top ten recordings ever made. Hale and Pace are another great team, as are Mel Smith and Griff Rhys Jones.

Star Rating: Three. Sometimes four. Sometimes five.

MALE HORSE

Horses demand a high level of integrity from those who they form friendships with and, ever practical, they do not get on well with daydreamers. Many Dragons have more dream power than logic, and this might easily form a barrier unless it is understood at the very beginning that both have quite different qualities to bring to a friendship. Neither are strangers to hard work and a business with Dragon and Horse forming a joint head is destined for success. In spite of the Horse sometimes becoming bored with even the closest things, including his friends, and the Dragon's hot-headed pursuit of any goal that brings him attention, this is a solid enough friendship. Again, a case of live and let live. Greatest ever songwriting team, Lennon and McCartney, were Dragon and Horse, and it was their inability to compromise their strongly held ideas that set them apart.

Star Rating: Four-ish.

MALE GOAT

All my experience indicates that this is a pair of chums who do not last the distance. Capricious as the day is long, the Goat simply needs more understanding than the short-fused Dragon is capable of. Short bursts in a creative field might help Dragon and Goat make something of their friendship. Although the Chinese Horoscopes are a little indifferent to this partnership, I have found it usually less than positive.

Star Rating: Two at most.

MALE MONKEY

This is an extremely auspicious relationship where both signs have all the cards, and know how to play them. A business with Dragon and Monkey is a sure bet as long as the Monkey is not too over ambitious or devious in his methods. But in the main, the Monkey's guile and adaptability, his sense of fun and quick wits, serve, and in turn are served by, the Dragon's brash originality. Should the two signs start a company, it is best that the Monkey keeps the books and the Dragon does the selling.

Star Rating: Five.

MALE ROOSTER

Another great partnership. The Dragon is not always helped by everyone telling him he is a great guy – a little criticism does him no harm at all and our old friend the candid Rooster is quick to pull the Dragon up short. In turn, the Dragon is quick to spot the Rooster's habit of building castles in the air, which he re-creates into something more attainable. Whereas the Monkey will let the Dragon carry the can when things go wrong, the Rooster will share all kinds of responsibility – personal and business. A clean relationship this, with much honest talk and the most positive side of both signs given a first rate chance of developing. The two geniuses behind the Spaghetti Western style of film making were a Dragon and Rooster. Director and writer Sergio Leone, a Rooster, dreamed up the plots and Dragon Ennio Mariccone created the music.

Star Rating: Five.

MALE DOG

The Chinese say Dog and Dragon have no understanding, and this is thought to be the least auspicious of all the Dragon's relationships. Dogs have a pessimistic streak, they worry over details and are genuinely concerned over the welfare of others less fortunate. Dragons are not so inclined. But Dragons admire the Dog's devotion, and once shown how, will readily return it. Any friendship involves good and bad times, and all friends have to work at putting the bad times right. This the Dog does instinctively, provided that he has not been treated poorly as a child; a kicked Dog may easily turn nasty. Dragons find forgiveness harder. This pair has more than a fair chance, but with reservations.

Star Rating: Three, and points up and down.

MALE PIG

Dragons are usually fine on their own. If they have to face life in their damp and dark caves, so be it. But Pigs are social creatures and adore to be in with the crowd. This means that a friendship between Pig and Dragon requires a centre, or a purpose of some kind, in order to make the most of it. Great in relationships, Pigs are willing and extremely honest in their dealings with those they like – which is practically everyone. A business partnership is a natural conclusion to a Pig and Dragon's friendship. Jeffrey Archer, a Dragon, had his major best-selling books edited by a Pig, Richard Cohen. Some have suggested it was the Pig who did most of the work, but I know for a fact it was shared evenly – the Dragon thinking up the plot and the Pig polishing up the prose.

Star Rating: Five.

COMPATIBILITY OF FEMALE DRAGONS IN FRIENDSHIP

FEMALE RAT

All the signs point to a strong and harmonious friendship, and so it will be. The female Dragon, though, has a strong masculine streak to her influence, which in a woman creates a set of sexual and emotional contradictions. The Rat recognises this and will let the Dragon do her own thing, which often means simply helping the Dragon calm down and get life back into perspective. In return, the Dragon will inspire the Rat and ease away her more anxious moments.

Star Rating: Five.

FEMALE BUFFALO

Difficult. Another case of male influence on female shoulders, with the result that the female side of these strong personalities are subjected to an invasion of unnatural masculine impulses. But where the negative sides of these influences cancel each other out, there is hope. The influence creates two ladies who prefer their own company – not the most auspicious pointer to lasting friendship. And the advice from the Chinese is not, should it be on the cards, to go into business without firm ideas about who does what.

Star Rating: One, sometimes one and a half.

FEMALE TIGER

Because Tigers are extremely strong willed and hot-headed in the face of authority, their chums must reflect these characteristics. Yet at the same time they must do so without detracting from the Tiger's need to run things. Not an easy task, but one which the Dragon is more than able to cope with. Admittedly there are a few nettles to grasp in terms of who does what, if the friendship involves business, but once decided, each sign backs the other up to the hilt. Faced with a tough problem, a Tiger and a Dragon are a force to be reckoned with and will not be taken for a ride. Both are generous to those around them and are always eager to help each other in the face of adversity. The female version is less auspicious than the male.

Star Rating: Four.

FEMALE CAT

Here's a couple of girls with a long future. The diplomatic Cat acts like blotting paper when the hot-headed Dragon blows her fuse, even if it is with the Cat. Both are two sides of the same coin, a perfect balancing act with one providing the other what she most lacks. No problems in sight here, as long as the Dragon remembers to say sorry once in a while.

Star Rating: Five all the way.

FEMALE DRAGON

This should be the most promising of all the Dragon relationships. Dragon females are up front and they hate pussyfooting around. They will certainly enjoy a sense of mutual respect, and it is a good idea to play to each other's strengths, not compete. But because the female Dragon has such a strong masculine side, there is always an internal confusion, which in many Dragon ladies is never fully resolved. If a couple of Dragon ladies are going to last the course, they must always remember to air their differences sooner rather than later, and try not to be too surprised when the other Dragon demands the same attention from those around. But even if the partnership is to succeed, no matter that it is business or pure friendship, the best is to be had at the beginning.

Star Rating: One or five. Seldom much in between.

FEMALE SNAKE

Given the good news in terms of marriage and love, this ought to be a stronger pairing. But there is a point in a Snake's life which leads her to become ineffective and incapable of making decisions. This is during their periodic spells of 'hibernation', a time when they have no direct control over their actions. Where a Snake male is concerned, a Dragon female might easily bide her time, but when it's a girlfriend, or worse, a business partner, then the lack of input will drive the Dragon up the wall. But during the positive spells, there is much in common and a great deal of subtle understanding takes place.

Star Rating: Three. Sometimes four. Sometimes five.

FEMALE HORSE

Horses demand a high level of integrity from those whom they form friendships with, and ever practical, they do not get on well with daydreamers. Many Dragons have more dream power than logic, and this might easily form a barrier

176

unless it is understood at the very beginning that both have quite different qualities to bring to a friendship. Neither are strangers to hard work and a business with Dragon and Horse forming a joint head is destined for success. In spite of the Horse sometimes becoming bored with even the closest things, including her friends, and the Dragon's reckless pursuit of any goal that brings her attention, this is a solid enough friendship. Again, a case of live and let live.

Star Rating: Four-ish

FEMALE GOAT

All my experience indicates that this is a pair of ladies who do not last the distance. Capricious as the day is long, the Goat simply needs more understanding than the short-fused Dragon is capable of. Short bursts in a creative field might help Dragon and Goat make something of their friendship. Although the Chinese Horoscopes are a little indifferent to this partnership, I have found it usually less than positive.

Star Rating: Two at most.

FEMALE MONKEY

This is an extremely auspicious relationship where both signs have all the cards and know how to play them. A business with Dragon and Monkey is a sure bet as long as the Monkey is not too over ambitious, or devious in her methods. But in the main, the Monkey's guile and adaptability, her sense of fun and quick wits, serve, and in turn are served by, the Dragon's brash originality. Should the two signs start a company, it is best that the Monkey keeps the books and the Dragon does the selling.

Star Rating: Five.

FEMALE ROOSTER

All the makings of a firm friendship, but there are a few problems. The Dragon female is not always helped by expecting everyone to be as perfect as they are – or think they are. She may not like it, but a little criticism does no harm. Our old friend the candid Rooster is quick to pull the Dragon up short. In turn, the Dragon is quick to spot the Rooster's habit of building castles in the air, which she re-creates into something more attainable. Whereas the Monkey will let the Dragon carry the can when things go wrong, the Rooster will share all kinds of responsibility – personal and business. A clean relationship this, with much honest talk and the most positive side of both signs given a first rate chance of developing. My mother is a Rooster, and enjoys a splendid relationship with a Dragon, a nurse she met while in hospital.

Star Rating: Five.

FEMALE DOG

The Chinese say Dog and Dragon have no understanding, and this is thought to be the least auspicious of all the Dragon's relationships. Dogs have a pessimistic streak, worry over details and are genuinely concerned over the welfare of others less fortunate than themselves. Dragons are not so inclined. But Dragons admire the Dog's devotion, and once shown how, will readily return it. Any friendship involves good and bad times, and all friends have to work at putting the bad times right. This the Dog does instinctively, provided that she has not been treated poorly as a child; a kicked Dog may easily turn nasty. Dragons find forgiveness harder. This pair has more than a fair chance, but with reservations. Female Dragon/female Dog are the best.

Star Rating: Three, and points up and down.

FEMALE PIG

Dragons are usually fine on their own. If they have to face life in their damp and dark caves, so be it. But Pigs are social creatures and adore to be in with the crowd. This means that a friendship between Pig and Dragon ladies requires a centre, or a purpose of some kind in order to make the most of it. Great in relationships, Pigs are willing and extremely honest in their dealings with those they like – which is practically everyone. A business partnership is a natural conclusion to a Pig and a Dragon's friendship.

Star Rating: Five.

THE SNAKE

1905	February 4th to January 24th	1906
1917	January 23rd to February 10th	1918
1929	February 10th to January 29th	1930
1941	January 27th to February 14th	1942
1953	February 14th to February 2nd	1954
1965	February 2nd to January 20th	1966
1977	February 18th to February 6th	1978
1989	February 6th to January 26th	1990

Eric Morecambe and Ernie Wise (Tiger and Buffalo).
Two strong and imaginative creatures have much to give each other.
(Times Newspapers Ltd).

Richard Burton and Elizabeth Taylor (Buffalo and Monkey).
Marriage complicates the issue . . .
(Gianni Bozzacchi, Rex Features Ltd)

Mick Jagger and Jerry Hall (Goat and Monkey).
The longer the relationship lasts the better this pair's chance of romantic
happiness. **(Times Newspapers Ltd)**

Prince Philip and Queen Elizabeth II (Rooster and Tiger).
Here's a rum couple . . . the male Rooster protects his deepest feelings by his cocksure stance.
(Times Newspapers Ltd)

Dr David Owen and David Steel (both Tigers).
The pits . . . **(Times Newspapers Ltd)**

Neil and Glenys Kinnock (Horse and Monkey).
The often manipulative Monkey will frequently infuriate the normally even-tempered
Horse . . . **(Times Newspapers Ltd)**

Mel Smith and Griff Rhys Jones (Dragon and Snake).
During the positive spells, there is much in common . . .
(Times Newspapers Ltd)

David Bailey and Jean Shrimpton (Buffalo and Horse).
Both signs demand great independence . . .
(Richard Young, Rex Features Ltd)

The Duke and Duchess of York (Rat and Pig). Marriage frequently creates the atmosphere in which a Rat and Pig can discover their most positive characteristics – both are social and enjoy good living. **(Times Newspapers Ltd)**

Princess Anne and Mark Phillips (Tiger and Rat). The Tiger sees herself as the boss of any team . . . **(Rex Features Ltd)**

The Prince and Princess of Wales (Rat and Buffalo). The Buffalo lady will increasingly dominate the home and the Rat will be left feeling more and more impotent.
(Rex Features Ltd)

Dennis and Margaret Thatcher (Cat and Buffalo). The Cat is not given to great ideals and does not share the Buffalo's power seeking . . .
(Times Newspapers Ltd)

Roger Law (left) and Peter Fluck (both Snakes).
An artistic base is a saving grace . . .
(Times Newspapers Ltd)

James Coburn and Lynsey de Paul (Dragon and Rat).
One of the great great relationships . . .
(Rex Features Ltd)

The earth doth like a Snake renew
Her winter weeds outworn:
Heaven smiles, and faiths and empires gleam,
Like wrecks of a dissolving dream.

Shelley

THE YEAR OF THE SNAKE

Snakes are born under the sign of wisdom. Unlike here, where they are thought of as evil, in the East Snakes are highly regarded. To be called a Snake in China is a compliment, and the term is applied only to someone acting with great insight or artistic skill. The Chinese also believe that a Snake in the family will help the rice to grow fat. In Western terms, this means a Snake will always have the ability to make money when needed.

Snakes are above all guided by their intuition. No other sign relies so much on their inner senses to help them perform even life's most simple acts. This is perhaps why the Snake is thought to have clairvoyant powers and the ability to bewitch. Snakes think deeply, pondering long before putting a plan into operation. But their thought process is not a case of logical progression. Snakes 'think' with their spirit, which is why so many excel in the fields of painting, sculpture and, above all, music; fields in which the romantic heart rules the clinical mind. Snakes are also blessed with a highly refined sense of humour, which like art depends on intuition in order to be successful. Furthermore, Snakes have a pronounced spiritual awareness which frequently expresses itself in a leaning towards the religious life.

If the Snake is given to great inner perception, they also suffer from long periods of inactivity. The word for 'lazy' in Chinese is the same as 'inactive', and it must be emphasised that all Snakes will undergo long periods in which they appear to be doing nothing. Do not be mistaken. It is at its most 'inactive' that the Snake is at its most productive. This usually takes place before the major changes which occur regularly in a Snake's life. In spite of periods of hibernation-like calm, Snakes have an active mind. But do not ask a

182

Snake to make up their mind in a hurry. Unless their intuition is running on all cylinders, Snakes will invariably make the wrong decision. As a result, the Snake makes a poor gambler. But once a Snake has set their mind on something, whether it be a new sexual partner or a new pair of shoes, nothing will stand in their way. Snakes are extremely possessive, especially in human relationships, and cling passionately to those they love.

The Snake sign is extremely feminine and as a result, men who are born in the Snake year are seldom aggressive, virile types. Snake men are often slightly reserved and well mannered. They have charisma, which they sometimes unconsciously exploit. Snake women, it is believed, love accessories and adore jewels. Snakes hate violence.

The three phases of a Snake's life are marked by what the East calls karma – a state whereby each action subtly yet inescapably influences the next. For the young Snake, life will be solitary and for the most part misunderstood. They grow painfully slowly, which will alienate all but the most dutiful parent. The Snake's mystical centre will produce plenty of tricky moments but there is comfort in old age. For the Snake who survives there is frequently great material wealth at the end of the road. The Chinese say that Snakes born in summer will find lasting happiness, but those born during a winter storm will always be in danger.

COMPATABILITY OF MALE SNAKES IN LOVE

FEMALE RAT

Rats are easily seduced by the Snake, who's natural sexuality promises so much excitement. This sometimes means the Rat will rush into the relationship, which might not always suit the Snake who is never at his best when forced into making a decision in a hurry. But there is a great deal of sexual chemistry on hand for Rat and Snake if they can overcome their most pronounced animal influences – aggressiveness in the case of the Rat, over-possessiveness in the case of the Snake. Of the two Rat/Snake combinations, lady Rat and male Snake is the most auspicious coupling.

Star Rating: Three, with a point lost or gained depending on the Rat's staying power.

FEMALE BUFFALO

Female Buffaloes are frequently intrigued by the male Snake's highly imaginative personality. The male Snake is humorous, artistic and wise. He has a form of sensuality which completely overwhelms the lady Buffalo. Using his subtle understanding of the senses, he winds his way into her most sheltered areas and cleverly soothes the female Buffalo's more complex emotions. The Buffalo's response is sometimes to be shocked by the depth of her own sensuality and at other times resistant. But she will give in fully at one stage to the Snake's bewitching charm. Of the two pairings, the female Buffalo and male Snake has less understanding and is the least common.

Star Rating: Two, sometimes three.

FEMALE TIGER

Tigers are very often captivated by the charm, subtle humour and quiet sexuality of the male Snake. Tiger ladies are usually quite fearless in love and once they decide, they act without hesitation. But even the most forward male Snake, and there are many, acts on a different set of impulses. They still need time to feel right about their actions, however exciting the prospect. Whereas the female Tiger is dominated by a male sign, the Snake is essentially a female sign. As you will have gathered, a pretty messy sort of relationship which promises more than is delivered by either side.

Star Rating: One at the very most.

FEMALE CAT

The female Cat has a soft nature, usually, and a highly tuned sense of what makes life worth living. They expect their partner to share their love of good food and fine wines, and the male Snake is quick to respond. The lady Cat can match his sexual expression and although the male Snake might easily become possessive and make demands the Cat is not always able to meet, she will nevertheless make plenty of hay while the sun shines, as it promises to do regularly during this affair. Much laughter, much love. But the possessive Snake does pose a bit of a problem in the long run.

Star Rating: Three, sometimes four. Sometimes even five! (but only for a very short romance).

FEMALE DRAGON

One of the really great sexual partnerships. The Chinese are quite emphatic about the female Dragon and male Snake relationship, which, they say, has the hallmarks of developing into a life long affair. The Dragon is, in fact, the distant cousin of the Snake, both of whom are members of the serpent family. Serpents are deeply connected with sex in our unconscious and with good reason. They are creatures who live in a world dominated by sexual instincts, and, it has to be said, few others. Added to this, the Chinese explain that in practically all circumstances, the Dragon can't help herself adoring the male Snake. Given this background, it is not surprising to find they score maximum points.

Star Rating: Five plus!

FEMALE SNAKE

Two Snakes are not thought to be ideal partners, least of all when in love. Possessive in love and, the Chinese add, unlucky, there is little or no future in these two bewitching animals. The biggest problem is that Snakes have no real say in what they feel, and as a result require a partner who is able to offset this sense of emotional unreality. I admit there is a very short term relationship on offer here, but it's only worth a candle when there's talk of a long term commitment. Leave two real snakes in a cage and the chances are that when driven by hunger, one will devour the other.

Star Rating: Big Zero.

FEMALE HORSE

Good news! This is an absolutely splendid love romp for the Snake, the Horse being a witty, delightful bed companion. Horse ladies are, in addition, independent and not likely to cling when it all blows over – unlike the Snake – and fall deeply, when smitten. Snake men are charismatic and Horse ladies are born to indulge their instinct for sexual freedom. And it gets better when the marriage vows are made. What else is there to say?

Star Rating: Four or five.

FEMALE GOAT

This should be an affair to savour but it leaves a lot to be desired. Goat ladies are notorious for their capricious heart, and no other sign is given to such temperamental outbursts. Snake men are not easy to please in the love stakes and are fussy with whom they share their considerable favours. They expect to exercise their bewitching sexual charm with minimum effort and with no shortage of takers. The restless sexual nature of the Goat will offer no great promise. But both signs share a love of beauty and there is hope for an artistic lady Goat and creative male Snake. An evening at the theatre and a nice supper is the order of the day, or night.

Star Rating: One at most.

FEMALE MONKEY

There are not many signs a Monkey can't win over and the Snake has few problems when it comes to really getting the object of their romantic desire. So, should the Monkey appeal to the Snake and vice versa, nothing should stand in the way of this being a top-hole affair. But there is a hidden E (erotic) additive that can have damaging side effects. Monkeys, it must be constantly remembered, are more interested in setting up the affair than the actual physical event. Snake chaps are more interested in the act than the preparation. There you have it, or rather, you might not.

Star Rating: Even Stevens. Three to five.

FEMALE ROOSTER

Not a lot of joy for this particular pair of signs. The Chinese offer a two star relationship but I disagree. All my experience has shown me that the Snake and the Rooster have nothing at all in common. True, the lady Rooster is fascinated by the Snake's inescapable sexual attraction. At their best, Snake men are genuinely charming and warm, qualities lady Roosters might fall for. But Rooster females do not throw themselves recklessly into romance, and should they step back and think they will probably be just a little suspicious of the Snake's overtures. And they would be right to think twice. Snake men can be highly unpredictable in the sex stakes. Male Snake/female Rooster is the better of the couples.

Star Rating: Zero. One at most.

FEMALE DOG

This is a common relationship in spite of its low rating. The loyal and idealistic Dog lady is easily bewitched by the male Snake, who is quick to respond to his partner's open show of affection. And let it be understood that Dog ladies have devoted hearts, which they give without asking much in return. But they do ask something, and it is usually more than Snake men can give. Snakes have long periods when they simply hibernate and their emotions, including their sexuality, are in flux. Dogs require stability once they fall in love and to be rejected, even temporarily, can create incurable scars.

Star Rating: Two.

FEMALE PIG

Pigs adore Snakes, both female and male alike. Big-hearted and affectionate in the extreme, Pig ladies find the wise and sexually attractive Snake a real catch. My experience is that this is a very common pairing, with the honest and easy going Pig creating a near perfect partner for the subtle and charismatic charms of the Snake. Marriage makes it an even better bet, which is why in love the couple rate only a relatively mediocre score.

Star Rating: Three.

COMPATIBILITY OF FEMALE SNAKES IN LOVE

MALE RAT

On first meeting, Rat males view Snakes not unlike the way they view the Dragon, who is a distant cousin of the snake family. The Snake lady appears to offer all the same sexual delights as the Dragon lady, but there is a big difference. Snakes are not impulsive and they tend to bewitch from a far more passive standpoint. Because Rats are easily seduced by the female Snake, whose often mysterious sexuality promises so much, this sometimes means that the Rat will rush the relationship. But female Snakes take ages before putting their toes in the deep end and could be put off by the Rat's aggression, which is never far from the surface. Matters are not helped by the fact that once the female Snake has committed herself she might want to possess the Rat. Fatal! The Rat will be off in a flash.

Star Rating: Three, with a point lost or gained depending on the Rat's staying power.

MALE BUFFALO

Male Buffaloes are frequently seduced by the female Snake's highly bewitching personality. The lady Snake is humorous, artistic and wise. She has an endless well of sensuality which completely overwhelms the Buffalo. Using her subtle understanding of the senses, she winds her way into his most sheltered areas and cleverly soothes the male Buffalo's more complex emotions. The Buffalo's response is sometimes to be shocked by the depth of this own sensuality and at other times resistant. But he will give in fully at one stage to the Snake's bewitching charm. Of the two pairings, the male Buffalo and female Snake has by far the greater understanding and is the most common.

Star Rating: Three, sometimes four.

MALE TIGER

Tigers are very often captivated by the bewitching charms of the female Snake. They behave in stark contrast to the Tiger's own volatile and often aggressive romantic antics. Cool in the first stages, and watchful of the predator's advances, Snakes must be truly certain of the man they choose to love before they let go. As so frequently happens in the case of the male Tiger, the female Snake is put off by his lack of subtlety and, in a sense, bites him out of fear. As you will have gathered, a pretty messy sort of relationship, which promises more than is delivered by either side.

Star Rating: One at the very most.

MALE CAT

The Cat has a soft nature, usually, and a highly tuned sense of what makes life worth living. They expect their partner to share their love of good food and fine wines, and the female Snake is quick to respond. She can match his sexual expression and although the lady Snake might easily become possessive and make demands the Cat is not always able to meet, he will nevertheless make plenty of hay while the sun shines, as it promises to do regularly during this affair. Much laughter, much love. But the possessive Snake does pose a bit of a problem in the long run.

Star Rating: Three, sometimes four. Sometimes even five! (but only for a very short romance).

MALE DRAGON

One of the really great sexual partnerships. The Chinese are quite emphatic about the male Dragon and female Snake relationship, which, they say, has the hallmarks of developing into a life-long affair. The Dragon is, in fact, the distant cousin of the Snake, both of whom are members of the serpent family. Serpents are deeply connected with sex in our unconscious, and with good reason. They are creatures who live in a world dominated by sexual instincts, and, it has to be said, few others. Added to this, the Chinese explain that in practically all circumstances, the Dragon can't help himself adoring the female Snake. Given this background, it is not surprising to find they score maximum points.

Star Rating: Five plus!

MALE SNAKE

Two Snakes are not thought to be ideal partners, least of all when in love. Possessive in love and, the Chinese add, unlucky, there is little or no future in these two bewitching animals. The biggest problem is that Snakes have no real say in what they feel, and as a result require a partner who is able to offset this sense of emotional unreality. I admit there is a very short term relationship on offer here, but it's only worth a candle when there's talk of a long term commitment. Leave two real snakes in a cage and the chances are that when driven by hunger, one will devour the other.

Star Rating: Big Zero.

MALE HORSE

Good news! This is an absolutely splendid love romp for the Snake, the Horse being a witty, delightful sexual companion. Horse men are, in addition, independent and not likely to cling when it all blows over – unlike the Snake – and fall deeply, when smitten. Snake ladies are charismatic and Horse males are born to indulge their instinct for sexual free-

191

dom. And it gets better when the marriage vows are made. What else is there to say?

Star Rating: Four or five.

MALE GOAT

This should be an affair to savour but it leaves a lot to be desired. Goat chaps are notorious for their capricious heart, and no other sign is given to such wandering. Snake females are not easy to please in the love stakes and are fussy with whom they share their considerable favours. They expect to exercise their bewitching sexual charm with minimum effort and with no shortage of takers. The restless sexual nature of the Goat will offer no great promise. But both signs share a love of beauty and there is hope for an artistic male Goat and creative female Snake. An evening at the theatre and a nice supper is the order of the day, or night.

Star Rating: One at most.

MALE MONKEY

There are not many signs a Monkey can't win over and the Snake has few problems when it comes to really getting the object of their romantic desire. So, should the Monkey appeal to the Snake and vice versa, nothing should stand in the way of this being a top hole affair. But there is a hidden E (erotic) additive that can have damaging side effects. Monkeys, it must be constantly remembered, are more interested in setting up the affair than the actual physical event. Snake women are more interested in the act than the preparation. There you have it, or rather, you might not.

Star Rating: Even Stevens. Three to five.

MALE ROOSTER

Not a lot of joy for this particular pair of signs. The Chinese offer a two-star relationship but I disagree. All my experience has shown me that the Snake and Rooster have nothing in common as lovers. True, the male Rooster is fascinated by the female Snake's inescapable sexual attraction. At their best, Snake women are genuinely charming and warm, qualities Roosters might fall for. But Rooster males do not usually throw themselves recklessly into romance, and should they step back and think, they will probably be just a little suspicious of the Snake's overtures. And they would be right to think twice. Snake ladies can be highly unpredictable in the sex stakes. This is the worst of the pairings.

Star Rating: Zero.

MALE DOG

This is a common relationship in spite of its low rating. The loyal and idealistic Dog is easily bewitched by the female Snake, who is quick to respond to her partner's open show of affection. And let it be understood that although ever anxious, Dog fellows have devoted hearts which they give without asking much in return. But they do ask something, and it is usually more than Snake ladies can give. Snakes have long periods when they simply hibernate and their emotions, including their sexuality, are in flux. Dogs require stability once they fall in love and to be rejected, even temporarily, can create incurable scars.

Star Rating: Two.

MALE PIG

Pigs adore Snakes, both female and male alike. Big-hearted and affectionate in the extreme, Pig chaps find the wise and sexually attractive Snake a real catch. My experience is that this is a very common pairing, with the honest and easy-going Pig creating a near perfect partner for the subtle and charismatic charms of the Snake. Marriage makes it an even better bet, which is why in love the couple rate only a relatively mediocre score. Female Snake/male Pig is the best. Jackie Kennedy's open and heady relationship with Aristotle Onassis gives you some idea of the power these two signs generate in love.

Star Rating: Four.

COMPATIBILITY OF MALE SNAKES IN MARRIAGE

FEMALE RAT

The early experiences in a Rat and Snake relationship largely determine how long it lasts. If the Rat can curb her excitement and slow her delight in life at a pace that the subtle Snake can tolerate, then marriage is a reasonable idea. Both Rats and Snakes have a very strong sexual inner core, but it has to be remembered that marriages, however successful, tend to become more like business partnerships the longer they continue. It is here that the problems arise. A business requires an abundance of thrift, and although the Snake can provide bundles of it, most Rats spend without thinking. There are difficulties at every level and quarrels about trivial matters remain an ever present symbol of that which divides them. But the Snake's deep reluctance to give up and the Rat's sharp wits will help keep the show on the road.

Star Rating: Three

FEMALE BUFFALO

There's something about the male Snake which female Buffaloes find very difficult to resist. Not quite as passionate as the Rat, whom the Buffalo invariably falls for, the Snake has great sexual power. In marriage these two animal signs have a more than average chance of success. The lady Buffalo may well offer a unique view of life which the subtle male Snake will find absorbing. But the lady Buffalo must remember that

Snakes demand much understanding, especially during moments of 'hibernation', those periods in which he is found inescapably listening to his ever present inner voice for direction. Here, alas, the active and often demanding female Buffalo will not be as sympathetic as the situation requires. Mark Thatcher, a Snake, is married to a Buffalo, Diane – same sign as his mum. TV's Sue Cook is a buffalo, and *was* married to guitarist John Williams, a Snake.

Star Rating: Two, with a point up or down depending on the Buffalo's sensitivity.

FEMALE TIGER

Snakes, in the main, love deeply and usually focus their love on only one person at a time. The object of their desire will certainly know about it, often feeling possessed by her Snake partner. This is bad news for the Tiger, who feels such love as a form of being caged. And some male Snakes shift their affections, and are driven by sensual urges they have no control over. This heralds more bad news for the short-fused Tigress. The odds are that from the affair stage to the marriage something very serious will have got lost between male Snake and female Tiger, and in spite of the many attractions, if such a relationship continues to hold out, it will certainly end in disaster. The Chinese advise against it.

Star Rating: Zero.

FEMALE CAT

Ever graceful and often mysterious the Cat finds a long term partnership with the equally humorous and sensuous Snake irresistible. Male Snakes are generally gentle husbands, and the Cat lady will adore his inner strengths and appreciative nature. A business might easily grow from such a marriage, especially since both are generally good with money. Plenty of support for each other in the bleaker moments points to a perfect duo. Humorist Miles Kington, famous for his *Let's Parlais Franglais*, is married to a Cat, Caroline.

Star Rating: Five and more.

FEMALE DRAGON

Dragon ladies are often bewitched by male Snakes and it does not take a great leap of the imagination to see that a marriage of some substance might easily develop. But there is a tiny word of warning. Snake males fall into two camps: those who cling possessively to the woman in their life, who are the greater in number, and those who can't resist any woman who hoves into view. Provided Mr Snake is a one girl man, little can go wrong, apart from the Dragon feeling a bit hemmed in – another red alert, by the way.

Star Rating: Four or five.

FEMALE SNAKE

All the evidence suggests that although two Snakes are easily bewitched by each other's deeply sensual powers, the fact of the matter is that marriage will do nothing to expand the inner core of either Snake partner. The chances are, at best, that both snakes will learn to realise that the long periods of inactivity and uncertainty do end eventually and to make hay while the sun shines. But there is seldom room for real growth together and the instinct to devour and possess the object of their love is an ever present threat. John F. Kennedy was a Snake and so is his former wife, Jackie.

Star Rating: One, maybe two. Usually zero.

FEMALE HORSE

This is a high-rating relationship with plenty of scope for the Snake male to discover the delights of having a practical and independent partner. The bright and sociable Horse lady makes a perfect hostess and needs little from others to achieve her full potential. Good with children and a strong support in times of stress and trouble, the Horse lady is certain to respond to the subtle Snake. But the Snake must remember not to be too possessive, and any attempt at 'ownership' of his lovely Horse wife will be firmly resisted. Clinging to a Horse is a recipe for disaster.

Star Rating: Three bottom, four tops.

FEMALE GOAT

A rich social life, plenty of good food and much appreciation of the world of art is the order for a Snake male and female Goat – yes sir! These animal signs are destined for a positive if sometimes emotionally rocky life together, with the Goat given ample opportunity to exercise all her domestic skills. This will be achieved against the Snake's humorous and sensual nature, one which, it must be remembered, has a nasty habit of occasionally turning introspective and difficult. But the Snake can easily tether the capricious heart and mind of the Goat. Children here are a mixed blessing. Actor John Thaw is a Snake and his wife, Sheila Hancock, is a Goat.

Star Rating: Three or Four.

FEMALE MONKEY

There is really nothing very special in this relationship, which marriage either helps or hinders. The sexual side is good, if just a little off-hand at times in respect of the Monkey's input. But there's always plenty of good humour around the place, and as long as the Snake doesn't feel outwitted by the super sharp Monkey, there shouldn't be too many problems. Both are good company and there should be plenty of family friends to keep them feeling they are a useful couple. Kids might be a good idea.

Star Rating: Three.

FEMALE ROOSTER

This is a better marriage than could have been dreamed of at the romance stage. Love affairs are not what Roosters, especially the female of the species, go in for. They are deeply conservative and only really open up when there is a strong sense of moral decency in the air. In a marriage, the sensual and sexual Snake might well provide this dimension; on the other hand, he might not. Snakes cannot be relied on for emotional stability. In which case there won't be a silver wedding, or indeed a first anniversary. But if both signs are willing to accept the faults in the other, they *might* just end up as good companions. No bets taken on it, though. My mother is a Rooster and my father was a Snake. A tough middle period saw them great pals in the last years.

Star Rating: Three is the max.

FEMALE DOG

This is a very common relationship and a large number of this particular pairing would vouch for it being better than the low rating the Chinese give it. Loyal and idealistic, the Dog certainly benefits from the Snake's positive qualities: they are wise, extremely thoughtful and give their time freely without asking for anything in return. But there is always the Dog's more negative streak to contend with – their anxiety. Dogs worry over details and can be very stubborn, sometimes for no apparent reason. This causes tension, and in turn will lead to much misunderstanding.

Star Rating: Two, but there are a few extra points when the Dog partner is less fretful.

FEMALE PIG

A high scoring marriage where we find both signs totally at one with each other. The Pig is a perfect partner to most signs, often preferring to work in conjunction with another than by themselves, and the Snake is quick to respond. Easy going and warm, the Pig lady has practically all the qualities a male Snake looks for, and in return the Snake offers his wise counsel and humour. Children should be happy in the home of a Pig and a Snake. But as always, there is a side of the Snake, his inner mystery, which might upset the applecart. Pig females must make a note to avoid confrontation during a Snake's 'quiet periods', as they are easily upset at these times and might bite.

Star Rating: Four.

COMPATIBILITY OF FEMALE SNAKES IN MARRIAGE

MALE RAT

The early experiences in a Rat and Snake relationship largely determine how long it lasts. If the Rat can curb his opportunism and slow his delight in life to a pace that the subtle Snake can tolerate, then marriage is a reasonable idea. Both Rats and Snakes have a very strong sexual inner core, but it has to be remembered that marriages, however successful, tend to become more like business partnerships the longer they continue. It is here that the problems arise. A business requires an abundance of thrift, and although the subtle Snake can provide bundles of it, most Rats spend without thinking. There are difficulties at every level, even in the kitchen. Whereas the Rat is fond of his tummy, the Snake is seldom interested in food. Obviously, petty differences about cuisine are not enough to lead to a divorce, but they'll remain an ever present reminder of what divides them.

Star Rating: Three

MALE BUFFALO

There's something about the female Snake which Buffaloes find very difficult to resist. Not quite as openly passionate as the Rat, whom the Buffalo invariably falls for, the Snake has the power to bewitch, and to cling to those she adores. In marriage these two animal signs have a more than average chance of success, especially when the male is a Buffalo. He

199

may well offer a unique view of life, which the female Snake, in her quiet wisdom, will find absorbing. But she demands much understanding, especially during her moments of 'hibernation', those periods in which she is listening to her inner voice for direction. Here, alas, the male Buffalo will not be sympathetic.

Star Rating: Two, with a point up or down depending on the Buffalo's sensitivity.

MALE TIGER

Lady Snakes, in the main, love deeply and usually focus their love on only one person at a time. The object of their desire will certainly know about it, often feeling possessed by his Snake partner. Bad news for the Tiger, who will feel caged. However, there are female Snakes who are able, without quite knowing how and with apparent ease, to shift their affections from one to another. This kind of Snake is not what the male Tiger is looking for and heralds more bad news. But should the Snake restricted to a love for just one other happen on a less than ebullient Tiger, then there is a tiny, tiny chance that the marriage will last. However, the odds are that from the affair stage to the marriage something very serious will have been lost between female Snake and male Tiger, and in spite of the many attractions, if such a relationship continues to hold out, it will almost certainly end in disaster. The Chinese advise against it.

Star Rating: Zero.

MALE CAT

Ever diplomatic, often mysterious and given the ability to surprise his noisiest critics with his sharp wit, the Cat finds a long term partnership with the equally subtle, humorous and deeply sensuous Snake irresistible. The Chinese place a high premium on the female Snake, saying she will make the rice grow fat. Her sexuality will, I am certain, do much to keep her Tom in trim, and the Cat will enjoy every second. A business might easily grow from such a marriage, especially since both are generally good with money. Plenty of support for each other in the bleaker moments points to a perfect duo. Sir Michael Levey, former director of London's National Gallery, is married to a Snake, the authoress Brigid Brophy.

Star Rating: Five and more.

MALE DRAGON

Dragon men are bewitched by female Snakes and it does not take a great leap of the imagination to see that a marriage of some substance might easily develop. But there is a tiny word of warning. Snake ladies fall into two camps: those who cling possessively to the man in their life, who are the greater in number, and those who can't resist any man who hoves into view. Providing Miss Snake is a one man girl, little can go wrong, apart from the Dragon feeling a bit hemmed in – another red alert, by the way. The great literary couple, Virginia Woolf and her husband, Leonard, were a Snake and a Dragon. Pakistan's beautiful Bhenazir Bhutto is also a Snake and, I am reliably informed, has happily married a Dragon.

Star Rating: Four or five.

MALE SNAKE

All the evidence suggests that although two Snakes are easily bewitched by each other's deeply sensual powers, the fact of the matter is that marriage will do nothing to expand the inner core of either Snake partner. The chances are, at best, that both snakes will learn to realise that the long periods of inactivity and uncertainty do end eventually and to make hay while the sun shines. But there is seldom room for real growth together and the instinct to devour and possess the object of their love is an ever present threat. John F. Kennedy was a Snake and so is his former wife, Jackie. Dramatist Harold Pinter is a Horse and his former actress wife Vivien Merchant was a Snake. Harold ran off with Lady Antonia Fraser. (See Monkeys and Horses).

Star Rating: One, maybe two. Usually zero.

MALE HORSE

This is a high rating relationship with plenty of scope for the Snake female to discover the delights of having a practical and independent partner. Male Horses have, as a rule, a quick appreciation of what's useful in a relationship, but more important, they have the ability to bring out the more positive side of their Snake wives. Good with children and a strong support in times of stress and trouble, the Horse male is certain to respond to the subtle Snake lady at all levels. But the Snake must remember not to be too possessive, and any attempt at 'ownership' of her independent Horse husband will be firmly resisted. Clinging to Horses is a recipe for disaster. Paul McCartney is a Horse, and he seems extremely happy in his choice of Linda, a Snake, as a full and complete partner. On the other hand, Fire Horse Mike Tyson had a less than happy marriage with Snake Robin Givens.

Star Rating: Three bottom, four tops.

MALE GOAT

A rich social life, plenty of good food and much appreciation of the world of art is the order for a Snake female and Male Goat – yes sir! These animal signs are destined for a positive if sometimes emotionally rocky life together, with the male Goat given ample opportunity to exercise all his clever social skills. This will be achieved against the Snake's humorous and sensual nature, one which, it must be remembered, has a nasty habit of occasionally turning introspective and difficult. But the Snake female can easily tether the capricious heart and mind of the Goat. Children here are a mixed blessing.

Star Rating: Three or four.

MALE MONKEY

There is really nothing very special in this relationship, which marriage either helps or hinders. The sexual side is good, if just a little off-hand at times in respect of the Monkey's input. But there's always plenty of good humour around the place and as long as the Snake doesn't feel threatened by the Monkey's sharper wit and artfulness, there should not be too many problems. Money shouldn't be a big problem either, providing the Monkey adds freely to the family kitty from time to time. Both are good company and there should be plenty of family friends to keep them feeling they are a useful couple. Kids might be a good idea.

Star Rating: Three

MALE ROOSTER

This is a better marriage than could have been dreamed of at the romance stage. Love affairs are not what Roosters go in for, although the male Rooster is more prone than the female (at least, they boast more about it). They are deeply conservative and only really open up when there is a strong whiff of moral decency in the air. In a marriage, the sensual and sexual Snake might well provide this dimension; on the otherhand, she might not. Snakes cannot be relied on for emotional stability. In this case there won't be a silver wedding, or indeed a first anniversary. But if both signs are willing to accept the faults in the other, they *might* just end up as good companions. No bets taken on it, though. Theatrical impresario and former Coronation Street star Bill Kenwright is a Rooster, and was once married to actress beauty and Snake Anouska Hempel.

Star Rating: Three is the max.

MALE DOG

This is a very common relationship and a large number of this particular pairing would vouch for it being better than the low rating the Chinese give it. Loyal and idealistic, the Dog certainly benefits from the Snake's positive qualities: they are wise, extremely thoughtful and give their time freely without asking for anything in return. But there is always the Dog's more negative streak to contend with – anxiety. Dogs worry over details and can be very stubborn, sometimes for no apparent reason. This causes tension, and in turn will lead to much misunderstanding. Dog male/Snake female is the best pairing.

Star Rating: Two, but there are a few extra points when the Dog partner is less fretful.

MALE PIG

A high scoring marriage where we find both signs totally at one with each other. The Pig is a perfect partner to most signs, often preferring to work in conjunction with others than by themselves, and the Snake is quick to respond. Easy going and warm, the big hearted Pig fellow has practically all the qualities a female Snake looks for, and in return, the Snake offers her wise council and humour. Children should be happy in the home of a Pig and Snake. But as always, there is a side of the Snake, her inner mystery, which might upset the applecart. Pig males must make a note to avoid confrontation during a Snake's 'quiet periods' as they are easily upset at these times and might bite. Pig chaps and lady Snakes have the highest rating. When Jackie Kennedy remarried, she did so with a Pig – Aristotle Onassis.

Star Rating: Four, or even five.

COMPATIBILITY OF MALE SNAKES IN FRIENDSHIP

MALE RAT

Not much to recommend this friendship. In a romantic relationship there's a degree of mileage, but as friends pure and simple, Rat and Snake do not enjoy much in common. Without the physical expression of their attraction they are two signs with directions pointing away from each other.

Star Rating: One, at a pinch.

MALE BUFFALO

It is commonly said that Buffaloes are solitary beasts who do not offer love or friendship easily. On the surface Snake people might be thought to be quite the opposite as many seem to possess an easy way with strangers and friends alike. But neither sign truly enjoys casual relationships and is only really happy when they dig deep emotionally. The Snake clings to whomever or whatever he cares deeply about, sometimes strangling the object of his possessiveness in the process. The Buffalo, once their demand for loyalty is thwarted, is slow to forgive – if ever. The same is true of Snakes. So the problems of Snakes and Buffaloes in friendship are highlighted by the constant threat of high voltage temperaments clashing. Friendship is a case of giving and taking, two of these signs' weakest points. Van Gogh was a Buffalo and his faithful brother Theo, a Snake. Theo clung to Vincent and a year after the great artist committed suicide in 1890, Theo died of a broken heart.

Star Rating: Three is average. Seldom more, often less.

MALE TIGER

This is a real non-starter. The slow moving Snake, with his deep intuition often disguised by a brash surface, has nothing in common with the fast thinking, ever changing Prince of the Jungle. Tigers charge about the place, emotionally, physically and just about every way there is. And they get results. Snakes sit and wait for the right moment to act – then they pounce and their bite is for keeps. It is the tortoise and the hare all over again.

Star Rating: Zero-0-0-0.

MALE CAT

Cats and Snakes are just fine. In a friendship which includes some sort of business deal there would be few better partnerships. Both are cautious with money as a rule, and both Cat and Snake have a terrific sense of what is beautiful, and what is not. Supportive and understanding of each other's need for inner peace, there is not a lot that can go wrong with this pairing. Ken Tynan was a Cat and, apart from being the first person to say f**k on TV, was one of the most influential theatre critics of the fifties. It was he who became the central figure in promoting the name of the 'Angry Young Man' playwright, John Osborne, a Snake. Tynan said once, 'I doubt if I could love anyone who did not wish to see *Look Back in Anger.*'

Star Rating: Five at least.

MALE DRAGON

Given the good news in terms of marriage and love, this ought to be a stronger pairing. But there is a point in a Snake's life which leads him to become ineffective and incapable of making decisions. This is during their periodic spells of 'hibernation', a time when they have no direct control over their actions. Where a Snake lady is concerned, a Dragon male might easily bide his time, but when it's a mate or, worse a business friend, then the lack of input will drive the Dragon up the wall. But during the positive spells, there is much in common and a great deal of subtle understanding takes place. One of the great musical partnerships of all time existed between Sir Edward Elgar, a Snake, and the boy Dragon genius, Sir Yehudi Menuhin. Their recording of the composer's violin concerto, recorded when Menuhin was only sixteen, is considered among the top ten recordings ever made. Hale and Pace are another great team, as are Mel Smith and Griff Rhys Jones.

Star Rating: Three. Sometimes four. Sometimes five.

MALE SNAKE

This is not one of the most auspicious of friendships and in nine cases out of ten ends up with one Snake coming out of it badly damaged. The law of two Snakes in a relationship decrees that life can only be made tolerable as long as there are quite distinct areas in which each will be free to work, play and *think* at their own pace. An artistic base is a saving grace, especially if there is a business involvement, but money will always prove a stumbling block. The brilliant model makers responsible for the *Spitting Image* puppets, Peter Fluck and Roger Law, are both Snakes, and so are long time Shadows, Hank Marvin and Bruce Welch. So there is hope.

Star Rating: Zero most times. Other times one, rising to two maximum, but very rarely.

MALE HORSE

A good middle of the road friendship for the Snake and Horse. The independent Horse never likes to have fussy friends and a Snake is usually happy to live his life without being led. Although sometimes possessive in relationships, a Snake dealing with a Horse seems to find this less of a problem. In fact, both sides are remarkably capable of doing their own thing and yet remaining closely in touch. But there is always the ever present threat of the Snake demanding too much of the Horse. Art Garfunkel is a Snake, and his one time partner, Paul Simon, is a Horse. Ditto Ronnie Barker and Ronnie Corbett.

Star Rating: Three or four.

MALE GOAT

A gentle social life, shared equally between the Snake and the Goat, might just be the recipe for these two quite different signs. Peace lovers, the cross-over points are their mutual love of beauty and appreciation of all things well made. A fine wine, a splendid meal, a perfectly cut suit, all could be the conversational meeting ground for the wayward Goat and the subtle Snake. Business partners might consider a wine bar or high class boutique. Not a robust relationship, it must be said, and Goats do tend to wander.

Star Rating: Two-ish.

MALE MONKEY

Not much chance of a lasting friendship between the intuitive Snake and the sharp as a knife Monkey. Monkeys are really very clever without necessarily being the fount of originality. Snakes are nothing if not original and are wise into the bargain. They are not, in the Monkey sense, clever. The relationship could work in that the Monkey would get his best lines from the Snake, but without the Snake being fully aware of it. As long as this doesn't worry the Snake, no problem. Two giants of modern jazz and co-founders of the forties Bebop craze were a Snake and Monkey, Dizzy Gillespie and Charlie Parker. But they ended up fighting on stage.

Star Rating: One.

MALE ROOSTER

The candid and outspoken Rooster, if he is also the spend-thrift type of bird, has almost nothing at all in common with the subtle and thrifty Snake. It is really difficult to discover where a Rooster and Snake friendship could go. Snakes can be very funny, in an original and very personal way, and most male Roosters love to be the centre of attention. There's mileage in a comedy partnership, perhaps. But these two signs are not meant to be. Sorry.

Star Rating: One at the very most.

MALE DOG

Snakes and Dogs do have a habit of forming strong friend-ships in all departments but only truly succeed where there is deep love and affection. Two chums having a pint in the pub will not be enough to bring this pair of signs close enough to form a lasting relationship. The Dog will be constantly anxious in the face of the Snake's long periods of inner silence and neither can help themselves break the tension.

Star Rating: Two at most.

MALE PIG

A solid sort of friendship for two signs who, on the surface would not appear to have a great deal in common. But the Pig is a good and open hearted fellow who genuinely admires the Snake's wisdom and sensitivity. Lacking initiative, or, to put it another way, better in partnership, the Pig enjoys his role as the Snake's ally. In turn the Snake is not slow to appreciate the Pig's gift for keeping the party going and, if there is a business to consider, his talent for making money. The snag in business may be that Pigs are easily duped, and the Snake, it is said, has a tight fist. Dean Martin and Jerry Lewis, the great Hollywood comic film duo of the fifties, were a Snake and Pig respectively.

Star Rating: Three

COMPATIBILITY OF FEMALE SNAKES IN FRIENDSHIP

FEMALE RAT

An unusual relationship in the female species of the sign. Both have deep sexual drives and unless they can find a way of channelling them into something that they can share, lady

Rat and lady Snake are not likely to find much in common. The Rat moves quickly and is seldom still, the Snake slides through life, acting on their intuition. In some senses, they are too much alike for real friendship, which is often most fruitful when there are two contrasting views.

Star Rating: One – just.

FEMALE BUFFALO

Marriage and love offer Snake and Buffalo hope but not in the less passionate realm of day to day friendship. Passion is what binds these two animal signs and without it there is not a great deal left in common. The subtle Snake becomes increasingly difficult for the Buffalo, who likes her friendships cut and dried. Men are what Snake ladies understand best, and what Buffalo ladies understand least. The females of both species are better off without each other's company for more than a few hours at a time.

Star Rating: None. Maybe a teeny weeny one at a pinch.

FEMALE TIGER

This is usually a real non-starter. The slow moving Snake, with her deep intuition often disguised by a brash surface has nothing in common with the fast thinking, ever changing Princess of the Jungle. Tigers charge about the place, emotionally, physically and just about every way there is. And they get results. Snakes sit and wait for the right moment to act – then they pounce and their bite is for keeps. It is the tortoise and the hare all over again. But with two females, since the Tiger is so masculine and the Snake so feminine, there is a tiny chance of a short relationship with just the hint of success. Julie Walters is a Tiger, and her erstwhile partner, Victoria Wood, a Snake.

Star Rating: Zero sometimes – most times, but one now and again.

FEMALE CAT

Cats and Snakes are just fine. In a friendship which includes some sort of business deal there would be few better partnerships. Both are cautious with money as a rule, and both Cat and Snake have a terrific sense of what is beautiful, and what is not. Supportive and understanding of each other's need for inner peace, there is not a lot that can go wrong with this pairing.

Star Rating: Five at least.

FEMALE DRAGON

Given the good news in terms of marriage and love, this ought to be a stronger pairing. But there is a point in a Snake's life which leads her to become ineffective and incapable of making decisions. This is during their periodic spells of 'hibernation', a time when they have no direct control over their actions. Where a Snake male is concerned, a Dragon female might easily bide her time, but when it's a girlfriend or, worse a business partner, then the lack of input will drive the Dragon up the wall. But during the positive spells, there is much in common and a great deal of subtle understanding takes place.

Star Rating: Three. Sometimes four. Sometimes five.

FEMALE SNAKE

This is not one of the most auspicious of friendships and in nine cases out of ten ends up with one Snake coming out of it badly damaged. The law of two Snakes in a relationship decrees that life can only be made tolerable as long as there are quite distinct areas in which each will be free to work, play and *think* at their own pace. An artistic base is a saving grace, especially if there is a business involvement, but money will always prove a stumbling block.

Star Rating: Zero most times. Other times one, rising to two maximum, but very rarely.

211

FEMALE HORSE

A good middle of the road friendship for the female Snake and Horse. The independent Horse never likes to have fussy friends and a Snake is usually happy to live her life without being led. Although sometimes possessive in relationships, a Snake dealing with a Horse seems to find this less of a problem. In fact, both sides are remarkably capable of doing their own thing and yet remaining closely in touch. But there is always the ever-present threat of the Snake demanding too much of the Horse.

Star Rating: Three or four.

FEMALE GOAT

A gentle social life, shared equally between the Snake and Goat, might just be the recipe for these two quite different signs. Peace lovers, the cross-over points are their mutual love of beauty and appreciation of all things well made. A fine wine, a spendid meal, a perfectly designed outfit, all could be the conversational meeting ground for the wayward Goat and subtle Snake. Business partners might consider a wine bar or high-class boutique. Not a robust relationship, it must be said, and Goats do tend to wander.

Star Rating: Two-ish.

FEMALE MONKEY

Not much chance of a lasting friendship between the intuitive Snake and the sharp as a knife Monkey. Monkeys are really very clever without necessarily being the fount of originality. Snakes are nothing if not original and are wise into the bargain. They are not, in the Monkey sense, clever. The relationship could work in that the Monkey would get her best lines from the Snake, but without the Snake being fully aware of it. As long as this doesn't worry the Snake, no problem.

Star Rating: One.

FEMALE ROOSTER

The candid and outspoken Rooster, if she is also the spend-thrift type of bird, has almost nothing at all in common with the subtle and thrifty Snake. It is really difficult to discover where a Rooster and Snake friendship could go. Snakes can be very funny, in an original and very personal way, and most male Roosters love to be the centre of attention. There's mileage in a comedy partnership, perhaps. But these two signs are not meant to be. Sorry.

Star Rating: One at the very most.

FEMALE DOG

Snakes and Dogs do have a habit of forming strong friend-ships in all departments but only truly succeed where there is deep love and affection. Two girls sipping hock in the wine bar will not be enough to bring this pair of signs close enough to form a lasting relationship. The Dog will be constantly anxious in the face of the Snake's long periods of inner silence and neither can help themselves break the tension.

Star Rating: Two at most.

FEMALE PIG

A solid sort of friendship for two signs who, on the surface, would not appear to have a great deal in common. But the Pig is a generous soul who genuinely admires the Snake's wisdom and sensitivity. Lacking initiative, or, to put it another way, better in partnership, the Pig enjoys her role as the Snake's ally. In turn the Snake is not slow to appreciate the Pig's gift for keeping the party going, and if there is a business to consider, her surprising talent for making money. The snag in business may be that Pigs are easily duped, and the Snake, it is said, has a tight fist.

Star Rating: Three.

THE HORSE

馬

1906*	January 25th to February 12th	**1907**
1918	February 11th to January 31st	**1919**
1930	January 30th to February 16th	**1931**
1942	February 15th to February 4th	**1943**
1954	February 3rd to January 23rd	**1955**
1966*	January 21st to February 8th	**1967**
1978	February 7th to January 27th	**1979**
1990	January 27th to February 14th	**1991**

*FIRE HORSE

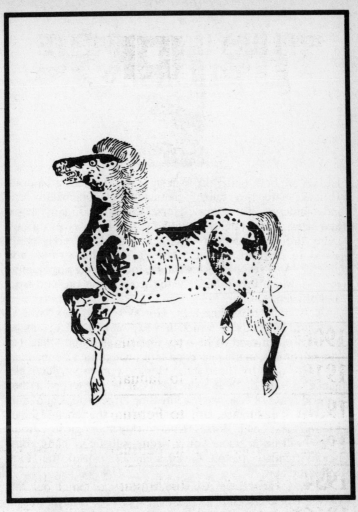

*When I consider the most wonderful work of
God in the creation of the Horse, endowing it
with a singular body and a noble spirit, the
principal whereof is a loving and dutiful
inclination to the service of man.*

Topsell

THE YEAR OF THE HORSE

Horses are born under the twin signs of elegance and ardour. Horses share two salient characteristics, practicality and independence. But because Horses come in so many shapes and sizes, these traits frequently express themselves through many different channels. After all, a Shetland pony is not asked to perform the same tasks as a highly strung show jumper. As a result, Horses will be found doing any number of jobs, which they'll tackle with the emphasis on hard work and efficiency.

A strongly masculine sign, Horses of both sex have an easy going personality, which they exploit to good advantage. Horse women tend to be witty and sociable and what they just might lack in obvious good looks will always be made up for twice over by sheer style. Horses, remember, have elegance as one of their twin signs. Male horses, with their natural sense of ease when addressing large groups and inner reserves of endurance, also usually mirror the female Horse's wit and clear head. Horses think quickly and logically. And a Horse will never quote you a wrong statistic or hand you a woolly-minded opinion. Given a chance to lead, the Horse will jump at it.

Slow to anger, the Chinese Horoscopes point out that once a Horse is seen in a rage, the experience is never forgotten. Horses also become easily bored, and not only with people. A Horse quickly changes jobs and hobbies and generally tends not to plan long term. They might *think* they have found a job or partner for life, but in reality it will be just another passing phase. However, once 'settled' in a family, the Horse will automatically become the key figure. But even then, they will probably invest more time in their work than their children.

216

As a rule, Horses are not possessive or jealous about those they love. They require freedom above all else, and usually acknowledge that their partners might require the same. But Horses fall in love easily, and although they seldom get bitter or twisted should it not work out, they do become extremely weak once smitten. Love is not logical and the practical minded Horse never learns this simple fact. They think each new romance is the Big One, forgetting they have thought this a hundred times before.

The three phases of a Horse's life will be determined by their need for freedom. Young Horses tend to leave the stable early and the middle years will see many changes. It is also said that a Horse born in the summer has an easier life than those born in the winter. However, old age is kinder to all Horses, with their need to be independent at all costs finding a more flexible level of expression.

A word about the Fire Horse. Occurring every sixty years, the Year of the Fire Horse has a powerful effect on all those born under its sign. The Chinese believe that Fire Horses suffer either great good fortune or sheer bad luck; sometimes they are dished out helpings of both. In short, nothing in a Fire Horse's life will ever be moderate.

COMPATIBILITY OF MALE HORSES IN LOVE

FEMALE RAT

The female Rat is undeniably attracted by the male Horse's wit, charm and elegance. Although the Horse is a fiercely practical creature, they become terribly weak when they fall in love. As a result they need a sexual partner who will not take advantage of this frequently occurring state. This partner is not the lady Rat, who will milk the affair dry. Following a sexually active start the Horse will quickly recover his composure and it will be a 'no calls situation' for the Rat. Olivia Newton-John is a Rat and John Travolta a Horse, and the relationship is very much a case of Saturday Night Fever.

Star Rating: Two minimum, with a few additional percentage points for what might have been.

FEMALE BUFFALO

The male Horse holds many attractions for the female Buffalo. He is a natural leader of any group, witty and full of personality. But he isn't one to be pushed around by the female Buffalo's often highly imperious temperament and there's something about the long, moody silences that stem from her complex nature which alienates him. Both signs demand great independence in order to function properly, which is hardly the best of platforms to launch a loving union from. Not exactly a no-no, this is not, however, a relationship which collects Oscars for long term understanding.

Star Rating: One, and even two at a pinch.

FEMALE TIGER

This is a relationship worth pursuing. There is something in the practical influence of a male horse which balances the Tiger's often fluctuating temperament. Socially at ease, the Horse has an instinct for the Tigress's deepest passion. Ever amorous, the danger-loving side of the Tiger is excited by her elegant Horse lover and there are no limits to the relationship. But there is a tiny word of warning. Horses and Tigers both tire easily. Horses become bored for no reason and Tigers run out of puff.

Star Rating: Five with reservations. Three would be the lowest.

FEMALE CAT

Plenty to keep the Cat and Horse happy. Both have a pronounced sense of humour – an essential ingredient for any romantic affair – and strong sexual personalities. And there'll be hours spent wandering around designer clothes shops as an alternative to the bedroom. Both signs are skilful at human relationships and enjoy many different types of people, each for their own individual personalities. The Horse in particular is not stable in love and, of the two, will probably be the first to move out of the relationship – one which marriage will neither help nor hinder. It will or it won't happen. TV Cat David Frost, whose fling with actress Lynne Frederick, a Horse, was more like a long affair than a short marriage, proves the point.

Star Rating: Four big ones.

FEMALE DRAGON

The fourth animal sign in a row of six which offer hundred per cent love relationships for the sexually energetic and forceful Dragon. Full of self confidence, the Dragon has better partnerships when her lovers are not put off by her sometimes rather masculine character. In fact, the signs the Dragon has strongest links with are, in the main, a touch on the vain side themselves. This means the Dragon and Horse look at each other as mirror images. They love each other's best points and, in a short affair, overlook the weakest. A little helpless in love, should the Horse commit himself to a love affair with a Dragon, it will really go with a bang – in every sense. However the Horse will eventually grow tired of his fiery lover, bored even, as they do with everyone. But while it lasts – oh boy! And again, the Dragon will not be too downcast.

Star Rating: Five all the way.

FEMALE SNAKE

Good news! This is an absolutely splendid love romp for the Horse and Snake, the Horse being a witty, delightful sexual companion. Horse men are, in addition, independent and not likely to cling when it all blows over – unlike the Snake – and fall deeply, when smitten. Snake ladies are charismatic and Horse males are born to indulge their instinct for sexual freedom. And it gets better when the marriage vows are made. What else is there to say?

Star Rating: Four or five.

FEMALE HORSE

This is not an easy relationship to pin down. Horses of both sexes are notoriously unreliable in love, falling under the spell of dear old Cupid at the drop of a hat, and deeply into the bargain. The trick is to find another Horse who is feeling the need for a bit of fun and just let it all hang out. A long term partnership is not usually seen as part of the deal, unless the two Horses in question decide to outline quite definite boundaries and stick within them. Vain and witty, the Horse lovers will find much to enjoy in each other's company, even if there is a touch of one Horse providing the mirror for the other's good looks. Fire Horses, however, keep well clear of each other.

Star Rating: Zero or five, or anything.

FEMALE GOAT

One of the great relationships of all time. Horses and Goats hit it off in just about every department. The Goat's wayward and capricious heart is for once happy to be tethered, and it would seem that only the male Horse, with his strong personality and natural affinity with the female Goat, is capable of this somewhat difficult task. A perfect recipe for a long, constructive and socially full marriage, with only just the minutest hint of trouble from the lady Goat. But she'll come trotting home to the stable ninety-nine times out a hundred.

Star Rating: Five, plus-plus-plus!

FEMALE MONKEY

Here's a puzzler. The Chinese offer not a single jot of understanding between the independent Horse male and the ever
sharp and adaptable Monkey female. But there are many
seemingly successful relationships between these two signs.
Perhaps it is again the old point about the attraction of opposites, but clearly something makes a Monkey and a Horse
tick. Having said that, it is easy to see why a Monkey, so
unreliable as a lover, might outwit the Horse, who himself is
desperately unsure of his own feelings when smitten by
romance. Two drifters in a sea of romantic uncertainty, one
might say. When you are both drifting, it helps to have one
who knows where the shore is. It is, in this case, usually the
Monkey.
   Star Rating: Zero. Sorry.

FEMALE ROOSTER

There are some very odd relationships in Chinese Horoscopes which on the surface leave the signs involved a little
confused. Horses and Roosters have a very high rating in
marriage but almost nothing in common in a purely romantic
relationship. Horse men have a strong physical nature and
fall in love heavily and often. Lady Roosters step carefully
into a sexual relationship and the over amorous male Horse
is sometimes a turn off – at least for the Rooster female. She
is after long term, committed love and a home and a garden.
Sex is OK, but the Horse is so much more attractive when
part of the whole domestic set up.
   Star Rating: One. Check the marriage section for a big
improvement.

FEMALE DOG

In the farmyard, the horse and the dog do different jobs and
seldom meet. But when they do they have much in common,
if only in their help to mankind. Horse and Dog signs benefit
from a mutual interest outside any particular hobby or field

of endeavour. Sex is a useful starting point and all that goes with it. Socially active, the Horse male provides the lady Dog with masses of opportunities to free herself from the nagging need to be loved and appreciated. The Horse is great fun to be with and his free spirit acts to sooth the sometimes anxious Dog lady. She in return provides much genuine and, a bonus for the Horse, undemanding love. Paul McCartney, a Horse, was *very* much in love with Dog lady Jane Asher and desperately wanted to marry her.

Star Rating: Four or five.

FEMALE PIG

Curious how poor this relationship promises to be. Pigs get on with just about everyone except the Horse. Try as I might, I cannot work it out and rely on the fact the Chinese have been doing their horoscopes for three thousand years and I have only been studying them for fifteen. Perhaps the Horse's vanity conflicts with the Pig's sometimes high self-esteem. Maybe the kind of Pig lady who leaves the home like a sty meets more Horses who expect their stable to be swept beautifully clean. Maybe there isn't one reason but lots of little niggling factors that leave the Horse and Pig in a position where their most positive attributes conflict. I don't know. Just accept the Chinese verdict.

Star Rating: Zero. Perhaps just one.

COMPATIBILITY OF FEMALE HORSES IN LOVE

MALE RAT

This is not as bad as the one star rating suggests, though it must be said that no great understanding exists between the two signs. The male Rat is undeniably attracted to the female Horse's wit, charm and elegance. But the lady Horse is a fiercely practical creature who is not greatly impressed by what she sees as the Rat's general lack of purpose. Because a Horse in love tends to lose their way, a wild romantic relationship can only leave both Rat and Horse emotionally adrift. Sex should be good but the lady Horse will quickly recover her composure and it will be *adiós* Ratty.

Star Rating: One. Maybe another half mark in some cases.

MALE BUFFALO

The female Horse holds many attractions for the male Buffalo. She is bright, witty and full of personality. But she isn't one to be pushed around by the male Buffalo's imperious temperament and there's something about the long silences that stem from his complex nature which alienates her. Both signs demand great independence in order to function properly, which is hardly the best of platforms to launch a loving union from. Not exactly a no-no, this is not, however, a relationship which collects Oscars for long term understanding. David Bailey is a Buffalo and in the swinging sixties he spent a while with model Jean Shrimpton, a Horse.

Of all Bailey's long term women (he's had four wives), 'The Shrimp' was the only one he didn't marry.
Star Rating: One.

MALE TIGER

This is a relationship worth pursuing. There is something in the influence of a Horse woman which brings out the more stable side to a Tiger's temperament. Horse ladies have a pronounced practical streak which bodes well for the long term problem of keeping the Tiger going through his bleaker moments. But she also enjoys a delightfully adoring heart which in the first throes of a love affair, excites all but the most stony-hearted. Ever amorous, the Tiger is warmed by his Horse lover and there are no limits to the relationship. But there is a tiny word of warning. Horses and Tigers both tire easily. Horses become bored for no reason and Tigers run out of puff.
Star Rating: Five with reservations. Three would be the lowest.

MALE CAT

Plenty to keep the Cat and Horse happy. Both have a pronounced sense of humour, an essential ingredient for any romantic affair, and strong sexual personalities and there'll be hours spent wandering around designer clothes shops as an alternative to the bedroom. Both signs are skilful at human relationships and enjoy many different types of people, each for their own individual personalities. The Horse in particular is not stable in love, and of the two, she will probably be the first to move out of the relationship – one which marriage will neither help nor hinder. It will or it won't happen.
Star Rating: Four big ones.

MALE DRAGON

The fourth animal sign in a row of six which offer a hundred per cent love relationships for the sexually energetic and forceful Dragon. Full of self-confidence, the Dragon has better partnerships when her lovers are not put off by her sometimes rather masculine character. In fact, the signs the Dragon has the strongest links with are, in the main, a touch on the vain side themselves. This means the Dragon and Horse look at each other as mirror images. They love each other's best points and, in a short affair, overlook the weakest. A little helpless in love, should the Horse commit himself to a love affair with a Dragon, it will really go with a bang – in every sense. However the Horse will eventually grow tired of his fiery lover, bored even, as they do with everyone. But while it lasts – oh boy! And again, the Dragon will not be too downcast.

Star Rating: Five all the way.

MALE SNAKE

Good news! This is an absolutely splendid love romp for the Horse and Snake, the Horse being a witty, delightful bed companion. Horse ladies are, in addition, independent and not likely to cling when it all blows over – unlike the Snake – and fall deeply, when smitten. Snake men are charismatic and Horse ladies are born to indulge in their instinct for sexual freedom. And it gets better when the marriage vows are made. What else is there to say?

Star Rating: Four or five.

MALE HORSE

This is not an easy relationship to pin down. Horses of both sexes are notoriously unreliable in love, falling under the spell of dear old Cupid at the drop of a hat, and deeply into the bargain. The trick is to find another Horse who is feeling the need for a bit of fun and just let it all hang out. A long term partnership is not usually seen as part of the deal, unless the two Horses in question decide to outline quite definite boundaries and stick within them. Vain and witty, the Horse lovers will find much to enjoy in each other's company, even if there is a touch of one Horse providing the mirror for the other's good looks. Fire Horses, however, keep well clear of each other.

Star Rating: Zero or five, or anything.

MALE GOAT

One of the great relationships of all time. Horses and Goats hit if off in just about every department. The Goat's wayward and capricious heart is for once happy to be tethered, and it would seem that only the female Horse, with her clear cut personality and natural affinity with the male Goat, is capable of this somewhat difficult task. A perfect recipe for a long, constructive and socially full marriage, with only just the minutest hint of trouble from Billy Goat. But he knows the grass is always greener in the Horse lady's field.

Star Rating: Five, plus-plus-plus!

MALE MONKEY

Here's a puzzler. The Chinese offer not a single jot of under-standing between the independent Horse female and the ever sharp, often scheming and adaptable Monkey male. But there are many seemingly successful relationships between these two signs. Perhaps it is again the old point about the attraction of opposites, but clearly something makes a Monkey and Horse tick. Having said that, it is easy to see why a Monkey, so unreliable as a lover, might outwit the Horse, who herself is desperately unsure of her own feelings when smitten by romance. Two drifters in a sea of romantic uncertainty, one might say. When you are both drifting, it helps to have one who knows where the shore is. It is, in this case, usually the Monkey.

Star Rating: Zero. Sorry.

MALE ROOSTER

There are some very odd relationships in Chinese Hor-oscopes which on the surface leave the signs involved a little confused. Horses and Roosters have a very high rating in marriage but almost nothing in common in a purely romantic relationship. Horse ladies have a strong physical nature and fall in love heavily and often. Male Roosters step carefully into a sexual relationship, in spite of the frequently self created impression that they are super studs, and the over amorous Horse is sometimes a turn off. Long term relationships are what male Roosters prefer.

Star Rating: One. Check the marriage section for a big improvement.

MALE DOG

In the farmyard, the horse and dog do different jobs and seldom meet. But when they do they have much in common, if only in their help to mankind. Horse and Dog signs benefit from a mutual interest outside any particular hobby or field of endeavour. Sex is a useful starting point and all that goes with it. Socially active, the Horse female provides the male Dog with masses of opportunities to free himself from the nagging need to be loved and appreciated. The Horse is great fun to be with and her free spirit acts to soothe the sometimes anxious Dog. He in return provides much genuine and, a bonus for the Horse, undemanding love.

Star Rating: Four or five.

MALE PIG

Curious how poor this relationship promises to be. Pigs get on with just about everyone except the Horse. Try as I might, I cannot work it out and rely on the fact the Chinese have been doing their horoscopes for three thousand years and I have only been studying them for fifteen. Perhaps the Horse's vanity conflicts with the Pig's sometimes high self-esteem. Maybe the kind of Pig male who leaves the home like a sty meets more Horses who expect their stable to be beautifully swept and clean. Maybe there isn't one reason but lots of little niggling factors that leave the Horse and Pig in a position where their most positive attributes conflict. I don't know. Just accept the Chinese verdict.

Star Rating: Zero. Perhaps just one.

COMPATIBILITY OF MALE HORSES IN MARRIAGE

FEMALE RAT

Born under the sign of charm, Rats achieve much of their success by a mixture of quick wits and warmth. Some signs fall easily under the spell of the exciting Rat, but the Horse is not one. Although they fall in love far too quickly and too often for their own good, male Horses do not like to be charmed into action. It might be OK for one night, but in the long term a Horse wants reason and logic to rule the roost. The Rat will for ever be cast in the role of spendthrift and her every action criticised.

Star Rating: Zero.

FEMALE BUFFALO

The love affair which just about scraped home now blows up in a puff of wind. Independence is the key to the Horse's soul and you will always find that the Horse is his own boss, regardless of whom he chooses to walk life's path with. Female Buffaloes are incapable of genuinely sharing their position as head of the family, a fault which will drive the male Horse into a sudden rage, another common trait in those born under their sign. Marriage has to be a shared partnership and here are two animal signs simply not capable of doing so, no matter what the circumstances.

Star Rating: Zero.

FEMALE TIGER

Again we find two signs filled with mutual attraction. They both have great personalities and enjoy a full social life. The problem that continually faces the Tiger is her sudden loss of inner belief and when she is low she will need much in the way of gentle ego nursing. Male Horses are witty, sociable and independent. They might fancy a spell at nursing; there again, they might not. The chances of a marriage between a female Tiger and male Horse working out depend entirely on how much give and take the Horse is prepared to offer. Male Horses, remember, fall in love at the drop of a hat, and Tiger females are seduced by danger. Both, then, face difficulties in and out of their marriage. Female Tiger and male Horse is the least auspicious pairing. Ali McGraw married three times. Two were Horses, Steve McQueen and production boss Bob Evans.

Star Rating: Three.

FEMALE CAT

Four five star marriages in a row for the refined and ever willing to listen Cat; and perhaps that's why she fares so well. Ever keen to let others have their say, by listening carefully the Cat eventually holds all the cards and can play them any way she wants. She loves the order and routine that married life offers, but there are moments in all marriages when she feels the need to explore her private sensual interior. Here, the willing and witty Horse provides a marvellous foil. Although not given to introspection, Cats are warm and gentle in their approach to family life and enjoy children. Horse gentlemen can please themselves *vis à vis* kids. Good in the bedroom, good in the garden, good in the dining room. A home of happiness.

Star Rating: Five.

FEMALE DRAGON

A love affair between these two amorous signs, being so strong, implies that a wedding looks a good bet. And if they are as headstrong as the two signs usually are, female Dragon and male Horse won't stop to think. But once married, there is a problem. Horse males are weakest when smitten by romance, and no matter how strong and appealing their Dragon partner might be, they tend to give in. And sadly, Dragon ladies can fall pretty heavily when given the opportunity. So, it is the old curse of fidelity, or the lack of it, which acts as the fly in this particular ointment. However, should both Dragon and Horse agree that the odd extra-marital fling is not serious enough to damage the marriage, it will work surprisingly well, and they will emerge as a very practical outfit.

Star Rating: Two through to five.

FEMALE SNAKE

This is high-rating relationship with plenty of scope for the Snake female to discover the delights of having a practical and independent partner. Male Horses have, as a rule, a quick appreciation of what's useful in a relationship, but more important, they have the ability to bring out the more positive side of their Snake wives. Good with children and strong support in times of stress and trouble, the Horse male is certain to respond to the subtle Snake lady at all levels. But the Snake must remember not to be too possessive, and any attempt at 'ownership' of her independent Horse husband will be firmly resisted. Clinging to a Horse is a recipe for disaster. Paul McCartney is a Horse, and he seems extremely happy in his choice of Linda, a Snake, as a full and complete partner. On the other hand, Fire Horse Mike Tyson had a less than happy marriage with Snake Robin Givens.

Star Rating: Three bottom, four tops.

FEMALE HORSE

No other relationship is so difficult to pin down as the marriage between two witty, independent and occasionally every so slightly vain Horses. But there is a way to turn a no-hoper into a five-star special and that's by both Horses defining specific boundaries in which they can explore their own very strong personalities. Being left to make the rules as they go along will find the Horse couple galloping in opposite directions. But with a firm fence, or, in other words, a common objective, two married Horses stand an even chance of staying that way. Failure to establish the personal limits is to court certain disaster. Lord Snowdon and Princess Margaret are both Horses, Chrissie Evert and John Lloyd are two others. A Goat daughter or Dragon son might help, but two Fire Horses must never marry.

Star Rating: Three most. Zero bottom, except for Fire Horses, who get a million below.

FEMALE GOAT

A vintage quality relationship, one of the all time greats! In love, both signs have already glimpsed the level of quite magical understanding that exists between these two lively and sociable animals. The male Horse is all stamina and the female Goat can be such a delightful tease. Long after the heady days of romance have faded into the sometimes dull routine of marriage there will always be a genuine understanding. A life of hard work and plenty of fun for two perfectly compatible signs. Goat Ian Botham is married to a Horse and in spite of rumours continues to illustrate that these two signs can survive in even the most difficult circumstances.

Star Rating: Five and more.

FEMALE MONKEY

Given the large number of Horse and Monkey marriages I have come across in my researches, I would have thought

231

that Monkey lady and male Horse would get a high rating. But the Chinese Horoscopes will have none of it. They say that the often manipulative Monkey will frequently infuriate the normally even tempered Horse. She will, they say, get her own way at his expense. Judged as a couple the Horse is by contrast reliable and steadfast, whereas the Monkey is mobile and quick to move away from testing moments. Having said that, the Monkey makes a first rate parent, when it suits her. A family, in spite of the prediction of a mismatch, is a good idea and a Dragon son is ideal. Neil Kinnock and his wife, Glenys, are a Horse and Monkey team. Prince and Princess Michael of Kent are another.

Star Rating: One. Two would be generous.

FEMALE ROOSTER

One of the great success stories. From a zero rating in romance the Horse and Rooster romp home to a really first class marriage. Both are natural partners in that they are happy, as animals, to use the farm as they feel. The picture I have is of the rooster sitting on the horse's fence. In human animal signs I believe the Rooster and Horse have such a relationship. A garden is important to the Rooster lady and a meadow is crucial to a Horse. Freedom combined with integrity forms the cornerstone to this auspicious marriage. A business relationship is also advised.

Star Rating: Five most times.

FEMALE DOG

The Dog's patience and understanding are seldom called on when the Horse is her married partner. His occasional rages are really few and far between and his love of hard work usually means a comfortable and somewhat fashionable life-style. The lady Dog offers warmth and true friendship, qualities on which every lasting marriage is founded. The Dog's anxieties are diminished in number by the Horse's clear-headed view of life. In return, the Horse's tendency to become suddenly bored and change direction, an act which can have quite serious repercussions, is often avoided by the

Dog's demand for honest simplicity in terms of family hopes and ideals. TV's 'Most Beautiful Bottom' winner and small-screen presenter, Anneka Rice, is a Dog who has married a Horse, Nick Allot.

Star Rating: Four.

FEMALE PIG

This is a marriage of what the two signs want it to be. The Horse and Pig have many options open as both are adaptable to internal and external changes. But the Horse is easily led off-course and the Pig lady, so the Chinese Horoscopes point out, a little too fond of her fun. In marriage, who you stay out late with is not usually a matter for breakfast discussion and should either Horse or Pig find themselves attracted to another outside their marriage they will do best to keep it quiet. The problem is, though, that the Pig is prone to boasting and the Horse falls heavily. But affairs to one side, this is a strong enough union with a warm home life and two reliable, unfussy and thoughtful parents.

Star Rating: Three.

COMPATIBILITY OF FEMALE HORSES IN MARRIAGE

MALE RAT

Born under the sign of charm, Rats achieve much of their success by a mixture of quick wits and warmth. Some signs fall easily under the spell of the exciting Rat, but the Horse is not one. Although they fall in love far too quickly, and too often for their own good, female Horses do not like to be charmed into action. It might be OK for one night, but in the long term a Horse wants reason and logic to rule the roost. The Rat will for ever be cast in the role of spendthrift and his every action criticised for its opportunist horizons.

Star Rating: Zero.

MALE BUFFALO

The love affair which just about scraped home now blows up in a puff of wind. Independence is the key to the Horse's soul and you will always find that the lady Horse is her own boss, regardless of whom she chooses to walk life's path with. Male Buffaloes are incapable of genuinely sharing their position as head of the family, a fault which will drive the lady Horse into endless rages. Marriage has to be a shared partnership and here are two animal signs simply not capable of doing so, no matter what the circumstances. Peter Sellers was a Buffalo and once married Britt Eckland. Ms Eckland is a Horse and it was a very short marriage. On the other hand, a longer marriage for Buffalo Rod Steiger and Horse Claire Bloom.

Star Rating: Zero. But where there's a Buffalo, anything is possible.

MALE TIGER

Again we find two signs filled with mutual attraction. They both have great personalities and enjoy a full social life. The problem that continually faces the Tiger is his sudden loss of inner belief and when he is low he will need much in the way of gentle ego nursing. Lady Horses are witty, sociable and independent. They might fancy a spell at nursing; they might not. A marriage between a Tiger and Horse working out depends entirely on how much give and take the Horse is prepared to offer. Horses, remember, fall in love at the drop of a hat, and Tiger males are easily seduced. Both, then, face difficulties in and out of their marriage. Barbra Streisand is a Horse and her fast and furious marriage to Tiger Elliot Gould is about the norm.

Star Rating: Three.

234

MALE CAT

Four five star marriage years in a row for the refined, cultured and ever willing to listen Cat; and perhaps that is why he fares so well. Ever keen to let others have their say, by listening carefully the Cat builds up a strong picture of those he can trust and those he can't. Cats love the order and routine that married life offers, but there are moments in all marriages when he feels the need to explore his private sensual interior. Here, the willing and witty Horse provides a marvellous foil. Although not given to introspection, Cats are warm and gentle in their approach to family life and enjoy children. Horse ladies can please themselves *vis à vis* kids. Good in the bedroom, good in the garden, good in the dining room. A home of happiness.

Star Rating: Five.

MALE DRAGON

A love affair between these two amorous signs, being so strong, implies that a wedding looks a good bet. And if they are as headstrong as the two signs usually are, male Dragon and female Horse won't stop to think. But once married, there is a problem. Horse ladies are easily seduced and no matter how strong and appealing their Dragon partner might be, they tend to give in. And sadly, Dragons are a push over for any bright little thing in a short skirt. So, it is the old curse of fidelity, or lack of it, which acts as the fly in this particular ointment. However, should both Dragon and Horse agree that the odd extra-marital fling is not serious enough to damage the marriage, it will work surprisingly well, and they will emerge as a very practical outfit. For instance, kids won't be a problem and, if anything, might help bond the union.

Star rating: Two through to five.

MALE SNAKE

This is a high rating relationship with plenty of scope for the Snake male to discover the delights of having a practical and independent partner. The bright and social Horse lady makes

235

a perfect hostess and needs little from others to achieve her full potential. Good with children and a strong support in times of stress and trouble, the Horse lady is certain to respond to the subtle Snake. But the Snake must remember not to be too possessive, and any attempt at 'ownership' of his lovely Horse wife will be firmly resisted. Clinging to Horses is a recipe for disaster.

Star Rating: Three bottom, four tops.

MALE HORSE

No other relationship is so difficult to pin down as the marriage between two witty, independent and occasionally ever so slightly vain Horses. But there is a way to turn a no-hoper into a five star special and that's by both Horses defining quite specific boundaries in which they can explore their own very strong personalities. Being left to make the rules as they go along the Horse couple will find themselves galloping in opposite directions. But with a firm fence, or, in order words, a common objective, two married Horses stand an even chance of staying that way. Failure to establish the personal limits is to court certain disaster. Lord Snowdon and Princess Margaret are both Horses, Chrissie Evert and John Lloyd are two others. A Goat daughter or Dragon son might help, but two Fire Horses must never marry.

Star Rating: Three at most. Zero bottom, except for Fire Horses, who get a million below.

MALE GOAT

A vintage quality relationship, one of the all time greats! In love, both signs have already glimpsed the level of quite magical understanding that exists between these lively and sociable animals. The female Horse is full of sound sense and the male Goat can be such a delightful indulgent creature, even after the heady days of romance have faded into the sometimes dull routine of marriage, that there will always be a genuine understanding between them. Hard work and plenty of fun for two totally compatible signs.

Star Rating: Five and more.

MALE MONKEY

Given the large number of Horse and Monkey marriages I have come across in my researches, I would have thought that Monkey male and female Horse would get a high rating. But the Chinese Horoscopes will have none of it. They say that the often manipulative Monkey will frequently infuriate the normally even tempered Horse. Monkeys get their own way no matter what, regardless of whose expense it's at. Judged as a couple the Horse is by contrast reliable and steadfast, whereas the Monkey is mobile and quick to move away from testing moments. Having said that, the Monkey makes a first rate parent, when it suits him. A family, in spite of the prediction of a mismatch, is a good idea and a Dragon son is ideal.

Star Rating: One. Two would be generous.

MALE ROOSTER

One of the great success stories. From a zero rating in romance the Horse and Rooster romp home to a really first-class marriage. Both are natural partners in that they are happy, as animals, to use the farm as they feel. The picture I have is of the rooster sitting on the horse's fence. In human animal signs I believe the Rooster and Horse have such a relationship. A garden is important to the male Rooster and a meadow is crucial to a Horse. Freedom combined with integrity forms the cornerstone to this auspicious marriage. A business relationship is also advised.

Star Rating: Five most times.

MALE DOG

The Dog's patience and understanding are seldom called on when the Horse is his married partner. The female Horse has bags of energy, wit and enthusiasm, plus a wonderful sense of style. This usually means a comfortable and elegant home. The male Dog offers warmth and true friendship, qualities on which every lasting marriage are founded. The male Dog's constant anxieties are diminished in number by the female

Horse's clear-headed view of life. In return, the Horse's tendency to become suddenly bored and change direction, an act which can have quite serious repercussions, is often avoided by the Dog's demand for an honest simplicity in terms of family hopes and ideals.

Star Rating: Four.

MALE PIG

This is a marriage of what the two signs want it to be. The Horse and Pig have many options open as both are adaptable to internal and external changes. But the Horse lady is easily led off course and the Pig male, so the Chinese Horoscopes point out is a little too fond of fun. In marriage, who you stay out late with is not usually a matter for breakfast discussion and should either Horse and Pig find themselves attracted to another outside their marriage they will do best to keep it quiet. The problem is, though, that the Pig is prone to boasting and the Horse falls heavily. But affairs to one side, this is a strong enough union with a warm home life and two reliable, unfussy and thoughtful parents.

Star Rating: Three.

COMPATIBILITY OF MALE HORSES IN FRIENDSHIP

MALE RAT

Of all the pairings open to the Rat, the one with the Horse presents the biggest obstacles. Neither fully understand the other's needs or departure points. The Horse works harder than most and it is often physical, whereas hard work for the Rat usually means using his wits. Graft is more what Horses do. A business partnership is out, and so is any other long term relationship.

Star Rating: Zero.

MALE BUFFALO

Every chance of a strong friendship here, with much mutual respect and understanding shown in the initial stages. But the Horse must have his freedom and must take important decisions on his own. The Buffalo's influence mirrors this aspect of the Horse's central trait. This means that working together ends up a fight for leadership, although if the boundaries can be clearly understood there is a chance that these two independent signs can form a friendship of lasting value. Goons Peter Sellers and Spike Milligan were Buffalo and Horse respectfully, but it must be said that they had little in common outside their wonderful working life together.

Star Rating: Three is usual, but with a point up for casual friends and two or more points for business partners.

MALE TIGER

I have never quite understood why this relationship should be so strong. Tigers live in the jungle and fight alone. Horses are seldom wild, and often helplessly domesticated. But perhaps that's the clue. In the wild, the Horse is more of a loner; certainly he enjoys a greater degree of independence. Tigers do need their friends to have guts and the ability to stick up two fingers at authority. The Horse is more than able to provide such back up to the Tiger's anti-authoritarian traits. And the Horse has a much slower fuse to his temperament, which creates a much needed balance. One of the best-selling author duos of the sixties consisted of a Tiger and a Horse. Now better known as Home Secretary, Douglas Hurd, a Horse, and Andrew Osmond, a Tiger, wrote a string of best sellers. *Smile on the Face of the Tiger* was the appropriate title of their most accomplished.

Star Rating: Four or five.

MALE CAT

No big setbacks here. Cats find the Horse an extremely sympathetic partner, and the feeling is mutual. As in all good friendships, it is essential that both bring different but harmonious qualities to bear. The Horse brings powerful leadership and the Cat, diplomacy and good taste. Lenin was a Horse, and his thoughtful revolutionary chum Trotsky, a Cat. Stalin was also a Cat and had Trosky assassinated, which, going back to the five star rating of two Cats, raises a doubt. It can only be explained, I think, by the fact that Stalin had everyone bumped off who threatened him, and even those who didn't. A more positive partnership existed between the creator of our most enduring children's character, Pooh Bear, and his illustrator. Writer A A Milne was a Horse and illustrator E H Shepard a Cat.

Star Rating: Four or five. Seldom less.

MALE DRAGON

Horses demand a high level of integrity from those with whom they form friendships and, ever practical, they do not get on well with daydreamers. Many Dragons have more power than logic, and this might easily form a barrier unless it is understood at the very beginning that both have quite different qualities to bring to a friendship. Neither are strangers to hard work and a business with Dragon and Horse forming a joint head is destined for success. In spite of the Horse sometimes becoming bored with even the closest things, including his friends, and the Dragon's hot-headed pursuit of any goal that brings him attention, this is a solid enough friendship. Again, a case of live and let live. Greatest ever song-writing team, Lennon and McCartney, are Dragon and Horse, and it was their inability to compromise their strongly held ideas that set them apart.

Star Rating: Four-ish.

MALE SNAKE

A good middle of the road friendship for the Snake and Horse. The independent Horse never likes to have fussy friends and a Snake is usually happy to live his life being led. Although sometimes possessive in relationships, a Snake dealing with a Horse seems to find this less of a problem. In fact, both sides are remarkably capable of doing their own thing and yet remaining closely in touch. But there is always the ever present threat of the Snake demanding too much of the Horse. Art Garfunkel is a Snake and his one time partner, Paul Simon, is a Horse. Ditto Ronnie Barker and Ronnie Corbett.

Star Rating: Three or four.

MALE HORSE

There is no point in beating around the bush; this is a relationship doomed to long term failure unless precautions are taken right at the start. Two Horses must define their roles and stick to them. In a love situation, there's every chance that two Horses, however independent and enthusiastic their personality, will make something solid, if not exactly lasting. A few beers in the pub is OK but starting a business, where so much depends on cooperation, is not; there's no possibility of a pair of Horses doing anything other than head off in entirely different directions. The off/on collaboration between Horse Stephen Sondheim and Leonard Bernstein is a fair indication of this pairing at its unusual best.

Star Rating: Zero, minus.

MALE GOAT

Every Horse should have at least one friend who is a Goat, and vice versa. The often capricious style of the Goat is a problem. They have a curious habit of saying the opposite of what everyone else has said and the Goat's way of over stating their view when forced into a corner is prone to drive some signs up the wall – the Dragon, for example. But the

Horse takes it all in his stride and turns these 'faults' into genuinely positive attributes. The Horse is influenced by the Goat's great social and artistic skills and the pair form a partnership which is hard to beat or break up. Ian Botham is a typical limelight-seeking, outspoken and constantly performing Goat, but the records show his finest hour for England was under the captaincy of Mike Brearley, a Horse leader if ever there was one.

Star Rating: Five.

MALE MONKEY

Try as I might I can not find any good reason why a Horse and Monkey should not make some kind of relationship work. But the Chinese give the pair a zero understanding and who am I to contradict them? The only time I can see why things might go wrong is when the Monkey tries to outwit the Horse. But there may never be a need for this. Neil Kinnock is a Horse and his deputy, Roy Hattersley is a Monkey. Mmmm . . . come to think of it, the Chinese might be right after all.

Star Rating: One for effort.

MALE ROOSTER

If a Horse born, say, in 1954 found life tough with someone born in 1956, a Monkey, then take the Chinese Horoscope's advice and move on a year. The next year's sign, the Rooster, is tailored to do business with the wit- and personality-rich Horse. Both signs are gifted in different skills: the Rooster has method and the Horse a strong work capacity. Combined, these qualities lead to the Horse and Rooster creating one of the all time great friendships. The brilliant pianist Daniel Barenboim is a Horse, and his recordings of Beethoven's five piano concertos under the great German conductor Otto Klemperer are considered by many experts to be the finest ever made. Otto was a Rooster, born in 1885.

Star Rating: Five.

MALE DOG

There's plenty of room for these two signs to move in and at the same time form a close understanding. The Dog's idealism is admired and taken up by the Horse and he, less anxious in the face of life's more troublesome moments, is helped by the Horse's good sense and logical judgement. Neither Dog or Horse is hypocritical, which means a relationship founded on honest endeavour and offered as a tool for others in less fortunate circumstances. It has been suggested that Horse Paul McCartney had the closest understanding of the Beatles' manager, Brian Epstein, a Dog who sadly took his own life when personal anxieties got on top of him.

Star Rating: Three or even four.

MALE PIG

This is not a totally bad idea. The Horse needs to express his independence, even in the firmest relationship, and it is said that a Pig only truly arrives at his full potential when in partnership. Perhaps it is this sense of being fettered by a relationship that hangs over the Horse and eventually disrupts it. The Chinese say this pair should steer well clear of a business relationship although one of the most successful men's Wimbledon doubles teams in recent times consists of a Horse and Pig. Respectively they are Peter Fleming and John McEnroe.

Star Rating: One usually. Three is the limit.

COMPATIBILITY OF FEMALE HORSES IN FRIENDSHIP

FEMALE RAT

The independence and practicality which mark the Horse also marks a friendship with the Rat a no-no of the first order. Both are witty and good company in a crowd, yet as attractive as the relationship might first appear, the Horse has no understanding of the Rat's spontaneous behaviour, nor does she approve. In more areas than is helpful to real friendship, both signs cancel each other out. Rats, though, are never ones to harbour grudges for long, finding them an obstruction to getting on with life. But they might make an exception in the case of the often vain and, as they might see it, over critical Horse.

Star Rating: Zero.

FEMALE BUFFALO

Every chance of a strong friendship here, with much mutual respect and understanding shown in the initial stages. But the Horse must have her freedom and must take important decisions on her own. The Buffalo's influence mirrors this aspect of the Horse's central trait. This means that working together ends up a fight for leadership, although if the boundaries can be clearly understood, there is a chance that these two independent signs can form a friendship of lasting value.

Star Rating: Three is usual, but with a point up for casual friends and two or more points down for business partners.

FEMALE TIGER

I have never quite understood why this relationship should be so strong. Tigers live in the jungle and fight alone. Horses are seldom wild, and in most cases are helplessly domesticated. But perhaps that's the clue. In the wild, the Horse is more of a loner; certainly she enjoys a greater degree of independence. Tigers do need their friends to have guts and the ability to stick up two fingers at authority. The Horse is more than able to provide such back-up to the Tiger's anti-authoritarian traits. And the Horse has a much slower fuse to her temperament, which creates a much needed balance.

Star Rating: Four or five.

FEMALE CAT

The Horse is a powerful leader, endowed with much independence. The influence of the Cat is less so, making her presence felt more in the quieter and less demanding moments. As in all good friendships, it is essential that both bring different but harmonious qualities to bear. The Horse brings thoughtful direction and the Cat, diplomacy and good taste.

Star Rating: Four or five. Seldom less.

FEMALE DRAGON

Horses demand a high level of integrity from those with whom they form friendships, and, ever practical, they do not get on well with daydreamers. Many Dragons have more dream power than logic, and this might easily form a barrier unless it is understood at the very beginning that both have quite different qualities to bring to a friendship. Neither are strangers to hard work and a business with Dragon and Horse forming a joint head is destined for success. In spite of the Horse sometimes becoming bored with even the closest things, including her friends, and the Dragon's reckless pursuit of any goal that brings her attention, this is a solid enough friendship. Again, a case of live and let live.

Star Rating: Four-ish.

FEMALE SNAKE

A good middle of the road friendship for the female Snake and Horse. The independent Horse never likes to have fussy friends and a Snake is usually happy to live her life without being led. Although sometimes possessive in relationships, a Snake dealing with a Horse seems to find this less of a problem. In fact, both sides are remarkably capable of doing their own thing and yet remaining closely in touch. But there is always the ever present threat of the Snake demanding too much of the Horse.

Star Rating: Three or four.

FEMALE HORSE

There is no point in beating around the bush: this is a relationship doomed to long term failure unless precautions are taken right at the start. Two Horses must define their roles and stick to them. In a love situation, there's every chance that two Horses, however independent and enthusiastic their personalities, will make something solid, if not exactly lasting. A few glasses of Chablis in the wine bar at lunch is OK but starting a business, where so much depends on cooperation, there's no possibility of a pair of Horses doing anything other than heading off in entirely different directions.

Star Rating: Zero, minus.

FEMALE MONKEY

Try as I might I cannot find any good reason why a Horse and Monkey should not make some kind of relationship work. But the Chinese give the pair a zero understanding and who am I to contradict them? The only time I can see why things might go wrong is when the Monkey tries to outwit the Horse. But there may never be a need for this. On the other hand, I can find no examples of this friendship in operation, either among my friends or on the wider world stage. So the Chinese could be right.

Star Rating: One for effort.

FEMALE ROOSTER

If a Horse born, say, in 1954 found life tough with someone born in 1956, a Monkey, then take the Chinese Horoscope's advice and move on a year. The next year's sign, the Rooster, is tailored to do business with the wit- and personality-rich Horse. Both signs are gifted in different skills; the Rooster has method and the Horse a strong work capacity. Combined, these qualities lead to the Horse and Rooster creating one of the all time great friendships. My wife is a Rooster and, typically, does not make friends easily. Yet all her long term friendships have been formed with Horses. In fact, it was this single instance of how accurate the Chinese Horoscopes are in terms of relationships that led me to study them as deeply as I have.

Star Rating: Five.

FEMALE DOG

There's plenty of room for these two signs to move in and at the same time form a close understanding. The Dog's ideal-ism is admired and taken up by the Horse and she is less anxious to face life's more troublesome moments, helped by the Horse's good sense and logical judgement. Neither Dog nor Horse is hypocritical, which means a relationship founded on honest endeavour and offered as a tool for others in less fortunate circumstances.

Star Rating: Three or even four.

FEMALE PIG

This is not a totally bad idea. The Horse needs to express her independence, even in the firmest relationships, and it is said that a Pig only truly arrives at her full potential when in part-nership. Perhaps it is this sense of being fettered by a relationship that hangs over the Horse and eventually disrupts it. Female Pig and female Horse have the least chance of lasting friendship and they should not form a bus-iness partnership under any circumstances. I still am not convinced so just take the Chinese Horoscope's word for it.

Star Rating: One at most.

THE GOAT

1907	February 13th to February 1st	1908
1919	February 1st to February 19th	1920
1931	February 17th to February 5th	1932
1943	February 5th to January 24th	1944
1955	January 24th to February 11th	1956
1967	February 9th to January 29th	1968
1979	January 28th to February 15th	1980
1991	February 15th to February 3rd	1992

My men, like Satyrs grazing on the lawns,
Shall with their Goat feet dance the antic hay.
Christopher Marlowe

THE YEAR OF THE GOAT

Goats are born under the sign of art and those born under her influence inherit the most feminine aspects of all the twelve signs. Respected for their shy and gentle manners, Goats are thought by the Chinese to be the Bringers of Peace. They are quick to react against conflict and only ever strike a militant pose in an attempt to restore harmony. However, it must be added that the Goat's love of a peaceful world is not based on some glorious universal idea of Utopia; quite the reverse is true. In general the Goat realises that only a harmonious world provides the socially pleasurable opportunities for which all Goats crave. The Japanese have an expression which sums up the Goat personality beautifully, *I-Shoku-Ju*, which roughly translated means a love of the senses: food, clothes and comfort. La dolce vita, in other, equally exotic words.

Because their sign is art, Goats make the most wonderful performers and it's impossible to stop a Goat from performing, no matter where. Should a Goat choose to turn his or her enormous artistic talent to anything that is even vaguely demanding of a show – it could be Hamlet at the Old Vic or tossing off an instant supper for two – we are likely to witness a performance of Oscar winning proportions. No one can dance or act as brilliantly as a Goat on form, and their great pleasure in performing provides an unexpected advantage when it comes to throwing a party. Although the Goat faces tough competition for the title of top hostess, namely from the Horse and Pig, they frequently run out the winner.

With the attention full on them Goats thrive, but it is here that they face the greatest danger. Goats need tethering to make the most of themselves and left to their own devices are prone to wander – usually in search of the next good time.

The Chinese describe Goats as capricious, which hits the nail since the word 'capricious' comes from the Italian for Goat, *capra*. They follow trends rather than create them. But once tethered, either to a task or ambition, a relationship or dream, a Goat will invariably hit the jackpot.

Although they might make money, in business Goats tend to overstate their case or choose the wrong moment to do so. They should avoid being salesmen unless working in a team. And should they take on supreme responsibility, Goats will do well to appoint advisers with a less fickle view of the world. No stranger to hard work, Goats usually spend what they earn – usually on beautiful objects, clothes and paintings.

The first of the three phases of a Goat's life finds the young Goat clinging to the family, and as throughout their lives using tears and tantrums to get their own way. Breaking parental ties is tough for a Goat and it is noted that Goats invariably live close to the family home. Driven by their senses, Goats experience a number of emotional ups and downs through the middle period, the heart always ruling the head. But Goats are quick to learn and seldom make the same mistake twice. Money, too, will bring its share of problems. But in the last phase, when the Goat realises that their own patch is truly worth cultivating, there will be peace and abundance.

COMPATIBILITY OF MALE GOATS IN LOVE

FEMALE RAT

Here's a relationship which on the surface, looks like a five star special all the way. Rats make no secret of the fact they love life. Sexuality is high on their list of priorities and capricious Goats can't keep away from the good life, in whatever shape or form it comes. But the problem is that the Rat and Goat, no matter which sex, are too much alike and the image that they reflect of each other is identical. Great love affairs are usually borne out of genuine opposing qualities and although many are doomed from the start, they do at least have a magnetic pull at the beginning. The most lasting affairs have that magnetism – all the time. Sexual success is a question of putting together the right kind of opposites.

Star Rating: Zero, with a chance in a hundred it could be five star fantastic for a few hours.

FEMALE BUFFALO

Buffalo women seldom view men as mere objects of physical love and relationships tend to be formed with the long term in mind. However, male Goats often have a strongly sexual side to their nature which can easily topple the straight-thinking female Buffalo into more fun and games than she bargained for. But the affair offers the Buffalo more than the Goat, who, strict to his sign's capricious influence, is unlikely to stick around for long, especially when the Buffalo gets one of her moods. As with all the female Buffalo's partners, the male Goat provides a stark contrast to her own highly individual personality and is therefore seen as a considerable temptation.

Star Rating: Zero as a rule, sometimes leaping to a surprising four.

FEMALE TIGER

No one is more capricious than the Goat. Proclaiming his undying love to one, he might easily be giving someone else the same story. As a result, Goat males need a firm hand to lead them through even the most casual relationship. The lady Tiger is one such sign, and certainly not a creature to be stood up or passed over for another. They don't like being lied to, ignored, or indeed upstaged. So what's in it for these two? The answer is that Goats have great artistry and when they make love, tend to give themselves completely to whomever they happen to be with. This suits the Tiger fine.

Star Rating: A tough one. Three at a pinch. Occasionally four.

FEMALE CAT

The Cat is a lucky lady even though luck is the Dragon's sign. Cats have the pick of the field to chose their partners from and apart from one (the Rooster), they hit it off with just about everyone. It is true they find some easier going than others, but the Goat is no problem. Together they share much of life's more agreeable aspects, especially when it includes la dolce vita. Faithfully inclined, in spite of their Tom-cat reputation, the Cat will not be over the moon when her Goat starts showing off to the other girls at the party. But as long as the Cat puts her foot (paw?) down, Master Goat will not cause too many upsets.

Star Rating: Four. It depends on the Goat's capricious heart.

FEMALE DRAGON

Here's a love affair that's doomed from the start, but then most love affairs usually are. So what's in it for the Dragon and Goat? The answer is found in the Goat, who, with his capricious heart and wayward nature, has a strong sense of the sexually mischievous quality the Dragon lady can't resist. This adds up to the easily seduced Dragon being taken for a bit of a ride, which in the opening stages is delightful. Goats are sensuous and giving in sexual matters, but they wander, always aware that it is possible the grass is greener somewhere else. Poor Dragon, she might be having fun but she'll pay the price of a wayward lover. And for sure she'll not be the only one enjoying the Goat's good time favours. And pity the poor Goat when the Dragon lady finds out!

Star Rating: Four and dropping. . .

FEMALE SNAKE

This should be an affair to savour but it leaves a lot to be desired. Goat chaps are notorious for their capricious hearts, and no other sign is given to such wandering. Snake females are not easy to please in the love stakes and are fussy about whom they share their considerable favours with. They expect to exercise their bewitching sexual charm with minimum effort, and with no shortage of takers, the restless sexual nature of the Goat will offer no great promise. But both signs share a love of beauty and there is hope for an artistic male Goat and creative female Snake. An evening at the theatre and a nice supper is the order of the day, or night.

Star Rating: One at most.

FEMALE HORSE

One of the great relationships of all time. Horses and Goats hit it off in just about every department. The Goat's wayward and capricious heart is for once happy to be tethered, and it would seem that only the female Horse, with her clear cut personality and natural affinity with the male Goat is capable of this somewhat difficult task. A perfect recipe for a long, constructive and socially full marriage, with only just the minutest hint of trouble from Billy Goat. But he knows the grass is always greener in the Horse's field.

Star Rating: Five, plus-plus-plus!

FEMALE GOAT

Love and a pair of Goats provide the student of Chinese Horoscopes with a considerable dilemma. On the one hand these are sensuous creatures capable of a strong emotional attachment, but at the same time Goats require a firm hand from their partner in order to realise their fullest potential. Love can be fun and uncomplicated, the way that most Goats prefer, yet true love demands a deeper commitment than many Goats are prepared to give. Time and again, they see the grass growing greener somewhere else. Not the basis for a long standing love affair. OK, however, for the short term.

Star Rating: One, maybe more for the first night, so full of promise.

FEMALE MONKEY

A big buzz at the start for Goats and Monkeys, who frequently find the wit and social skills of each other's animal influence sexually compelling and highly appealing. The Monkey lady can never say no to a good thing, or even a bad one – she *has* to try everything once – and the male Goat has great charm and promises plenty. But the Monkey has a low horizon when it comes to fidelity and the male Goat is no stranger to a fickle heart. A great opening with a fair chance that the longer the relationship lasts the better this pair's chance of romantic happiness. Goat Mick Jagger has promised marriage to Monkey model Jerry Hall. But that's as far as it has got.

Star Rating: Three is about average.

FEMALE ROOSTER

After a great deal of give and take, mostly on the Rooster's behalf, this pair of lovers just might get it together. But the chances are very slight. In some relationships, such as same-sex friendships, Goat and Rooster could even be said to have a fair understanding of each other. In romance, however, Goat male and lady Rooster rarely have anything in common. Rooster women are sexually deeply private and rarely promiscuous. Male Goats have no such self control. The big non-starter.

Star Rating: Zero.

FEMALE DOG

Dogs are faithful, loyal and totally self-deprecating in the face of a true loving relationship, seeing themselves as the partner who must always win approval, rather than expecting it. Dog ladies are the reverse side of the romantic coin to the capricious and often self centred Goat. Although generous and witty, male Goats are trendsetters at heart, and they love to perform and be the centre of attention. They also change their minds more quickly than any other sign, a trait which Dog ladies simply find hard to keep up with. And Goats are no idealists, in bed or out. Sara Keays was born in a Dog year and Cecil Parkinson in the Year of the Goat.

Star Rating: One at the most. Usually Zero.

FEMALE PIG

Female Pigs are great fun, as a rule, and the male Goat is quick to cash in on the Pigette's good nature and warm open love. Like so many affairs, though, the best is at the beginning. In this case, the reason is to be found in the Goat and Pig sharing too much in common. There is no real drama outside the clash between the decision about where to eat and what club to go to after. Sexual relationships need a degree of tension, and there is not enough in the love affair of a Goat and Pig to keep it bubbling.

Star Rating: Two, three or even four (for a very short affair).

COMPATIBILITY OF FEMALE GOATS IN LOVE

MALE RAT

Here's a relationship which, on the surface, looks like a five star special all the way. Rats make no secret of the fact they love life and sexuality is high on their list of priorities. Lady Goats are warm, sensuous and can't keep away from the good life, in whatever shape or form it comes. And in keeping with the Rat's view, lady Goats see sex as something to be experienced in large long happy doses. But the problem is that Rat and Goat are too much alike, which means that they reflect the same image of each other. Great love affairs are often born out of genuine opposing qualities, and although many are doomed from the start, they do at least have a magnetic pull at the beginning. The very best affairs have that magnetism all the time. Sexual success is a question of putting together the right kind of opposites.

Star Rating: Zero, with a chance in a hundred it could be five-star-fantastic for a few hours!

MALE BUFFALO

Buffalo men seldom view women as mere sex objects and relationships tend to be formed with the long term in mind. However, lady Goats often have a coquettish side to their nature which can easily topple the straight thinking Buffalo into more fun and games than he bargained for. But the affair offers the Buffalo more than the Goat, who, strict to her sign's capricious influence, is unlikely to stick around for long, especially when the Buffalo gets one of his moods. As with all the male Buffalo's partners, the lady Goat provides a stark contrast to his own highly individual personality and is therefore seen as a considerable temptation.

Star Rating: Zero as a rule, sometimes leaping to a surprising four.

MALE TIGER

No one is more capricious than Miss Goat. Proclaiming love to one, she might easily be giving someone else the same story. Wayward and a tease, Goat ladies need a firm hand to lead them through even the most casual relationship. The Tiger is one such sign, and certainly not a creature to be stood up or passed over for another. They don't like being lied to, ignored, or indeed upstaged. So what's in it for these two? The answer is that Goats have great artistry and when they make love, tend to give themselves completely to who they happen to be with. This suits the Tiger fine.

Star Rating: A tough one. Three at a pinch. Occasionally four.

MALE CAT

The Cat is a lucky fellow – even though luck is the Dragon's sign. Cats have the pick of the field to choose their partners from and apart from (the Rooster), they hit it off with just about everyone. It is true they find some easier going than others, but the Goat is no problem. Together they share much of life's more agreeable aspects, especially when in includes la dolce vita. Faithfully inclined, in spite of their Tom-cat reputation, the Cat will not be over the moon when his lady Goat starts showing off to the other guys at the party. But as long as the Cat puts his foot (paw?) down, Miss Goat will not cause too many upsets.

Star Rating: Four. It depends on the Goat's capricious heart.

MALE DRAGON

Here's an intense love affair that's doomed from the start, but then, most such love affairs usually are. So what's in it for the Dragon and the Goat? The answer is found in the Goat, who with her fickle heart and wayward nature, has such a strong sense of the mischievous – a quality the Dragon can't resist. This adds up to the easily seduced Dragon being taken for a bit of a ride, which in the opening stages is delightful. Goats are sensuous and giving in sexual matters, but they wander, ever aware that it is possible the grass is greener somewhere else. Poor old Dragon, he might be having fun but he'll pay the price of a wayward mistress. And sure as eggs are eggs he'll not be the only one enjoying Miss Goat's favours.

Star Rating: Four.

MALE SNAKE

This should be an affair to savour but it leaves a lot to be desired. Goat ladies are notorious for their capricious heart, and no other sign is given to such temperamental outbursts. Snake men are not easy to please in the love stakes and are fussy about with whom they share their considerable favours. They expect to exercise their bewitching sexual charm with minimum effort, and with no shortage of takers, the restless sexual nature of the Goat will offer no great promise. But both signs share a love of beauty and there is hope for an artistic lady Goat and creative male Snake. An evening at the theatre and a nice supper is the order of the day, or night.

Star Rating: One at most

MALE HORSE

One of the great relationships of all time. Horses and Goats hit it off in just about every department. The Goat's wayward and capricious heart is for once happy to be tethered, and it would seem that only the male Horse, with his strong personality and natural affinity with the female Goat, is capable of this somewhat difficult task. A perfect recipe for a long, constructive and socially full marriage, with only just the minutest hint of trouble from the lady Goat. But she'll come trotting home to the stable ninety-nine times out of a hundred.

Star Rating: Five, plus-plus-plus.

MALE GOAT

Love and a pair of Goats provide the student of Chinese Horoscopes with a considerable dilemma. On the one hand these are sensuous creatures capable of a strong emotional attachment, but at the same time Goats require a firm hand from their partners in order to realise their fullest potential. Love can be fun and uncomplicated, the way that most Goats prefer, yet true love demands a deeper commitment than many Goats are prepared to give. Time and again, they see the grass growing greener somewhere else. Not the basis for a long standing love affair. OK, however, for the short term.

Star Rating: One, maybe more for the first night, so full of promise.

MALE MONKEY

A big buzz at the start for Goats and Monkeys, who frequently find the wit and social skills of each other's animal influence sexually compelling and highly appealing. The Monkey male can never say no to a good thing, or even a bad one – he *has* to try everything once – and the female Goat has great charm and promises plenty. But the Monkey has a low horizon when it comes to fidelity and the female Goat is no stranger to a fickle heart. A great opening with a fair chance that the longer the relationship lasts the better this pair's chance of romantic happiness. Male Monkey/female Goat have the best chance.

Star Rating: Three is about average.

MALE ROOSTER

After a great deal of give and take, mostly on the Rooster's part, this pair of lovers just might get it together. But the chances are very slight. In some relationships, such as same-sex friendships, Goat and Rooster could even be said to have a fair understanding of each other. In romance, however, Ms Goat and Mr Rooster rarely have anything in common. Rooster men are curiously self-conscious sexually and, in spite of the image they often tend to create, are almost never promiscuous. Female Goats have no such self-control. The big non starter.

Star Rating: Zero.

MALE DOG

Dogs are faithful, loyal and totally self-deprecating in the face of a true loving relationship, seeing themselves as the partner who must always win approval, rather than expecting it. Dog men are the reverse side of the romantic coin to the capricious and often self-centred Goat. Although generous and witty, female Goats are often trend followers at heart, and they love to perform and be the centre of attention. They also change their minds more quickly than any other sign, a trait which Dog men simply find hard to keep up with. And Goats are no idealists, in bed or out.

Star Rating: One at the most. Usually zero.

MALE PIG

Male Pigs are great fun, as a rule, and the female Goat is quick to cash in on the Pig's good nature and warm open heart. Like so many affairs, though, the best is at the beginning. In this case, the reason is to be found in the Goat and Pig sharing too much in common. There is no real drama outside the clash between the decision about where to eat and what club to go to after. Sexual relationships need a degree of tension, and there is not enough in the love affair of a Goat and a Pig to keep it bubbling.

Star Rating: Two, three or even four (for a very short affair).

COMPATIBILITY OF MALE GOATS IN MARRIAGE

FEMALE RAT

Although the Rat and Goat pairing has a very low standing in terms of a casual relationship, there is a massive improvement when the couple decide to cement their love in a marriage. Out of wedlock, Rat and Goat have a habit of keeping an eye open for the next best thing. Goats require much tethering to make the most of their talents whereas the Rat, although giving sound advice, generally prefers to let the others decide for themselves. These influences are not the stuff from which marriages are made, at least not ones that run the course. But an agreement to marry is a statement about wanting to make their relationship work. In a sense the nuptials provide both a framework in which the Rat can operate and a tethering post for the capricious Goat. A rich social life is on the cards, which creates the pleasurable backdrop against which most Rats and all Goats prefer to perform.

Star Rating: Four – almost.

FEMALE BUFFALO

A better than average partner for the female Buffalo, and one which seems extremely popular by the number of male Goats who walk down the aisle with her. From a very low mark as lovers, the step into marriage seems the right one. With their mutual love of family life and the Goat's apparent acceptance of the tethering rope as a force for good in his life, it looks like full steam ahead. But the differences which divide them as romantic partners are ever present and there is always the likelihood that Billy Goat will wander, in the way that Goats do. And the Goat must remember that although some animal signs are quick to overlook his indiscretions, the female Buffalo is not one. Twiggy is a Buffalo lady and her latest husband, Leigh Lawson, is a Goat. They are said to be very happy.

Star Rating: Two, maybe three, depending on the Goat's level of capriciousness.

FEMALE TIGER

The Chinese don't have a strong view either way about this relationship. Marriage between these two signs is a statistical rarity, which doesn't rule it out. Goat men do have a tendency to wander, but they have great social graces and are wonderful hosts. Tiger ladies are not slow to appreciate positive qualities in others, especially those close to them. And Goats adore being loved. If there is a problem, it is in the fact that Goats can't help wanting the limelight and Tigers do not enjoy being ignored. You pays your money and takes your choice.

Star Rating: Two? Difficult, but two is about right.

FEMALE CAT

This is the best of the two pairings and in some cases, most, in fact, reaches top marks. The only cloud on the horizon is that neither Cats nor Goats suffers adversity well, and in many a marriage there are times when either the money gets low or the emotional well runs a bit dry. Then the Goat will tend to find his stimulation elsewhere, much to the Cat's sadness and even anger. But if there's money in the bank, plus time to enjoy it, Goat and Cat will find themselves with few if any rifts growing between them. The good life is what both tend to crave and a beautiful, well cared for home, well stocked with goodies, is what they'll produce.

Star Rating: Four to five.

FEMALE DRAGON

The male Goat is prone to an extremely fickle heart and loves the good life and all the many sensual experiences that good living brings. The Goat, for ever thinking that the grass is greener somewhere else, finds it difficult to say no to any new offer of excitement. For the Dragon, his changing moods are impossible to understand, let alone live with. All in all, not the kind of thing to appeal to a Dragon, who is only really interested in leading life's carnival and not being led up the garden path. Capricious Goats have their moments and some Dragons might even enjoy tethering them but most won't bother. Marriage is not a good idea.

Star Rating: One, creeping up to two.

FEMALE SNAKE

A rich social life, plenty of good food and much appreciation of the world of art is the order for a Snake female and a male Goat – yes sir! These animal signs are destined for a positive if sometimes emotionally rocky life together, with the male Goat given ample opportunity to exercise all his clever social skills. This will be achieved against the Snake's humorous and sensual nature, one which, it must be remembered, has a nasty habit of occasionally turning introspective and difficult. But the Snake female can easily tether the capricious heart and mind of the Goat. Children here are a mixed blessing.

Star Rating: Three or four.

FEMALE HORSE

A vintage quality relationship, one of the all time greats! In love, both signs have already glimpsed the level of quite magical understanding that exists between these two lively and sociable animals. The female Horse is all stamina and the male Goat can be such a delightful tease. Long after the heady days of romance have faded into the sometimes dull routine of marriage there will always be a genuine under-standing. A life of hard work and plenty of fun for two perfectly compatible signs. A classic Goat, Ian Botham is married to a Horse, and in spite of the rumours that they are not happy, their marriage continues to illustrate that these two signs can survive in even the most difficult circum-stances.

Star Rating: Five and more.

FEMALE GOAT

Whereas some animal signs have an introvert and extrovert side to their nature, Goats are, well, just Goats. They are bright, capricious and sensual people who adore romance. As long as one Goat is prepared to make the first move, much will happen, but Goats hate making that initial step. There's much fun to be had in the early days, and should wedding bells eventually ring, there is a more than even chance of some degree of permanence. And if both Goats are active in the arts or an arts-related subject, so much the better. As a matter of fact, I know no less than seven Goat couples, more than any other same sign pairing. Anna Ford and her late husband, cartoonist Mark Boxer, were both born in a Goat year.

Star Rating: One usually. Occasionally two or even three.

FEMALE MONKEY

The Goat and Monkey are capable of sharing a great deal in common, especially when there's a strong social undercurrent to their lives. Goat males make original, interesting homes and the female Monkey can adapt easily to any situation. In marriage, it is sometimes necessary to alter our outlook as there are often many pitfalls. The able Monkey is quick to side-step most of marriage's more dangerous hurdles and, with the Goat following her example, both signs can consider this a match well made. But their failure to be awarded the five star maximum is due to the long term effect of the Goat male's capricious heart and the Monkey female's ever present curiosity for new experiences. Shirley Conran is a Monkey and her former husband, Sir Terence Conran, is a Goat. Their marriage and subsequent divorce is a near perfect blueprint for Goats and Monkeys.

Star Rating: Four.

FEMALE ROOSTER.

Not much understanding ever exists between the Rooster female and Goat male, and any understanding that either can lay claim to comes only after a long hard slog. But is it worth it? The Goat, ever capricious, is often considered self-centred in the eyes of the ever critical female Rooster – not the most auspicious departure point for marital awareness. In addition Rooster ladies have a high moral standard and expect their husbands to follow suit. The Goat is not ideally suited to strait-jacket morality and a marriage of short tempers and long rows is the distinct scenario.

Star Rating: Zero. One at the very most.

FEMALE DOG

Goats and Dogs of both the male and female variety do not have much in common. When you look at the archetypal farmyard, where the origins of Chinese Horoscopes were first considered, goats do not normally bump into dogs – they have different functions, which are not usually linked. However, the female Dog wife is extremely devoted, even though her male Goat husband might not exactly return such blind devotion. But there is a strong element of the peace-maker in both signs and a marriage which included a religious or spiritual aspect would help. Drama man Jack Rosenthal is a Goat, married to actress Dog Maureen Lipman.

Star Rating: One at the most.

FEMALE PIG

One of the better marriages for both Pig and Goat. The high octane social activity is a pronounced feature of this couple's getting together and as long as there are plenty of friends, and enough money left for the free spending pair to entertain them, there is every chance of a long and bump-free marriage. Goat men are useful home-builders, and Pig ladies are in the main caring, jolly home-makers. Sexually compatible, this is a marriage to be given serious thought. The only very slight hint of danger is that both signs lack initiative and perform better in partnerships. Once in a while, even a deeply attached married partner must act on his or her own.

Star Rating: Four.

COMPATIBILITY OF FEMALE GOATS IN MARRIAGE

MALE RAT

Although the Rat and Goat pairing has a very low standing in terms of a casual relationship, there is a massive improvement when the couple decide to cement their love in a marriage. Out of wedlock, Rat and Goat have a habit of keeping an eye open for the next best thing. Goats require much tethering to make the most of their talents whereas the Rat, although giving sound advice, generally prefers to let others decide for themselves. These influences are not the stuff from which marriages are made, at least not ones that run the course. But an agreement to marry is a statement about wanting to make their relationship work. In a sense the nuptials provide both a framework in which the Rat can operate and a tethering post for the capricious Goat. A rich social life is on the cards, which creates the pleasurable backdrop against which most Rats and all Goats prefer to perform.

Star Rating: Four – almost.

MALE BUFFALO

A better than average partner for the male Buffalo, and one which seems extremely popular by the number of female Goats who walk down the aisle with him. From a very low mark as lovers, the step into marriage seems the right one.

With their mutual love of family life and the Goat's apparent acceptance of the tethering rope as a force for good in her life, it looks like full steam ahead. But the differences which divide them as romantic partners are ever present and there is always the likelihood that the lady Goat will wander, in the way that Goats do. And she must remember that although some animal signs are quick to overlook her indiscretions, the male Buffalo is not one. One of photographer David Bailey's four wives, Catherine, was born in a Goat year. It seemed an OK marriage while it lasted.

Star Rating: Three, maybe four, depending on the Goat's level of capriciousness.

MALE TIGER

The Chinese don't have a strong view either way about this relationship. Marriage between these two signs is a statistical rarity, which doesn't rule it out. Goat males do have a tendency to put themselves about a bit, even in marriage, but they are great company and warm and affectionate at heart. Tigers are not slow to appreciate positive qualities in others, especially those close to them. And Goats of both sexes adore being loved, to be the object of another's desire. If there is a problem, it is in the fact that female Goats can't help wanting the limelight and Tigers do not enjoy being ignored. On the other hand, the Tiger might be happy tethering the Goat. You pays your money and takes your choice.

Star Rating: Two? Difficult, but two is about right.

MALE CAT

This is the best of the two pairings and in some cases, most, in fact, reaches top marks. The only cloud on the horizon is that neither Cats or Goats suffer adversity well, and in many a marriage there are times when either the money gets low or the emotional well runs a bit dry. Then the Goat will tend to find her stimulation elsewhere, much to the Cats sadness and even anger. But if there's money in the bank, plus time to enjoy it, Goat and Cat will find themselves with few if any rifts growing between them. The good life is what both tend to crave and a beautiful, well cared for home, well stocked with goodies, is what they'll produce.

Star Rating: Four to five.

MALE DRAGON

The female Goat is prone to an extremely fickle heart and loves the good life and all the sensual experiences that good living brings. The Goat, for ever thinking that the grass is greener somewhere else, finds it difficult to say no to any new offer of excitement. For the male Dragon, her changing moods are impossible to understand, let alone live with. All in all, not the kind of thing to appeal to a Dragon, who is only really interested in leading life's carnival and not being led up the garden path. Capricious Goats have their moments and some Dragons might even enjoy tethering them, but most won't bother. Marriage is not a good idea.

Star Rating: One, creeping up to two.

MALE SNAKE

A rich social life, plenty of good food and much appreciation of the world of art is the order for a Snake male and female Goat – yes sir! These animal signs are destined for a positive if sometimes emotionally rocky life together, with the Goat given ample opportunity to exercise all her domestic skills. This will be achieved against the Snake's humorous and sensual nature, one which, it must be remembered, has a nasty habit of occasionally turning introspective and difficult. But the Snake can easily tether the capricious heart and mind of the Goat. Children here are a mixed blessing. Actor John Thaw is a Snake and his wife, Sheila Hancock, is a Goat.

Star Rating: Three or four.

MALE HORSE

A vintage quality relationship, one of the all-time greats! In love, both signs have already glimpsed the level of quite magical understanding that exists between these lively and sociable animals. The male Horse is full of sound good sense and the female Goat can be such a delightfully indulgent creature, even after the heady days of romance have faded into the sometimes dull routine of marriage. And there will always be a genuine understanding between them. Hard work and plenty of fun for two totally computable signs. A classic Goat, Ian Botham is married to a Horse, and in spite of the rumours that they are not happy, their marriage continues to illustrate that these two signs can survive in even the most difficult circumstances.

Star Rating: Five and more.

MALE GOAT

Whereas some animal signs have an introvert and extrovert side to their nature, Goats are, well, just Goats. They are bright, capricious and sensual people who adore romance, and as long as one Goat is prepared to make the first move lots will happen. But Goats hate making that initial step. There's much fun to be had in the early days, and should wedding bells eventually ring, there is a more than even chance of some degree of permanence. And if both Goats are active in the arts or an arts-related subject, so much the better. As a matter of fact, I know no less than seven Goat couples, more than any other same-sign pairing. Anna Ford and her late husband, cartoonist Mark Boxer, were both born in a Goat year.

Star Rating: One usually. Occasionally two or even three.

MALE MONKEY

The Goat and Monkey are capable of sharing a great deal in common, especially when there's a strong social undercurrent to their lives. Goat females make wonderful homes and the male Monkey can adapt easily to any situation. In marriage, it is sometimes necessary to alter our outlook as there are often many pitfalls. The able Monkey is quick to side-step most of marriage's more dangerous hurdles and with the Goat following his example, both signs can consider this a match well made. But their failure to be awarded the five star maximum is due to the long term effect of the Goat female's capricious heart and the Monkey male's ever present curiosity for new experiences.

Star Rating: Four.

MALE ROOSTER

Not much understanding ever exists between the Rooster male and the Goat female, and any understanding that either can lay claim to comes only after a long, hard slog. But is it worth it? The Goat, ever capricious, is often considered self-centred in the eyes of the frequently critical Rooster – not the most auspicious departure point for marital awareness. In addition Rooster men have, in spite of their tendency to lay boastful claims to the contrary, a high moral standard and expect their wives to follow suit. The Goat is not ideally suited to strait-jacket morality and a marriage of short tempers and long rows is the distinct scenario.

Star Rating: One at the very most.

MALE DOG

Goats and Dogs of both the male and female variety do not have much in common. When you look at the archetypal farmyard, where the origins of Chinese Horoscopes were first considered, goats do not normally bump into dogs – they have different functions, which are not usually linked. However, the male Dog husband is extremely devoted, even though his female Goat wife might not exactly return such blind devotion. But there is a strong element of the peacemaker in both signs and a marriage which includes a religious or spiritual aspect would help. But the male Dog's anxiety level might be stretched by the fickle female Goat's heart.

Star Rating: One at the most.

MALE PIG

One of the better marriages for both Pig and Goat. The high octane social activity is a pronounced feature of this couple's getting together and as long as there are plenty of friends and enough money left for the free spending pair to entertain themselves, there is every chance of a long and bump-free marriage. Goat females are decorative home makers, and Pig males are in the main caring, jolly home builders. Sexually compatible, this is a marriage to be given serious thought. The only very slight hint of danger is that both signs lack initiative and perform better in partnerships. Once in a while, even a deeply attached married partner must act on his or her own.

Star Rating: Four.

COMPATIBILITY OF MALE GOATS IN FRIENDSHIP

MALE RAT

As long as there's a wine bar or pub nearby, Rat and Goat should make out pretty well. Both enjoy life and neither sign finds 'no thanks' easy to say in the face of a good time. There's much good humour, although the Rat might tire a little of the Goat's more capricious side. There again, the Rat is no stranger to a changed plan or two himself. Good vibes on the whole for two fun-lovers. Rolling Stone Bill Wyman is a Rat and both Mick Jagger and Keith Richards are Goats.

Star Rating: Between three and four. Seldom less.

MALE BUFFALO

Although marriage between these two quite different signs stands a more than even chance of succeeding, in simple friendship the differences are exposed to a telling degree. The Buffalo is certainly able to tether the Goat's wayward-ness, but can he be bothered? Goats adore the good life and social intrigue whereas the Buffalo has little or no interest in what he usually sees as trivial pursuits. Not friends, not enemies, a non-starter if ever there was one, and try as I might, I can find no examples of a successful partnership between Buffalo and Goat.

Star Rating: Zero.

MALE TIGER

Tigers and Goats do not share much in common. However, it is sometimes the case that the Goat, ever in need of tether-ing, will respond to the Tiger's energetic nature. But there is always the difficulty that the capricious Goat will wander off when the friendship demands he stick around. The composer Richard Rodgers was a Tiger, and worked with two brilliant lyricists, both Goats. Oscar Hammerstein and Lorenz Hart aided Rodgers with his finest songs. The difficult genius, Lorenz Hart, could alter a lyric at a moment's notice, provid-ing he could be kept away from booze and his gay friends. Hammerstein preferred to write his lyrics in isolation, and found it a struggle even then.

Star Rating: Two minimum, four maximum.

MALE CAT

Another solid friendship for the Cat, who finds that life at a social level is much enhanced by the fun loving and lively minded Goat. These two signs share a genuine love of the arts at all levels and with the Cat's diplomacy acting as a gentle tether for the Goat's more wayward moments, there is every possibility this relationship could last a lifetime. Good fun and a deep understanding make this a winner. It has been noted that two of the Monty Python team, Eric Idle (Goat) and John Cleese (Cat), always get on really well.

Star Rating: Four to five.

MALE DRAGON

All my experience indicates that this is a pair of chums who do not last the distance. Capricious as the day is long, the Goat simply needs more understanding than the short-fused Dragon is capable of. Short bursts in a creative field might help Dragon and Goat make something of their friendship. Although the Chinese Horoscopes are a little indifferent to this partnership, I have found it usually less than positive.

Star Rating: Two at most.

MALE SNAKE

A gentle social life, shared equally between the Snake and Goat might just be the recipe for these two quite different signs. Peace lovers, the cross-over points are their mutual love of beauty and appreciation of all things well made. A fine wine, a splendid meal, a perfectly cut suit, all could be the conversational meeting ground for the wayward Goat and subtle Snake. Business partners might consider a wine bar or high class boutique. Not a robust relationship, it must be said, and Goats do tend to wander.

Star Rating: Two-ish.

MALE HORSE

Every Horse should have at least one friend who is a Goat, and vice versa. The often capricious style of the Goat is a problem. They have a curious habit of saying the opposite of what everyone else has said and the Goat's way of over stating their view when forced into a corner is prone to drive some signs up the wall – the Dragon, for example. But the Horse takes it all in his stride and turns these 'faults' into genuinely positive attributes. The Horse is influenced by the Goat's great social and artistic skills and the pair form a partnership which is hard to beat or break up. Ian Botham is a typical limelight-seeking, outspoken and constantly performing Goat, but the records show his finest hour for England was under the captaincy of Mike Brearley, a Horse leader if ever there was one.

Star Rating: Five.

MALE GOAT

Without the demands and benefits which the sexual aspect brings to a relationship, two Goats aiming at friendship pure and simple might find it hard going. Goat males are artistic and enjoy grazing in both the spiritual and social meadows, which would seem to suggest two Goats happy to string along with each other. But because the Goat's influence creates the ever-nagging desire to wander next door to where the grass appears to be greener, and because a Goat requires a great deal of tethering the news is not good. Goats find it extremely difficult to tether each other and firm friendships between two Goats are considered a rarity. Mick Jagger, a most typical example of his sign, and Keith Richards are both Goats. When not on the stage together, they live in quite separate worlds. And there are those who say, a little unkindly, that Keith has lived in his own world since 1963.

Star Rating: One.

MALE MONKEY

A genuine understanding exists between these two quite different chums, although when combined, the influencing signs of both Goat and Monkey find an interesting mutual path. Male Goat and male Monkey enjoy life's lighter moments, and with the Monkey making the running and the Goat making the most of what's on offer there is every chance that these two socially inclined and acquisitive signs will firm up their friendship for a long term arrangement. One of Britain's most brilliant animation studios, Grand Slam – the Paul McCartney/Rupert Bear video was theirs – is run by a Goat and Monkey team, Jeff Dunbar and Ginger Gibbons.

Star Rating: Three and four.

MALE ROOSTER

A non-sexual partnership is perhaps the only really possible partnership between Goat and Rooster. The males of both signs are capable of demanding more than their fair share of the limelight and it follows that if the friendship involves any kind of show business or public performance, there is a better than average chance that this pair of farmyard chums will get through the difficult early stages of understanding – or misunderstanding. Big spenders and a little full of themselves as a couple, Goat and Rooster males have a good platform for a successful relationship. Chas and Dave are a Goat and Rooster respectively, and a splendid example of the possibilities open to both signs.

Star Rating: Three at the most.

MALE DOG

Dog men are always a touch anxious. Wanting the best for everyone, they are idealists and loyal – sometimes to a fault. Goat men tend to please themselves as to how they behave. Kind, artistic and open minded they may be, but all Goat males are not blessed with large doses of reciprocal loyalty. Dog chums will put up with a lot but when the lake of dependability eventually runs dry, the Dog will finally turn and bite, so to speak. Frank Muir and Dennis Norden, one of post-war Britain's most successful script writers, are a Goat and Dog. They don't do too much together these days, except sit on opposing sides of panel games. An OK friendship over a short distance.

Star Rating: One through to three. Two average.

MALE PIG

Pigs get on with just about every sign and make no exception in the case of the Goat. Here we have two good friends, if a little too vain for their own good, who enjoy a night out, spend plenty of time discussing trends and getting into just about as many as there are on offer. Business relationships are secure in the multiple hoofs of these two signs. As long as the Goat pulls his weight and the Pig isn't too easily duped, any endeavour inspired by the peace loving, artistic Goat and hard working honest Pig is likely to last. Ronald Reagan is the Pig and Mikhail Gorbachov is a Goat.

Star Rating: Four.

COMPATIBILITY OF FEMALE GOATS IN FRIENDSHIP

FEMALE RAT

This pair of female friends are good news. Their mutual interests in good food, fashion and the latest trends create a really positive attitude towards keeping the friendship buoyant. Both signs have a natural flair for all things new and they could easily make a success of any business venture should Rat and Goat choose that particular path to express themselves. Lots of fun and games. And talking of games, one of the greatest ever tennis doubles partnerships was a Rat and Goat – Rosie Casals and Billie-Jean King. They were extremely close on and off the court. Rosie is a Rat.

Star Rating: Five most of the time.

FEMALE BUFFALO

Although marriage between these two quite different signs stands a more than even chance of succeeding, in simple friendship the differences are exposed to a telling degree. The Buffalo is certainly able to tether the Goat's waywardness, but can she be bothered? Goats adore the good life and social intrigue whereas the Buffalo has little or no interest in what she usually sees as trivial pursuits. Not friends, not enemies, a non-starter if ever there was one, and try as I might, I can find no examples of a successful partnership between lady Buffalo and Goat.

Star Rating: Zero.

FEMALE TIGER

Tigers and Goats do not share much in common. However, it is sometimes the case that the Goat, ever in need of tethering, will respond to the Tiger's energetic nature. But there is always the difficulty that the capricious Goat will wander off when the friendship demands she stick around. Here again, the dominant influence of the Tiger's masculine sign might fit well with the extremely female Goat.

Star Rating: Two minimum, four maximum.

FEMALE CAT

Another solid friendship for the Cat, who finds that life at a social level is much enhanced by the fun loving and lively minded Goat. These two signs share a genuine love of the arts at all levels and with the Cat's diplomacy acting as a gentle tether for the Goat's more wayward moments, there is every possibility this relationship could last a lifetime. Good fun and a deep understanding make this a winner.

Star Rating: Four to five.

FEMALE DRAGON

All my experience indicates that this is a pair of ladies who do not last the distance. Capricious as the day is long, the Goat simply needs more understanding than the short-fused Dragon is capable of. Short bursts in a creative field might help Dragon and Goat make something of their friendship. Although the Chinese Horoscopes are a little indifferent to this partnership, I have found it usually less than positive.

Star Rating: Two at the most.

FEMALE SNAKE

A gentle social life, shared equally between the Snake and Goat might just be the recipe for these two quite different signs. Peace lovers, the cross-over points are their mutual love of beauty and appreciation of all things well made. A fine wine, a splendid meal, a perfectly designed outfit, all could be the conversational meeting ground for the wayward Goat and subtle Snake. Business partners might consider a wine bar or high class boutique. Not a robust relationship, it must be said, and Goats do tend to wander.

Star Rating: Two-ish.

FEMALE HORSE

Every Horse should have a least one friend who is a Goat, and vice versa. The often capricious style of the Goat is a problem. They have a curious habit of saying the opposite of what everyone else has said and the Goat's way of over stating their view when in a tight corner is prone to drive some signs up the wall – the Dragon, for example. But the Horse takes it all in her stride and turns these 'faults' into genuinely positive attributes. The Horse is influenced by the Goat's great social and artistic skills and the pair form a partnership which is hard to beat or break up.

Star Rating: Five.

FEMALE GOAT

Without the demands and benefits which the sexual aspect brings to a relationship, two Goats aiming at friendship pure and simple might find it hard going. Goat females are artistic and enjoy grazing in both the spiritual and social meadows, which would seem to suggest two Goats happy to string along with each other. But because a Goat's influence creates the ever nagging desire to wander next door to where the grass appears greener, and because a Goat requires a great deal of tethering, the news is not good. Goats find it extremely difficult to tether each other and firm friendships between two Goats are considered a rarity. Two female Goats don't happen.

Star Rating: Zero.

FEMALE MONKEY

A genuine understanding exists between these two quite different chums, although when combined, the influencing signs of both Goat and Monkey find an interesting mutual path. Female Goat and female Monkey enjoy life's lighter moments, and with the Monkey making the running and the Goat making the most of what's on offer there is every chance that these two socially inclined and acquisitive signs will firm up their friendship for a long term arrangement.

Star Rating: Three and four.

FEMALE ROOSTER

A non-sexual friendship is perhaps the only really possible partnership between Goat and Rooster. The females of both signs are capable of demanding more than their fair share of the limelight and it follows that if the friendship involves any kind of show business or public performance, there is a better than average chance that this pair of farmyard chums will get through the difficult early stages of understanding – or misunderstanding. Big spenders and a little full of themselves as a couple, Goat and Rooster females have only a moderate platform for a successful relationship.

Star Rating: Three at the most.

FEMALE DOG

Dog ladies are always a touch anxious. Wanting the best for everyone, they are idealists and loyal – sometimes to a fault. Goat ladies tend to please themselves as to how they behave. Kind, artistic and open minded they may be, but Goat females are not over blessed with large doses of reciprocal loyalty. Dogs will put up with a lot but when the lake of dependability eventually runs dry, the Dog will finally turn and bite, so to speak. An OK friendship over a short distance.

Star Rating: One through to three. Two average.

FEMALE PIG

Pigs get on with just about every sign and make no exception in the case of the Goat. Here we have two good friends, if a little too vain for their own good, who enjoy a night out, spend plenty of time discussing fashion trends and getting into just about as many as there are on offer. Business relationships are strong in the multiple and well-manicured hoofs of these two signs. As long as the Goat pulls her weight and the Pig isn't too easily duped, any endeavour inspired by the peace loving, artistic Goat and hard working, honest Pig is likely to last.

Star Rating: Four

THE MONKEY

1908	February 2nd to January 21st	**1909**
1920	February 20th to February 7th	**1921**
1932	February 6th to January 25th	**1933**
1944	January 25th to February 12th	**1945**
1956	February 12th to January 30th	**1957**
1968	January 30th to February 16th	**1969**
1980	February 16th to February 4th	**1981**
1992	February 4th to January 22nd	**1993**

Some Monkey's queer grimaces,
Forestalling human faces,
Fill the gaps and spaces
That link two ancient races.

Leon Underwood

THE YEAR OF THE MONKEY

Monkeys are born under the sign of fantasy and of all twelve signs, Monkeys are the closest to man. They are blessed with all the very best that mankind offers, and unfortunately, many of his worst faults. On the credit side, Monkeys are endowed with great intelligence. They have a high regard for knowledge and are capable of thinking through even the most complex problems. This they do, seemingly, without effort. Charming and resourceful, Monkeys have a firm sense of their own value. They use a potent mixture of wit and wisdom to attain their goals, of which there are usually dozens.

Monkeys are nothing if not wheeler-dealers and in business they usually end up settling on the most profitable. As a rule, though, Monkeys are not originators. Brilliant at taking the ideas of others and skilfully adapting them to suit their own needs, they can turn dross into gold. A Monkey, it is said, will try anything once.

Monkeys have a cool head and a powerful memory, which tends to give them a great advantage in business. Coupled with a pronounced acquisitiveness, the Monkey's business acumen invariably leads to a healthy bank balance, which, the Chinese Horoscopes warn unkindly, is usually governed by a tight fist. However, there are few more generous with help or praise when it is genuinely needed. Highly organised, though sometimes prone to casting superficial judgements, Monkeys are gifted creatures with an extraordinary ability to make people believe whatever they say. The Chinese again warn against this, pointing out that since their sign is fantasy, Monkeys find it difficult to distinguish between fact and fiction.

Most Monkeys enjoy a highly sophisticated sense of

284

humour. This they might easily use to get out of a tight corner, more common for a Monkey than any other sign. Intrepid travellers, Monkeys see an open road both as a challenge and a route to new experiences. If the Monkey has one outstanding quality it is the power to adapt. But once a Monkey has decided on a course of action, they must act there and then. If not, they'll quickly move on to something else. And if a project turns sour you won't find a Monkey nursing their wounds. Quick to recover, they will be up and running in no time at all.

Because they have a constant need to develop new interests, Monkeys frequently find long term relationships elude them. No one person ever truly satisfies a Monkey, the reason being that Monkeys are not seeking satisfaction. It is the love of new experiences that the Monkey enjoys. The Chinese view of the Monkey states that they prefer intrigue to love itself.

The first phase of a Monkey's life will be dictated by an unsettled childhood in which there will be a constant brush with authority. A lack of stability at home and a trail of failed relationships will dominate the second phase. But usually there will be enough money to pay the rent and alimony. Old age is kinder to the inquisitive Monkey, in spite of the fact that the Chinese say that Monkeys are in danger of meeting a sudden end in a far place.

COMPATIBILITY OF MALE MONKEYS IN LOVE

FEMALE RAT

Monkeys have few moral horizons and even fewer scruples when it comes to sexual intrigue. The lady Rat is vulnerable when gripped by a sexual affair and few can resist the Monkey's tricks. Both signs have a great deal in common when it comes to pleasure. They like plenty of it, often at the expense of other, more edifying, activities. Give Monkey and Rat an open cheque and a week off and they will have a ball. But there are a few provisos. The Monkey is a cool lover and both signs always have one eye open for the main chance. So, if something better comes along . . . goodbye romance.

Star Rating: Five in some cases but usually four. It depends on how long they decide to stay interested in each other.

FEMALE BUFFALO

On the surface there doesn't seem much going for the fast thinking Monkey male, who lives off his wits, and the more dependable, conservative Buffalo lady. But there is moving poetry in the heart of the female Buffalo, even though she sometimes finds it hard to express. The Monkey male is a wizard at touching the sensual nerve of even the most reluctant female, and he might find the emotionally complex Buffalo something of a challenge. As far as a love affair goes, this is not at all bad. At best, however, the affair will be the on/off kind, with the Buffalo finding herself less in command that in other relationships.

Star Rating: Three, sometimes four.

FEMALE TIGER

This is a relationship very much created from a spirit of suck-it-and-see style optimism. Nothing can actually be said against it but however hard you look, it is not easy to find a lot to say in favour of the Tiger female and Mr Monkey letting it all hang out. Monkeys have never been heard to say no to a new experience and even the most feminine Tiger is no slouch when it comes to offering them. But there is something in the chemistry of both signs which does not sit comfortably when they are placed together. The Tiger is just a little too rebellious and active; the Monkey a teeny-weeny bit too open to other offers.

Star Rating: This is not a cop out, but this relationship is almost impossible to pin down. Two is average.

FEMALE CAT

Cats do not usually meet Monkeys in nature. One is domestic and the other a very intelligent creature of the wild. And to a certain extent, this is true of the relationship between these two Chinese animal signs. Cats like life cut and dried if they are to get the most from it, and this is also how they view romance. They like their lovers to arrive on time and when it is suggested they meet on Friday, they are not crazy about last minute cancellations. Monkeys are prone to living life to suit themselves and both sexes are emotional wheeler-deelers. However, there are a few points they have in common – wit and an appreciation of life's more subtle sides being high on the list. Lady Cat/male Monkey are the more likely to make it work.

Star Rating: Three tops.

FEMALE DRAGON

The last of the five star love relationships on the Dragon's list of six. And it is unlike the others because although, as in all love affairs, there is plenty of physical contact, there is also much meeting of the mind. Both sides are more than capable of taking themselves not at all seriously, and although the Dragon is prone to over heating, she tends to be more relaxed with the Monkey than with any other. He is a great reader of the Dragon's inner strengths, and weaknesses, and will manipulate his colourful lover almost any way he wants. And the Dragon won't mind one bit. In turn, she will push for the Monkey to act even more irresponsibly in matters of passion, and there will be no stopping these two positive signs. Many have commented on the praise Monkey Tim Rice has so often heaped on his Dragon star, Elaine Paige.

Star Rating: Five alive.

FEMALE SNAKE

There are not many signs a Monkey can't win over and the Snake has few problems when it comes to really getting the object of her romantic desire. So, should the Monkey appeal to the Snake and vice versa, nothing should stand in the way of this being a top hole affair. But there is a hidden E (erotic) additive that can have damaging side effects. Monkeys, it must be constantly remembered, are more interested in setting up the affair than the actual physical event. Snake women are more interested in the act than the preparation. There you have it, or rather, you might not.

Star Rating: Three from five.

FEMALE HORSE

Here's a puzzler. The Chinese offer not a single jot of under-standing between the independent Horse female and the ever sharp, often scheming and adaptable Monkey male. But there are many seemingly successful relationships between these two signs. Perhaps it is again the old point about the attraction of opposites, but clearly something makes a Monkey and Horse tick. Having said that, it is easy to see why a Monkey, so unreliable as a lover, might outwit the Horse, who herself is desperately unsure of her own feelings when smitten by romance. Two drifters in a sea of romantic uncertainty, one might say. When you are both drifting, it helps to have one who knows where the shore is. It is, in this case, usually the Monkey.

Star Rating: Zero. Sorry.

FEMALE GOAT

A big buzz at the start for Goats and Monkeys, who frequently find the wit and social skills of each other's animal influence sexually compelling and highly appealing. The Monkey male can never say no to a good thing, or even a bad one – he *has* to try everything once – and the female Goat has great charm and promises plenty. But the Monkey has a low horizon when it comes to fidelity and the female Goat is no stranger to a fickle heart. A great opening, with a fair chance that the longer the relationship lasts the better this pair's chance of romantic happiness. Male Monkey/female Goat have the best chance.

Star Rating: Three is about average.

FEMALE MONKEY

A love match between two Monkeys has a perfect ring to it. Complementary in just about every department, the Monkey lovers are quick to adapt to each other's moods, which are seldom given to extremes of emotional highs and lows. Quick to flatter the other and generous in their appreciation of the 'little things' that go to make up a relationship, love-struck Monkeys enjoy the experience of getting the relationship off the ground as much as the affair itself. The only problem is that Monkeys are destined to travel and to take on new friends. This means Monkeys must ensure they are in the same place at the same time with the same person.

Star Rating: Five all the way.

FEMALE ROOSTER

Here we're talking about the attraction of opposites, an often fatal attraction which is only too often discovered when it is too late to do anything to repair the damage. But happily, the days of wine and roses don't run into months. And it is an absolute certainty that both Monkey and Rooster will discover they have such diametrically opposed views on just about everything that the parting of the ways between moralist Rooster and artful Monkey will take place before the wedding bells chime.

Star Rating: One, and that's being generous.

FEMALE DOG

This is a relationship which looks good on paper but the reality often shows a different view. The Monkey is a bit of a trickster in every aspect of his life. He loves intrigue and games. He might even play off one friend against another, and one lover against the next. Dog ladies are warm if anxious about their love life and, once committed, will not enjoy being taken for granted, no matter how much the Dog's influence of loyalty and devotion is exercised. Too many tricks and not enough respect mark the Monkey in his love affair with the lady Dog as a non-starter, or a quick finisher.

Star Rating: Zero. Maybe half a point at best.

FEMALE PIG

Here's a fine romance. Monkeys and Pigs positively revel in each other's highly social and fun loving company. Pig ladies love getting dressed up for a night out and Monkey men will spare no effort in finding the right time and place to make everything go with a bang. Neither animal sign cares much about what others say about them, so expect an open and high stepping affair. Go for it.

Star Rating: Five of the best.

COMPATIBILITY OF FEMALE MONKEYS IN LOVE

MALE RAT

Lady Monkeys have few moral horizons and even fewer scruples when it comes to sexual intrigue. This is just too much for the Rat, who is bowled over by the Monkey's tricks. Both signs have a great deal in common when it comes to pleasure. They like plenty of it, often at the expense of other, more edifying, activities. Give Monkey and Rat an open cheque and a week off and they will have a ball. But the lady Monkey is the cooler lover and both signs have one eye open for the main chance. So, if something better comes along . . . goodbye romance. Prince Andrew is a Rat and his affair with Monkey Koo Stark probably tells us all we need to know about this particular partnership.

Star Rating: Four or five, depending on how long they stay interested in each other.

MALE BUFFALO

On the surface there doesn't seem much going for the fast thinking Monkey lady, who lives off her wits, and the solid, dependable Buffalo. But there is poetry in the heart of many a male Buffalo, even though they sometimes find it hard to express. The Monkey lady is a wizard at bringing out even the most repressed male, and she might well find the emotionally complex Buffalo something of a challenge. As far as a love affair goes, this is not at all bad. At best,

291

however, the affair will be the on/off kind, with the Buffalo finding himself less in command than in other relationships.

Star Rating: Three, sometimes four.

MALE TIGER

This is a relationship very much created from a spirit of suck-it-and-see style optimism. Nothing can actually be said against it but however hard you look, it is not easy to find a lot to say in favour of Tiger male and Miss Monkey letting it all hang out. Monkeys have never been heard to say no to a new experience and the Tiger is no slouch when it comes to offering them. But there is something in the chemistry of both signs which does not sit comfortably when they are placed together. The Tiger is just a little too rebellious and active; the Monkey a teeny-weeny bit too open to other offers.

Star Rating: This is not a cop out, but this relationship is almost impossible to pin down. Two is average.

MALE CAT

Cats do not usually meet Monkeys in nature. One is domestic and the other a very intelligent creature of the wild. And to a certain extent, this is true of the relationship between these two Chinese animal signs. Cats like life cut and dried if they are to get the most from it, and this is also how they view romance. They like their lovers to arrive on time and when it is suggested they meet on Friday, they are not crazy about last minute cancellations. Monkeys are prone to living life to suit themselves and both sexes are emotional wheeler-dealers. However, there are a few points they have in common – wit and an appreciation of life's more subtle sides being high on the list.

Star Rating: Three tops.

MALE DRAGON

The last of the five star love relationships on the Dragon's list of six. And it is unlike the others because although, as in all love affairs, there is plenty of physical contact, there is also much meeting of the mind. Both sides are more than capable of taking themselves not at all seriously, and although the Dragon is prone to over-heating, he tends to be more relaxed with the Monkey than with any other. She is a great reader of the Dragon's inner strengths, and weaknesses, and will manipulate her colourful lover almost any way she wants. And the Dragon won't mind one bit. In turn, he will push for the Monkey to act even more irresponsibly in matters of passion, and there will be no stopping these two positive signs. During his stay at Number Ten, it was often noted how close Premier Harold Wilson, a Dragon, worked with Marcia Williams, his Monkey secretary.

Star Rating: Five alive.

MALE SNAKE

There are not many signs a Monkey can't win over and the Snake has few problems when it comes to really getting the object to his romantic desire. So, should the Monkey appeal to the Snake and vice versa, nothing should stand in the way of this being a top hole affair. But there is a hidden E (erotic) additive that can have damaging side effects. Monkeys, it must be constantly remembered, are more interested in setting up the affair than the actual physical event. Snake chaps are more interested in the act than the preparation. There you have it, or rather, you might not.

Star Rating: Even Stevens. Three through to five.

MALE HORSE

Here's a puzzler. The Chinese offer not a single jot of understanding between the independent Horse and the ever sharp and adaptable Monkey female. But there are many seemingly successful relationships between these two signs. Perhaps it is again the old point about the attraction of opposites, but clearly something makes a Monkey and Horse tick. Having said that, it is easy to see why a Monkey, so unreliable as a lover, might outwit the Horse, who himself is desperately unsure of his own feelings when smitten by romance. Two drifters in a sea of romantic uncertainty, one might say. When you are both drifting, it helps to have one who knows the where the shore is. It is, in this case, usually the Monkey.

Star Rating: Zero. Sorry.

MALE GOAT

A big buzz at the start for Goats and Monkeys, who frequently find the wit and social skills of each other's animal influence sexually compelling and highly appealing. The Monkey lady can never say no to a good thing, or even a bad one – she *has* to try everything once – and the male Goat has great charm and promises plenty. But the Monkey has a low horizon when it comes to fidelity and the male Goat is no stranger to a fickle heart. A great opening with a fair chance that the longer the relationship lasts the better this pair's chance of romantic happiness. Goat Mick Jagger has promised marriage to Monkey model Jerry Hall. But that's as far as it has got.

Star Rating: Three is about average.

MALE MONKEY

A love match between two Monkeys has a perfect ring to it. Complementary in just about every department, the Monkey lovers are quick to adapt to each other's moods, which are seldom given to extremes of emotional highs and lows. Quick to flatter the other and generous in their appreciation of the 'little things' that go to make up a relationship, love-struck Monkeys enjoy the experience of getting the relationship off the ground as much as the affair itself. The only problem is that Monkeys are destined to travel and take on new friends. This means Monkeys must ensure they are in the same place at the same time with the same person.

Star Rating: Five all the way.

MALE ROOSTER

Here we're talking about the attraction of opposites, an often fatal attraction which is only too often discovered when it is too late to do anything to repair the damage. But happily, the days of wine and roses don't run into months. And it is an absolute certainty that both Monkey and Rooster will discover they have such diametrically opposed views on just about everything that the parting of the ways between candid Rooster and artful Monkey will take place before the wedding bells chime. Of the two pairings, male Rooster/ female Monkey stands the best chance.

Star Rating: One, and that's being generous.

MALE DOG

This is a relationship which looks good on paper but the reality often takes a different view. The Monkey is something of a trickster in every aspect of her life. She loves intrigue and games. She might even play off one friend against another, and one lover against the next. Dog males are warm if anxious about their love life and, once committed, will not enjoy being taken for granted, no matter how much the Dog's influence of loyalty and devotion is exercised. Too many tricks and not enough respect mark the Monkey in her love affair with the Dog as a non starter, or a quick finisher.

Star Rating: Zero. Maybe half a point at best.

MALE PIG

Here's a fine romance. Monkeys and Pigs positively revel in each other's highly social and fun loving company. Pig fellas love getting dressed up for a night out and Ms Monkey will spare no effort in finding the right time and place to make everything go with a bang. Neither animal sign cares much about what others say about them, so expect an open and high stepping affair. Go for it.

Star Rating: Five of the best.

COMPATIBILITY OF MALE MONKEYS IN MARRIAGE

FEMALE RAT

In the love category, female Rat and male Monkey are among the top handful of relationships. With no set limits, both animal signs are free to indulge their considerable appetites and a sexual affair is the perfect outcome. Marriage, on the other hand, demands a great many sacrifices which neither sign are particularly inclined towards. As a rule, the astute Monkey will prevent the family finances from slipping into the red, although the Rat won't be too bothered either way. But with Mr and Mrs Chancer under the same roof for any lengthy period, the question must be asked, when will their true nature creep through the marriage-vow barrier? But both Rat and Monkey make splendid parents and should they wed, a family, the larger the better, will go a long way to keep them together. Transport minister Peter Bottomley is a Monkey and his MP wife, Virginia, is a Rat.

Star Rating: Three. Sometimes a point less, sometimes a point more, but the male Rat/female Monkey partnership scores the highest points.

FEMALE BUFFALO

The male Monkey has few problems in any relationship, finding he can weave his clever spell, a mix of wit, cunning and flattery, on any animal sign. A love affair between male

Monkey and female Buffalo rates higher than average marks. His cool style and humour relaxes her and exposes the Buffalo's own highly individual personality. But marriage complicates the issue and the relationship has only a 50/50 chance of succeeding. Children are a good move in a Monkey and Buffalo marriage as they supply a focal point for both signs. Monkey males make first rate parents and the Buffalo female will always do her utmost, in a traditionalist kind of way, to insure her children's education is the best on offer. But the monkey loves tricks and intrigue and there is no room for either in the female Buffalo's home.

Star Rating: Two.

FEMALE TIGER

A very middle of the road kind of marriage which promises bags of fun and ends up with both partners a touch confused as to why the bright lights went out. Strong on ideas, the female Tiger is always quick to display her emotions whereas the male Monkey is much more select in what they let on. Lovers of intrigue, the skilful Monkey is the master of his own heart and prefers to play at love. Their attitude to marriage is similarly affected. But children figure strongly in both signs and a family will certainly make all the difference to this couple's life.

Star Rating: Two.

FEMALE CAT

Monkeys always live life the way they want it, although they have an uncanny knack of making you think you are in charge. Never one hundred per cent honest about their true feelings, Monkey men are nevertheless extremely perceptive. Female Cats are particularly fragile in terms of temperament, especially when compared with the easy adaptability and emotional self control of the Monkey. This difference might well create problems. In her favour, the Cat adores refinement, method and routine, and is frequently saved from being a victim of life's duller side by a sharp and sometimes snobbish sense of humour. The more acerbic the lady Cat, the more the bright Monkey male will want to make this marriage last. Kids will make a big difference in the couple's favour.

Star Rating: Two, maybe three. Seldom more.

FEMALE DRAGON

One of the best of all marriages, especially if there is a hint of professional or business interest involved. The Monkey has great skill when it comes to organisation and adaptability, and coupled with the Dragon's self confidence and imagination, the sky's the limit. Both Dragons and Monkeys do have the potential to experiment, and it is said that the Monkey finds it hard to turn down the offer of a new experience. This could mean the marriage is threatened by the Monkey suddenly deciding he wants to change his lifestyle. But there is usually so much mutual respect between Monkey husband and Dragon wife that whatever fate brings, they see it through together. And this is another marriage in which a review of the marriage vows, highlighting the one to be faithful, might not be a bad idea once in a while. The male Monkey/female Dragon is not the strongest of pairs, as Dragon Shirley Temple found when marrying her first husband, actor Monkey John Agar.

Star Rating: Five (most times).

FEMALE SNAKE

There is really nothing very special in this relationship which marriage either helps or hinders. The sexual side is good, if just a little off-hand at times in respect of the Monkey's input. But there's always plenty of good humour around the place and as long as the Snake doesn't feel threatened by the Monkey's sharper wit and artfulness, there should not be too many problems. Money shouldn't be a big problem either, providing the Monkey adds freely to the family kitty from time to time. Both are good company and there should be plenty of family friends to keep them feeling they are a useful couple. Kids might be a good idea.

Star Rating: Three.

FEMALE HORSE

Given the large number of Horse and Monkey marriages I have come across in my researches, I would have thought that Monkey male and female Horse would get a high rating. But the Chinese Horoscopes will have none of it. They saw that the often manipulative Monkey will frequently infuriate the normally even tempered Horse. Monkeys get their own way no matter what, regardless of whose expense it's at. Judged as a couple the Horse is reliable and steadfast, whereas the Monkey is mobile and quick to move away from testing moments. Having said that, the Monkey makes a first-rate parent, when it suits him. A family, in spite of the prediction of a mismatch, is a good idea and a Dragon son is ideal.

Star Rating: One. Two would be generous.

FEMALE GOAT

The Goat and Monkey are capable of sharing a great deal in common, especially when there's a strong social undercurrent to their lives. Goat females make wonderful homes and the male Monkey can adapt easily to any situation. In marriage, it is sometimes necessary to alter our outlook, as there are often many pitfalls. The able Monkey is quick to side-step most on marriage's more dangerous hurdles and with the Goat following his example, both signs can consider this a match well made. But their failure to be awarded the five star maximum is due to the long term effect of the Goat female's capricious heart and the Monkey male's ever-present curiosity for new experiences.

Star Rating: Four.

FEMALE MONKEY

A great romance that has every chance of developing into a great marriage, and that's the case nine times out of ten. A thrifty, carefully organised pair who are excellent with children and can handle most of what life has to throw. But there is a word of warning to which a couple of wedding-hopeful Monkeys might like to heed. All Monkeys find new sensations and experiences almost impossible to ignore. Marriage is usually better when there are no lovers hiding under the bed and all the cards are on the table. But Monkeys are such gifted story-tellers that should one or the other be tempted, the chain of confusion might end up strangling everyone. Mastermind-winner and taxi driver Fred Housego and his wife are both Monkeys. They're happy, I'm told.

Star Rating: Five (usually).

FEMALE ROOSTER

From a shaky and short-lived romance, the male Monkey and female Rooster really test the Chinese Horoscope to its limits when, or if, they stroll down the aisle. The prospects are really about as gloomy as could be. The female Rooster is an exceptionally private individual in spite of her glamorous looks, and the Monkey male, capable of charming the pants off anyone, has no time for dyed in the wool morality. Money, sex and the home will always be seen through opposing lenses. Kids will not help the marriage either and only under exceptional conditions – like they are the only couple left on earth – should Monkey and Rooster wed.

Star Rating: The pits, beggin' your pardon.

FEMALE DOG

From a no-no love affair, the element of promising a long term commitment adds an important dimension to the relationship. Put simply, over a period of time the Dog's high idealism and loyal outlook will transform her Monkey husband's general attitude to one of relatively honest endeavour. As a result the Monkey husband will frequently adopt an uncharacteristic single mindedness, thus providing this curious couple with more than an even chance of making the marriage work. Kids would be a good idea. Ray Davies, leader of one of the only original sixties pop groups still performing, The Kinks, is a Monkey. He enjoyed a long marriage to his Dog wife Rasa before divorcing her. Long by pop standards, that is.

Star Rating: Three, surprisingly.

FEMALE PIG

A really fun marriage this. After a splendid romance, the Pig lady and Monkey male who decide to settle down usually find there's still plenty in common and there's bags of laughs for everyone else. A strong circle of friends and a big bouncing family, with plenty of mum's cream cakes and dad's witty and talkative nature, suggest it is all systems go for Monkey and Pig. And so it is. Honest Pig and sharp Monkey combine to keep the party going, bringing the best out in each other.

Star Rating: Five.

COMPATIBILITY OF FEMALE MONKEYS IN MARRIAGE

MALE RAT

In the love category, male Rat and female Monkey are among the top handful of relationships. With no set limits, both animal signs are free to indulge their considerable appetites and a sexual affair is the perfect outcome. Marriage, on the other hand, demands a great many sacrifices which neither sign are particularly inclined towards. As a rule, the astute Monkey will prevent the family finances from slipping into the red, although the Rat won't be too bothered either way. But with Mr and Mrs Chancer under the same roof for any lengthy period, the question must be asked, when will their true nature creep through the marriage-vow barrier? Both Rat and Monkey make splendid parents, and should they wed, a family, the larger the better, will go a long way to keep them together.

Star Rating: Three. Sometimes a point less, sometimes a point more.

MALE BUFFALO

The female Monkey has few problems in any relationship, finding she can weave her clever spell, a mix of wit and flattery, on any sign. A love affair between female Monkey and male Buffalo rates high marks. She relaxes him and exposes his own highly individual personality. But marriage complicates the issue and the relationship has only a 50/50 chance of succeeding. Children are a good move in a Monkey and Buffalo marriage as they supply a focal point for both signs. Monkey ladies make first-rate parents and the Buffalo male will always do his utmost, in a traditionalist kind of way, to ensure his children's education is the best on offer. But the Monkey loves tricks and intrigue, and there is no room for either in the male Buffalo's home. Liz Taylor is a Monkey and her twice-husband, the late Richard Burton, a Buffalo. Nobody could say they didn't make a try of marriage or that they were closest when they weren't.

Star Rating: Two.

MALE TIGER

A very middle of the road kind of marriage which promises bags of fun and ends up with both partners a touch confused as to why the bright lights went out. Strong on ideas, the Tiger is always quick to display his emotions whereas the Monkey is much more selective in what she lets on. Lovers of intrigue, the bright and witty Monkey prefers to play at love and their attitude to marriage is similarly affected. But children figure strongly in both signs and a family will certainly make all the difference to this couple's life.

Star Rating: Two.

MALE CAT

Monkey ladies always live life the way they want to, although they have an uncanny knack of making you think you are the guy in charge. Never one hundred per cent honest about their true feelings, Monkey women are nevertheless extremely perceptive. Cats are particularly fragile in terms of their temperament, especially when compared with the easy adaptability and emotional self control of the Monkey. Male Cats like refinement, method and routine, and are frequently saved from being a victim of life's duller side by a sharp and sometimes snobbish sense of humour. The more acerbic the Cat, the better the sharp as a knife Monkey lady will want to stick around and make this marriage last. Kids will make a Big Difference in its favour. Actor Michael Denison was born in a Cat year, and his actress wife, Dulcie Gray, in the year of the Monkey.

Star Rating: Two, maybe three. Seldom more.

MALE DRAGON

One of the best of all marriages, especially if there is a hint of professional or business interest involved. The Monkey lady has a great skill when it comes to organisation, and coupled with the Dragon's drive and imagination, the sky's the limit. Both Dragons and Monkeys do have the potential to experiment, and it is said that the Monkey finds it hard to turn down the offer of a new experience. This could mean the marriage is threatened by the Monkey suddenly deciding she wants to change her lifestyle. But there is usually so much mutual respect between Monkey wife and Dragon husband that whatever fate brings, they see it through together. And this is another marriage in which a review of the marriage vows, highlighting the one to be faithful, might not be a bad idea once in a while. Fifties singing star Dragon Eddie Fisher married two Monkeys to prove the point – Debbie Reynolds and Elizabeth Taylor.

Star Rating: Five. Top whack.

MALE SNAKE

There is really nothing very special in this relationship which marriage either helps or hinders. The sexual side is good, if just a little off-hand at times in respect of the Monkey's input. But there's always plenty of good humour around the place, and as long as the Snake doesn't feel outwitted by the super sharp Monkey, there shouldn't be too many problems. Both are good company and there should be plenty of family friends to keep them feeling they are a useful couple. Kids might be a good idea.

Star Rating: Three.

MALE HORSE

Given the large number of Horse and Monkey marriages I have come across in my researches, I would have thought that Monkey lady and male Horse would get a high rating. But the Chinese Horoscopes will have none of it. They say that the often manipulative Monkey will frequently infuriate the normally even tempered Horse. She will, they say, get her own way at his expense. Judged as a couple the Horse is by contrast reliable and steadfast, whereas the Monkey is mobile and quick to move away from testing moments. Having said that, the Monkey makes a first-class parent, when it suits her. A family, in spite of the prediction of a mismatch, is a good idea and a Dragon son is ideal. Neil Kinnock and his wife, Glenys, are a Horse and Monkey team. Prince and Princess Michael of Kent another.

Star Rating: One. Two would be generous.

MALE GOAT

The Goat and Monkey are capable of sharing a great deal in common, especially when there's a strong social undercurrent to their lives. The Goat male makes original, interesting homes and the female Monkey can adapt easily to any situation. In marriage, it is sometimes necessary to alter our outlook, as there are often many pitfalls. The able Monkey is quick to side-step most of marriage's more dangerous hurdles and with the Goat following her example, both signs can consider this a match well made. But their failure to be awarded the five star maximum is due to the long term effect of the Goat male's capricious heart and the Monkey female's ever present curiosity for new experiences. Shirley Conran, is a Monkey and her former husband, Sir Terence Conran is a Goat. Their marriage and subsequent divorce is a near-perfect blueprint for Goats and Monkeys.

Star Rating: Four.

MALE MONKEY

A great romance that has every chance of developing into a great marriage, and that's the case nine times out of ten. A thrifty, carefully organised pair who are excellent with children and can handle most of what life has to throw. But there is a word of warning to which a couple of wedding hopeful Monkeys might like to heed. All Monkeys find new sensations and experiences almost impossible to ignore. Marriage is usually better when there are no lovers hiding under the bed and all the cards are on the table. But Monkeys are such gifted story-tellers that should one or the other be tempted, the chain of confusion might end up strangling everyone. Mastermind-winner and taxi driver Fred Housego and his wife are both Monkeys. They're happy, I'm told.

Star Rating: Five (usually).

MALE ROOSTER

From a shaky and short lived romance, the female Monkey and male Rooster really test the Chinese Horoscope to its limits when, or if, they stroll down the aisle. The prospects are really about as gloomy as could be. The male Rooster is an exceptionally private individual in spite of his strutting style, and the Monkey female, capable of charming the pants off anyone, has no time for priggish morality. Money, sex and the home will always be seen through opposing lenses. Kids will not help the marriage either and only under exceptional conditions – like they are the only couple left on earth – should Monkey and Rooster wed.

Star Rating: The pits, beggin' your pardon.

MALE DOG

From a no-no affair, the element of promising a long term commitment from the Monkey adds an important dimension to the relationship. Put simply, over a period of time the Dog's high idealism and loyal outlook will transform his Monkey wife's general attitude to one of relatively honest endeavour. As a result the Monkey wife will frequently adopt an uncharacteristic single mindedness, thus providing this curious couple with more than an even chance of making the marriage a success. Kids would be a good idea.

Star Rating: Three, surprisingly.

MALE PIG

A really fun marriage this. After a splendid romance, the Pig male and Monkey female who decide to settle down usually find there's still plenty in common and there's bags of laughs for everyone else. A strong circle of friends and a big bouncing family, with plenty of mum's funny stories and dad's warm and generous nature, suggest it is all systems go for Monkey and Pig. And so it is. Honest Pig and sharp Monkey combine to keep the party going, bringing the best out in each other.

Star Rating: Five.

COMPATABILITY OF MALE MONKEYS IN FRIENDSHIP

MALE RAT

A very reasonable friendship, with the best coming at the beginning. Monkeys are wheeler-dealers to a man and the Rat loves in-fighting, especially in business, and so a commercial union is something to aim at. The only setback is that they will finally find themselves trying to outwit each other. Andrew Lloyd Webber is a Rat and Tim Rice a Monkey.

Star Rating: Four most days.

MALE BUFFALO

Not much to write home about, I am sorry to say. Most Buffaloes are straight talkers and straight dealers. They work to their positive strengths and succeed in all walks of life by using the full weight of their powerful personal conviction to reach whatever goal they decide upon. In relationships they use the same criteria, never shilly-shallying and demanding a one hundred per cent fidelity. This is not how the clever and sometimes artful Monkey runs his life. Tricks are what Monkeys are good at, and playing the field – even though you will never find a Monkey to admit it. In terms of a pure friendship, a Buffalo and Monkey is one for the birds. Imagine Alex Higgins (Buffalo), partnering Stephen Hendry, (Monkey).

Star Rating: Zero.

MALE TIGER

Tigers and Monkeys can only ever expect a middle to average understanding, no matter what sex they are or type of relationship they form. As in every other case, the Monkey carves his own lifestyle in stark contrast to that of the Tiger. Where these differences, or strengths, depending on your interpretation, can be welded together, there's an even chance of friendship. But I wouldn't place bets. Britain's most famous jazz singer, George Melly, is a Tiger and his long standing trumpet-playing side-kick, John Chiltern, is a Monkey. A more traditional musical relationship was that between light operetta masters Gilbert and Sullivan. Sir William Gilbert was the Monkey, and relied heavily on Tiger Sir Arthur Sullivan's clever music for his inspiration. So there is hope.

Star Rating: Two maximum.

MALE CAT

This is not a good idea. The Cat looks for all kinds of stability in his relationships, or perhaps consistency would be a better word. The Monkey is a law unto himself, and although he may promise great friendship to one and all he will always end up by suiting himself. And this might mean a good chum, in this case the Cat, will be left hanging around.

Star Rating: One at the most.

MALE DRAGON

This is an extremely auspicious relationship where both signs have all the cards, and know how to play them. A business with Dragon and Monkey is a sure bet as long as the Monkey is not too over-ambitious, or devious in his methods. But in the main, the Monkey's guile and adaptability, his sense of fun and quick wits, serve, and in turn are served by, the Dragon's brash originality. Should the two signs start a company, it is best that the Monkey keeps the books and the Dragon does the selling.

Star Rating: Five.

MALE SNAKE

Not much chance of a lasting friendship between the intuitive Snake and the sharp as a knife Monkey. Monkeys are really very clever without necessarily being the fount of originality. Snakes are nothing if not original and are wise into the bargain. They are not, in the Monkey sense, clever. The relationship could work in that the Monkey would get his best lines from the Snake, but without the Snake being fully aware of it. As long as this doesn't worry the Snake, no problem. Two giants of modern jazz and co-founders of the forties Bebop craze were a Snake and Monkey, Dizzy Gillespie and Charlie Parker. But they ended up fighting on stage.

Star Rating: One.

MALE HORSE

Try as I might I cannot find any good reason why a Horse and Monkey should not make some kind of relationship work. But the Chinese give the pair a zero understanding and who am I to contradict them? The only time I can see why things might go wrong is when the Monkey tries to outwit the Horse. But there may never be a need for this. Neil Kinnock is a Horse and his deputy, Roy Hattersley, is a Monkey. Mmmm . . . come to think of it, the Chinese might be right after all.

Star Rating: One for effort.

MALE GOAT

A genuine understanding exists between these two quite different chums, and when combined, the influencing signs of both Goat and Monkey find an interesting mutual path. Male Goat and male Monkey enjoy life's lighter moments, and with the Monkey making the running and the Goat making the most of what's on offer there is every chance that these two socially inclined and acquisitive signs will firm up their friendship for a long term arrangement. One of Britain's most brilliant animation studios, Grand Slam – the Paul McCartney/Rupert Bear video was theirs – is run by a Goat and Monkey team, Jeff Dunbar and Ginger Gibbons.

Star Rating: Three and four.

MALE MONKEY

Whereas the relationship between two Monkeys reaches high marks in love and marriage, it drops a point or two when there is no physical involvement. Monkeys, particularly if they are engaged in a business partnership, will end up with one trying to outsmart the other. That is not to say that Monkey mates will not find plenty in common. They have much to enjoy together, especially in the exchange of knowledge. Not exactly friends in the conventional sense, Lord Forte and his son Rocco behave more like chums than father and son. Both are Monkeys.

Star Rating: Two to four.

MALE ROOSTER

The Rooster male is something of an enigma, being both thrifty and spendthrift, boastful and private. None of the Rooster's strengths or weaknesses fit into any of the Monkey's. The Monkey *can* adapt to suit another's personality, but all in all the Rooster's demands do not appeal. Having said that, one of the great tennis doubles partnerships, that of John Newcombe and Tony Roche, was a Monkey and Rooster. A sporting outlook seems to be the solution.

Star Rating: Love all. Maybe one at a pinch.

MALE DOG

A no go area if ever there was one. Dog blokes are straightforward in their dealings and care about those who are less well off. They don't like the cunning outwitting the stupid, however much it might be deserved. Given that the Monkey has no such scruples he always, no matter what he might say to the contrary, suits himself in life. Not much to add, apart from the warning not to go into business either.

Star Rating: None.

MALE PIG

Plenty of opportunities here for Pig and Monkey to create something useful in terms of a lasting friendship. The Monkey is full of schemes and the hard working Pig, a little slower when left to work outside of a relationship, finds extra zest in this one. Monkeys and Pigs look for a good time and their friendship promises one of good humour and genuine understanding.

Star Rating: Five.

COMPATIBILITY OF FEMALE MONKEYS IN FRIENDSHIP

FEMALE RAT

A first-rate friendship with great intimacy. Neither sign is modest about their feelings and love to let their hair down. If gossip is the order of the day you can count on the Rat and the Monkey making the most of it. Both signs enjoy emotional freedom and are not likely to make heavy demands on each other. A good intrigue is what this pair enjoy and if there isn't one in the offing, they'll be quick to create it.

Star Rating: Five.

FEMALE BUFFALO

A non starter. The Buffalo has little time for the easy going and over flexible attitudes of the Monkey. As in many of the Buffalo's relationships, the reasons why they don't work out are often so deep and complex, that no one, not even the Buffalo herself, can explain it. But nearly always, the Buffalo is capable of distant although quite sincere admiration for another's abilities. It is just tough for the Buffalo to pay lip service to them. Lady Monkeys are quick to make friends of almost anyone, but they will not find a great reward in their attempts to get close to the Buffalo.

Star Rating: An iddy-biddy one at most.

FEMALE TIGER

Tigers and Monkeys can only ever expect a middle to average understanding, no matter what sex they are or type of relationship they form. As in every other case, the Monkey carves her own lifestyle in stark contrast to that of the Tiger. Where these differences, or strengths, depending on your interpretation, can be welded together, there's an even chance of friendship. But I wouldn't place bets. A Tiger, The Queen's relationship with Monkeys, the late Duchess of Windsor, Koo Stark and Princess Michael of Kent (who HRH calls Princess Pushy), gives the game away to this couple's true chances. On the other hand, one of Wimbledon's sharpest women's doubles pairs in recent years was Pam Shriver (Tiger) and Martina Navratilova (Monkey).

Star Rating: Two maximum.

FEMALE CAT

This is not a good idea. The Cat looks for all kinds of stability in her relationships, or perhaps consistency would be a better word. The Monkey is a law unto herself, and although she may promise great friendships to one and all she will always end up by suiting herself. And this might mean a good companion, in this case the Cat, will be left hanging around.

Star Rating: One at most.

FEMALE DRAGON

This is an extremely auspicious relationship where both signs have all the cards, and know how to play them. A business with Dragon and Monkey is a sure bet as long as the Monkey is not too over ambitious, or devious in his methods. But in the main, the Monkey's guile and adaptability, his sense of fun and quick wits, serve, and in turn are served by, the Dragon's brash originality. Should the two signs start a company, it is best that the Monkey keeps the books and the Dragon does the selling.

Star Rating: Five.

FEMALE SNAKE

Not much chance of a lasting friendship between the intuitive Snake and the sharp as a knife Monkey. Monkeys are really very clever without necessarily being the fount of originality. Snakes are nothing if not original and are wise into the bargain. They are not, in the Monkey sense, clever. The relationship could work in that the Monkey would get her best lines from the Snake, but without the Snake being fully aware of it. As long as this doesn't worry the Snake, no problem

Star Rating: One.

FEMALE HORSE

Try as I might I cannot find any good reason why a Horse and Monkey should not make some kind of relationship work. But the Chinese give the pair a zero understanding and who am I to contradict them? The only time I can see why things might go wrong is when the Monkey tries to outwit the Horse. But there may never be a need for this. On the other hand, I can find no examples of this friendship in operation, either among my friends or on the wider world stage. So the Chinese could be right.

Star Rating: One for effort.

FEMALE GOAT

A genuine understanding exists between these two quite different chums, and combined, the influencing signs of both Goat and Monkey find an interesting mutual path. Female Goat and female Monkey enjoy life's lighter moments, and with the Monkey making the running and the Goat making the most of what's on offer there is every chance that these two socially inclined and acquisitive signs will firm up their friendship for a long term arrangement.

Star Rating: Three and four.

FEMALE MONKEY

Whereas the relationship between two Monkeys reaches high marks in love and marriage, it drops a point or two when there is no physical involvement. Monkeys, particularly if they are engaged in a business partnership, will end up with one trying to outsmart the other. That is not to say that Monkey companions will not find plenty in common. They have much to enjoy together, especially in the exchange of knowledge.

Star Rating: Two to four.

FEMALE ROOSTER

The Rooster female is something of an enigma, being both thrifty and spendthrift, boastful and private. None of the Rooster's strengths or weaknesses fits into any of the Monkey's. The Monkey *can* adapt to suit another's personality, but all in all the Rooster's demands do not appeal. Of the two pairings, Monkey and Rooster female are not entirely without hope and there is a slight chance of a relationship. But it will not last a lifetime.

Star Rating: One. Maybe one and a half at a pinch.

FEMALE DOG

A no go area if ever there was one. Dog lasses (or should it be Lassies?) are straightforward in their dealings and care about those who are less well off. They don't like the cunning outwitting the stupid, however much it might be deserved. Given that the Monkey has no such scruples she always, no matter what she might say to the contrary, suits herself in life. Not much to add, apart from the warning not to go into business either.

Star Rating: None.

FEMALE PIG

Plenty of opportunities here for Pig and Monkey to create something really useful in terms of a lasting friendship. The Monkey is full of schemes and the hard working Pig, a little slower when left to work outside of a relationship, finds extra zest in this one. Monkeys and Pigs look for a good time and their friendship promises one of good humour and genuine understanding.

Star Rating: Five.

THE ROOSTER

1909	January 22nd to February 9th	1910
1921	February 8th to January 27th	1922
1933	January 26th to February 13th	1934
1945	February 13th to February 1st	1946
1957	January 31st to February 17th	1958
1969	February 17th to February 5th	1970
1981	February 5th to January 24th	1982
1993	January 23rd to February 9th	1994

The crown of red
set on your little head
is charged with all your fighting blood.

Elizabeth Bishop

THE YEAR OF THE ROOSTER

Roosters are born under the sign of candour and the Chinese say that there are two basic Rooster groups. Those born between 5 and 7 in the morning and between 5 and 7 in the evening are called sunup/sundown Roosters, and are usually distinguished by their cock-sure bluntness. For these Roosters, money is for spending and having an overdraft is just something they learn to live with. The reverse side of the coin is the save-every-penny Rooster, who form the second group. These birds are the kind to spend all morning walking round the supermarket looking for the day's bargain. But even the hard saving Rooster is tainted with the spendthrift influence. Once they have saved a tidy pile it is frequently squandered in a flash, usually on something quite un-expected.

Roosters are no nonsense folk. They are generally easy to spot in a crowd, being self assured, talkative and frank. Male Roosters are usually just plain boastful. No other sign is more outspoken or moral. Whereas some animals have an in-fluence which produces a low moral horizon and few if any scruples, the high-minded Rooster has more than enough to go round. Getting attention is a natural function of the Rooster influence and the Chinese say that their sign has a military significance. Indeed, with all those wonderful feathers and red crown it is easy to see why.

Conservative with a small c, and often with a big one, Roosters are exceptionally methodical. They adore keeping notebooks and are forever writing all manner of things on bits of paper which are then filed and put away. They also tend to build castles in the air, which leads to another prom-inent feature of their personality; to promise more than they can deliver. A little short of initiative at times, once Roosters find a task that fits their rigid temperament nothing will stand in a Rooster's way.

For all their conceit and candour, Roosters are deeply secretive about their private relationships. Although they may lack tact, there can be no doubting a Rooster's honesty and in a relationship it would be a very rare Rooster indeed who would be the first to wander. This is especially the case in female Roosters. Quick to point out the faults in others, Roosters of both sexes are not so happy about being criticised or even teased themselves. Although naturally good mixers, Roosters might be just as contented with their own company. However, female Roosters are more than happy to spend a night out with the girls.

The first of a Rooster's three phases, childhood, is thought to be the most auspicious. Rooster children are bright and attentive and make the most of their youthful exuberance. Middle years are often dogged by money matters and their over the top morality tends to break up rather than heal marriage difficulties. Old age finds the Rooster, more often than not, a rather solitary creature. Happy in their gardens (which all Roosters love) they will at least have their dreams.

COMPATIBILITY OF MALE ROOSTERS IN LOVE

FEMALE RAT

Some animal signs are attracted by sexual opposites but this pair isn't one of them. There is only the faintest chance that a Rat and Rooster will survive the first few moments. The high minded and often boastful Rooster has absolutely no under-standing of the majority of Rats, and although the lady Rat warms to most signs, she will not find the candid Rooster remotely interesting sexually. But there are some Rooster males she'll go for, in particular the introvert, who is sensitive and thoughtful. These, however, are in the minority and most Roosters are a mixture of deep conservative and bar room braggart. Not for Rats

Star Rating: One, drifting out to zero.

FEMALE BUFFALO

Jackpot time. Only two signs are completely compatible with the female Buffalo and the male Rooster is one. Neither is looking for a short term relationship and the love affair will soon establish itself as a winner and it won't be long before there's an announcement in the paper and a wedding list on display at the local big store. Both animal signs are deeply conservative, usually with a big and small C, and neither cares to fool around when there's been a genuine commit-ment given. As a romance it's short and sweet and quickly down the aisle.

Star Rating: Five big ones.

FEMALE TIGER

Up-front Rooster male meets exciting female Tiger and is usually left wondering what to do about it. It looks great on paper but the reality is not the five star relationship that's promised. However, there are compensations. The Tiger is intrigued by the Rooster's candour, and sees his openness as a quality sympathetic to her own sometimes rebellious instincts. But love affairs are not usually enhanced by the Tiger's sense of rebellion, or helped by the often cocksure stance the male Rooster uses to protect his deepest feelings. But they do quite enjoy a mutual frankness, which gives these two animal signs a slight chance of making it. Overall, though, not much future.

Star Rating: One.

FEMALE CAT

A big hiccup for the Rooster and Cat. All the other signs love Pussy, but not the Rooster, at least not usually. The problem arises from the fact that Roosters do not usually go in for casual affairs, although there is the odd one who behaves more in keeping with his Cock reputation. Most Rooster males are deeply personal, private, conservative men and even if the idea of a bit of stray sex with a beautiful Cat lady comes up, they will not be as quick as some to react. The point is that these two signs fare slightly better when married, should this event ever take place. The Chinese give this pair no marks, but I must say that I have found one or two couples who have made surprisingly good friends.

Star Rating: Zero. But sometimes one or two.

FEMALE DRAGON

This is a case of putting the cart before the horse, or should it be the Dragon before the Rooster, or even sex before marriage? The point is that Roosters and Dragons are one of the best marriage partners of all the sign combinations, but the male Rooster, in spite of his boasts to the contrary, is not given to wild romances. He is a deeply conservative creature who is not inspired to open demonstrations of his innermost feelings. He builds romantic castles in the air, but that, for the Dragon, is no place for a castle, as appreciative as she might well be of the effort. The course of action here is for both female Dragon and male Rooster to get themselves hitched pronto.

Star Rating: Two, seldom more, seldom less.

FEMALE SNAKE

Not a lot of joy for this particular pair of signs. The Chinese offer a two star relationship but I disagree. All my experience has shown me that the Snake and Rooster have nothing in common as lovers. True, the male Rooster is fascinated by the female Snake's inescapable sexual attraction. At their best, Snake women are genuinely charming and warm, qualities Roosters might fall for. But Rooster males do not usually throw themselves recklessly into romance, and should they step back and think, they will probably be just a little suspicious of the Snake's overtures. And they would be right to think twice. Snake ladies can be highly unpredictable in the sex stakes. This is the worst of the pairings.

Star Rating: Zero.

FEMALE HORSE

There are some very odd relationships in Chinese Horoscopes, which on the surface leave the signs involved a little confused. Horses and Roosters have a very high rating in marriage but almost nothing in common in a purely romantic relationship. Horse ladies have a strong physical nature and fall in love heavily and often. Male Roosters step carefully into a sexual relationship, and in spite of the frequently self created impression that they are super studs, the over amorous Horse is sometimes a turn off. Long term relationships are what male Roosters prefer.

Star Rating: One. Check the marriage section for a big improvement.

FEMALE GOAT

After a great deal of give and take, mostly on the Rooster's behalf, this pair of lovers just might get it together. But the chances are very slight. In some relationships, such as same sex friendships, Goat and Rooster could even be said to have a fair understanding of each other. In romance, however, Ms Goat and Mr Rooster rarely have anything in common. Rooster men are curiously self conscious sexually and in spite of the image they often tend to create, are almost never promiscuous. Female Goats have no such self control. The big Non Starter.

Star Rating: Zero.

FEMALE MONKEY

Here we're talking about the attraction of opposites, an often fatal attraction which is only too often discovered when it is too late to do anything to repair the damage. But happily, the days of wine and roses don't run into months. And it is an absolute certainty that both Monkey and Rooster will discover they have such diametrically opposed views on just about everything that the parting of the ways between candid Rooster and artful Monkey will take place before the wedding bells chime. Of the two pairings, male Rooster/ female Monkey stands the best chance.

Star Rating: One, and that's being generous.

FEMALE ROOSTER

The only really good thing to be said for two Roosters billing and cooing is that they have the presence of mind to realize that the only way the affair can go is forward. Never the animal sign to leave loose ends undone – the way many Roosters view a casual relationship – marriage has to be the answer. It is a case of cementing the genuine concern that two Roosters will show to each other, or ending it and flying off in different directions. Sexuality is important to a Rooster, but it has to be earned through love and devotion. So one night stands are out. Marriage is in.

Star Rating: One or two. Big improvement after the wedding.

FEMALE DOG

Once again, there is a problem confronting both these animal signs. Neither really enjoys casual relationships and a commitment to long term loving definitely broadens the possibilities. Rooster males are often very demanding in the sense that they are not very flexible, especially in terms of personal feelings. The same, but for different reasons, is also true of the Dog lady. Rooster men are conservative in outlook, Dog ladies are anxiously liberal. The chances of true understanding is therefore extremely remote. But it is possible. The worst scenario is that one's negativity will corrupt the other, as it did in the case of Bonny (Dog) and Clyde (Rooster).

Star Rating: One or two.

FEMALE PIG

Roosters and Pigs are not a common mix, which is curious because their star rating is quite high. Perhaps it is because the relationship succeeds through praising the absence of negative qualities in the union, rather than acknowledging the fewer positive points. The truth is that the fun loving Pigette poses no threat to the Rooster, who nevertheless might be quick to take advantage of her easy virtue. And the male Rooster/female Pig partnership is undoubtedly the better of the two couplings. Once up and running, this pair might have fun, it might not. Depends on what each sees as the long term outcome. Marriage is not advised.

Star Rating: One or three.

COMPATIBILITY OF FEMALE ROOSTERS IN LOVE

MALE RAT

Some animal signs are attracted by sexual opposites but this pair isn't one of them. An all time no-hoper, there is only the faintest chance that a Rat and the candid Rooster will survive the first few moments. The high minded lady Rooster has absolutely no understanding of the majority of Rats, in particular their eagerness to live life without planning or moral codes. The Rat's charm might keep the lady Rooster from being too critical for a while, but there's little chance of a long term relationship unless marriage is the outcome.

Star Rating: Zero, zero, zero.

MALE BUFFALO

Jackpot time. Only two signs are completely compatible with the male Buffalo and the female Rooster is one. Neither is looking for a short term relationship and the love affair will soon establish itself as a winner and it won't be long before there's an announcement in the paper and a wedding list on display at the local big store. Both animal signs are deeply conservative, usually with a big and small C, and neither cares to fool around when there's been a genuine commitment given. As a romance it's short and sweet and quickly down the aisle.

Star Rating: Five big ones.

MALE TIGER

Private Rooster lady meets vigorous male Tiger and is usually left wondering what to do about it? However, there are compensations. The Tiger is intrigued by the Rooster lady's candour, and sees her openness as a quality sympathetic to his own rebellious instincts. But love affairs are not usually enhanced by the Tiger's sense of rebellion, or helped by the censorious wall the female Rooster places around her deepest feelings. But they do quite enjoy a mutual frankness, which gives these animal signs a slight chance of making it. Overall, though, not much future.

Star Rating: One.

MALE CAT

A big hiccup for the Cat and Rooster. All the other signs love tom, but not the Rooster, at least not usually. The problem arises from the fact that Roosters do not like casual affairs – ever. They are deeply personal, private, conservative ladies and the idea of a bit of randy tom-style slap and tickle is not normally for them. Of course, not all Cats behave that way; in fact, very few do. But the point is that these two signs fare slightly better when married, should this event ever take place. Some Cats, though, can be too well mannered and sexy for the prudish Rooster to resist. The Chinese give this pair no marks, but I must say that I have found one or two couples who have made surprisingly good friends. Female Rooster/male Cat rates the better pair.

Star Rating: One or two.

MALE DRAGON

This is a case of putting the cart before the horse, or should it be the Dragon before the Rooster, or even sex before marriage? The point is that Roosters and Dragons are one of the best marriage partnerships of all the sign combinations, but the lady Rooster is not given to wild romances. She is a deeply conservative creature who is not inspired to open demonstrations of her innermost feelings. She builds romantic castles in the air, but that, for the Dragon, is no place for a castle, as appreciative as he might well be of the effort. The course of action here is for both male Dragon and female Rooster to get themselves hitched pronto.

Star Rating: Two.

MALE SNAKE

Not a lot of joy for this particular pair of signs. The Chinese offer a two star relationship but I disagree. All my experience has shown me that the Snake and Rooster have nothing in common. True, the lady Rooster is fascinated by the Snake's inescapable sexual attraction. At their best, Snake men are genuinely charming and warm, qualities lady Roosters might fall for. But Rooster females do not throw themselves recklessly into romance, and should they step back and think, they will probably be just a little suspicious of the Snake's overtures. And they would be right to think twice. Snake men can be highly unpredictable in the sex stakes. Male Snake/female Rooster is the better of the couples.

Star Rating: Zero. One at most.

MALE HORSE

There are some very odd relationships in Chinese Horoscopes, which on the surface leave the signs involved a little confused. Horses and Roosters have a very high rating in marriage but almost nothing in common in a purely romantic relationship. Horse men have a strong physical nature and fall in love heavily and often. Lady Roosters step carefully into a sexual relationship and the over amorous male Horse is sometimes a turn off – at least for the Rooster female. She is after long term, committed love and a home and garden. Sex is OK, but the Horse is so much more attractive when part of the whole domestic set up.

Star Rating: One. Check the marriage section for a big improvement.

MALE GOAT

After a great deal of give and take, mostly on the Rooster's part, this pair of lovers might get it together. But the chances are very slight. In some relationships, such as same-sex friendships, Goat and Rooster could even be said to have a fair understanding of each other. In romance, however, Goat male and lady Rooster rarely have anything in common. Rooster women are sexually deeply private and rarely promiscuous. Male Goats have no such self control. The big non-starter.

Star Rating: Zero.

MALE MONKEY

Here we're talking about the attraction of opposites, an often fatal attraction which is only too often discovered when it is too late to do anything to repair the damage. But happily, the days of wine and roses don't run into months. And it is an absolute certainty that both Monkey and Rooster will discover they have such diametrically opposed views on just about everything that the parting of the ways between moralist Rooster and artful Monkey will take place before the wedding bells chime.

Star Rating: One, and that's being generous.

MALE ROOSTER

The only really good thing to be said for two Roosters billing and cooing is that they have the presence of mind to realise that the only way the affair can go is forward. Never the animal sign to leave loose ends undone – the way many Roosters view a casual relationship – marriage has to be the answer. It is a case of cementing the genuine concern that two Roosters will show to each other, or ending it and flying off in different directions. Sexuality is important to a Rooster, but it has to be earned through love and devotion. So one-night stands are out. Marriage is in.

Star Rating: One or two. Big improvement after the wedding.

MALE DOG

Once again, there is a problem confronting both these animal signs. Neither really enjoys casual relationships and a commitment to long term loving definitely broadens the possibilities. Rooster females are often very demanding in the sense that they are not very flexible, especially in terms of personal feelings. The same, but for different reasons, is also true of the Dog. Rooster ladies are conservative in outlook, Dog chaps are anxiously liberal. The chances of true understanding are therefore extremely remote. But it is possible.

Male Dog/female Rooster couples have the best chance of the two pairs.

Star Rating: One or two.

MALE PIG

Roosters and Pigs are not a common mix, which is curious because their star rating is quite high. Perhaps it is because the relationship succeeds through praising the absence of negative qualities in the union rather then acknowledging the fewer positive points. The truth is that the robust Pig poses no threat to the female Rooster, who nevertheless might be quick to take offence at his sometimes blunt advances. Once up and running, this pair might have fun; it might not. Depends on what each sees in the long term as to the outcome. Woody Allen is a Pig and Diane Keaton is a Rooster. Their affair didn't work out. And there's the much-publicised affair between Pig Michael Winner and the beautiful Rooster Jenny Seagrove. Marriage is not advised.

Star Rating: One or three.

COMPATIBILITY OF MALE ROOSTERS IN MARRIAGE

FEMALE RAT

A big shift in gear in the unusual partnership of Rat and Rooster. In love, which is an equally rare relationship, there are zero marks for understanding and minus zero for compatibility. But as sometimes happens if signs of markedly different temperament can agree on the boundaries of married life, setting down at the outset what is expected of each other, matters greatly improve. From zero, Rat and Rooster stand a very good chance indeed of making a marriage blossom. Much depends on the type of Rooster. If he is the more tolerant Rooster, with less than the normal dose of high moral fortitude that normally comes with his sign, there is a distinct possibility that the marriage could survive. But it is never easy and there will be times when the Rat regrets having such a candid creature around the place. Jill Ireland is a Rat, married to Rooster Charles Bronson. Former presidential candidate Michael Dukakis is another Rooster with a Rat wife, Kitty.

Star Rating: Three, which is a one star increase for the female Rat/male Rooster over the male Rat/female Rooster pairing.

FEMALE BUFFALO

A hundred per cent in love and now a hundred and one for marriage. Of all the choices open to the Buffalo and Rooster, this combination wins hands down. The conservative backbone of both animal signs is strengthened in partnership and their mutual support creates a solid and totally reliable unit. A family will help provide an even stronger base and should Buffalo wife and Rooster husband decide to go into business there will be few able to match them. A great natural relationship, it is none the less not as common a marriage as it should be, at least not first time round. One reason for this is that the Buffalo male is headstrong and his complex heart is too easily turned by signs that are not compatible, notably the Rat.

Star Rating: Five plus.

FEMALE TIGER

Here's a rum couple. On the surface, the hot-headed Tiger and candid Rooster seem to have nothing in common but a long row about who's right and who's wrong. But from a poor romance grows a much better marriage. If the Tiger has a streak of reason in her make up, and there is nothing to suggest she hasn't, and the Rooster is not a spendthrift, then the couple stand a fair chance of a fruitful and happy life together. Method and madness meet in the middle. With the Rooster in charge of the house keeping and the Tiger firing on all cylinders (hopefully), these two can achieve a great deal together. But family life will not enhance their understanding of each other. Male Rooster is better with female Tiger, as in the relationship between HRH The Queen and Prince Philip.

Star Rating: Three. Not more, not less.

FEMALE CAT

Only two marriage partners are truly unsuitable for the Cat – the Rooster and the Rat. Roosters, although illustrating a tendency towards poor understanding with a Cat in love, do make a slightly better impression when marriage is involved. One of the many areas of poor mutual understanding lies in the Rooster's open frank response, which contrasts badly with the Cat's quieter, more reserved approach. Married life is full of tense moments, and it is during these times that Cat and Rooster fail to see eye to eye. Children will not make it easier, nor will a healthy bank balance, something most spendthrift Roosters have never known.

Star Rating: Normally zero, but there are two on offer for real triers.

FEMALE DRAGON

A terrific marriage for the lucky Dragon, who does seem to have more than her fair share of options when it comes to stepping down the aisle with the right goods. Unlike the

Monkey husband, who is prone to over-indulge the Dragon's weakest points, the morally incorruptible Rooster makes it clear there will be no hanky-panky while he's around. Sometimes both Dragon and Rooster are over-critical of each other. In the negative, this could prove disastrous, and sometimes it is. But when Rooster husband and Dragon wife are faced with a genuine threat, especially one which contains an abuse of power, there is no couple more able to cope. No pair is better capable of putting up a fight, or starting one!

Star Rating: Five all the way.

FEMALE SNAKE

This is a better marriage than could have been dreamed of at the romance stage. Love affairs are not what Roosters go in for, although the male Rooster is more prone than the female (at least, they boast more about it). They are deeply conservative and only really open up when there is a strong whiff of moral decency in the air. In a marriage, the sensual and sexual Snake might well provide this dimension; – on the other hand she might not. Snakes cannot be relied on for emotional stability. In this case there won't be a silver wedding, or indeed a first anniversary. But if both signs are willing to accept the faults in the other, they *might* just end up as good companions. No bets taken on it, though. Theatrical impresario and former Coronation Street star Bill Kenwright is a Rooster, and was once married to actress beauty and Snake Anouska Hempel.

Star Rating: Three is the max.

FEMALE HORSE

One of the great success stories. From a zero rating in romance the Horse and Rooster romp home to a really first class marriage. Both are natural partners in that they are happy, as animals, to use the farm as they feel. The picture I have is of the Rooster sitting on the Horse's fence. In human animal signs I believe the Rooster and Horse have such a relationship. A garden is important to the Rooster lady and a meadow is crucial to a horse. Freedom combined with integrity forms the corner stone to this auspicious marriage. A business relationship is also advised.

Star Rating: Five most times.

FEMALE GOAT

Not much understanding ever exists between the Rooster male and Goat female, and any understanding that either can lay claim to comes only after a long, hard slog. But is it worth it? The Goat, ever capricious, is often considered self centred in the eyes of the frequently critical Rooster – not the most auspicious departure point for marital awareness. In addition Rooster men have, in spite of their tendency to lay boastful claims to the contrary, a high moral standard and expect their wives to follow suit. The Goat is not ideally suited to strait-jacket morality and a marriage of short tempers and long rows is the distinct scenario.

Star Rating: Zero. One at very most.

FEMALE MONKEY

From a shaky and short lived romance, the female Monkey and male Rooster really test the Chinese Horoscope to its limit when, or if, they stroll down the aisle. The prospects are really about as gloomy as could be. The male Rooster is an exceptionally private individual in spite of his strutting style, and the Monkey female, capable of charming the pants off anyone, has no time for priggish morality. Money, sex and the home will always be seen through opposing lenses. Kids will not help the marriage either and only under exceptional conditions – like they are the only couple left on earth – should Monkey and Rooster wed.

Star Rating: The pits, beggin' your pardon.

FEMALE ROOSTER

A big improvement in the future success of this pair when the banns are read. But it must be underlined that there are no smooth paths in love or marriage for the Rooster, and although the relationship of two Roosters improves with the commitment of marriage, it is still a very tough one. The Chinese say, pointedly, that two Roosters under one roof might well suit each other, but they are likely to make life extremely difficult for everyone else. So there you have it. Happy or not with each other, spare a thought for the rest of us. Nick Faldo is a Rooster and divorced his former Rooster wife on October 17, 1984. Points for this one are a mess.

Star Rating: One through to four. Usually one.

FEMALE DOG

Male Rooster and female Dog have not had a particularly deep engagement; that is to say, there have not been a great many inner revelations. Marriage tends to demand that honest folk, who include both Dogs and Roosters, come clean about what they really care about. This could mean that the loyal Dog and candid Rooster might well find they do not share quite as much in common as they had previously imagined. But there is still plenty of scope for understanding and although the Chinese hand these two signs a poor mark for marriage, my experience is that it holds up rather well.

Star Rating: Three, but drifting down a few stars in some cases; for example, an over anxious Dog.

FEMALE PIG

Lady Pigs do like to enjoy themselves, and usually with no holds barred. In and out of marriage, a Pig lady plays as hard as she works and her view of morality is not high. Certainly, she does not share the Rooster's somewhat morally imperious attitude towards fun and games. Roosters demand an organised world and are straightforward in their thinking, in spite of the impression they give to the contrary. Roosters can spend with the best, but a deeply conservative interior often prevents them from falling off the edge. The Pig/Rooster pair will need to martial their resources, deal carefully with their finances and invest all spare energies into home and garden if they are to stick together.

Star Rating: Two or three.

COMPATIBILITY OF FEMALE ROOSTERS IN MARRIAGE

MALE RAT

A big shift in gear in the unusual partnership of Rat and Rooster. In love, which is an equally rare relationship, there are zero marks for understanding and minus zero for compatibility. But as sometimes happens, matters greatly improve if signs of markedly different temperament can agree on the boundaries of married life, setting down at the outset what is to be expected of each other. From zero, Rat and Rooster stand a very good chance indeed of making a marriage blossom. Much depends on the type of Rooster. If she is the outgoing Rooster, with less than the normal dose of high moral fortitude that comes with her sign, there is a distinct possibility that the marriage could survive. But it is never easy and there will be times when the Rat regrets sharing the perch in the hen house.

Star Rating: Two, which in this instance is really good.

MALE BUFFALO

A hundred per cent in love and now a hundred and one in marriage. Of all the choices open to the Buffalo and Rooster, this combination wins hands down. The conservative backbone of both animal signs is strengthened in partnership and their mutual support creates a solid and totally reliable unit. A family will help provide an even stronger base and should Buffalo husband and Rooster wife decide to go into business there will be few able to match them. A great natural relationship, it is none the less not as common a marriage as it should be, at least not first time round. One reason for this is that the Buffalo male is headstrong and his complex heart is too easily turned by signs that are not compatible, notably the Rat.

Star Rating: Five plus.

MALE TIGER

Here's a rum couple. On the surface, the hot-headed Tiger and candid Rooster seem to have nothing in common but a long row about who's right and who's wrong. But from a poor romance grows a much better marriage. It the Tiger has a streak of controlled reason in his make up, and there is nothing to suggest he hasn't, and the Rooster is not a spendthrift, then the couple stand a fair chance of a fruitful and happy life together. Method and madness meet in the middle. With the Rooster in charge of the house-keeping and the Tiger firing on all cylinders (hopefully), these two can achieve a great deal together. But family life will not enhance their understanding of each other.

Star Rating: Three. Not more, not less.

MALE CAT

Only two marriage partners are truly unsuitable for the Cat – the Rooster and the Rat. Roosters, although illustrating a tendency towards poor understanding with a Cat in love, do make a slightly better impression when marriage is involved. One of the many areas of poor mutual understanding lies in the Rooster's open, frank response, which contrasts badly with the Cat's quieter, more reserved approach. Married life is full of tense moments, and it is during these times that Cat and Rooster fail to see eye to eye. Children will not make it easier, and nor will a healthy bank balance, something most spendthrift Roosters have never known.

Star Rating: Normally zero, but there are two stars on offer for real triers.

MALE DRAGON

A terrific marriage for the Rooster and lucky Dragon, who does seem to have more than his fair share of options when it comes to stepping down the aisle with the right goods. Unlike the Monkey wife, who tends to over indulge the Dragon's weakest points, the morally incorruptible Rooster makes it clear there will be no hanky-panky while she's around. Sometimes both Dragon and Rooster are over critical of each other, and here I speak from personal experience (Mrs Fantoni/mum and Mrs Fantoni/wife are both Roosters). But when Rooster wife and Dragon husband are faced with a genuine threat, especially one which contains an abuse of power, there is no couple more able to cope. No pair is better capable of putting up a fight, or of starting one! Jeffrey Archer is a Dragon and his wife, Mary, is a Rooster. Remember the way they saw off the blackmailing callgirl, and a dubious Fleet Street?

Star Rating: Five all the way.

MALE SNAKE

This is a better marriage than could have been dreamed of at the romance stage. Love affairs are not what Roosters, especially the female of the species, go in for. They are deeply conservative and only really open up when there is a strong sense of moral decency in the air. In a marriage, the sensual and sexual Snake might well provide this dimension; on the other hand he might not. Snakes cannot be relied on for emotional stability. In this case there won't be a silver wedding, or indeed a first anniversary. But if both signs are willing to accept the faults in the other, they *might* just end up as good companions. No bets taken on it, though. My mother is a Rooster and my father was a Snake. A tough middle period saw them great pals in the last years.

Star Rating: Three is the max.

MALE HORSE

One of the great success stories. From a zero rating the Horse and Rooster romp home to a really first class marriage. Both are natural partners in that they are happy, as animals, to use the farm as they feel. The picture I have is of the Rooster sitting on the Horse's fence. In human animal signs I believe the Rooster and Horse have such a relationship. A garden is important to the Rooster lady and a meadow is crucial to a Horse. Freedom combined with integrity forms the cornerstone to this auspicious marriage. A business relationship is also advised.

Star Rating: Five most times.

MALE GOAT

Not much understanding ever exists between the Rooster female and Goat male, and any understanding that either can lay claim to comes only after a long, hard slog. But is it worth it? The Goat, ever capricious, is often considered self centred in the eyes of the ever critical female Rooster – not the most auspicious departure point for marital awareness. In addition Rooster ladies have a high moral standard and expect their husbands to follow suit. The Goat is not ideally suited to strait-jacket morality and a marriage of short tempers and long rows is the distinct scenario.

Star Rating: One at the very most.

MALE MONKEY

From a shaky and short lived romance, the male Monkey and female Rooster really test the Chinese Horoscopes to the limits when, or if, they stroll down the aisle. The prospects are really about as gloomy as could be. The female Rooster is an exceptionally private individual in spite of her glamorous looks, and the Monkey male, capable of charming the pants off anyone, has no time for dyed in the wool morality. Money, sex and the home will always be seen through opposing lenses. Kids will not help the marriage either and only under exceptional conditions – like they are the only couple left on earth – should Monkey and Rooster wed.

Star Rating: The pits, beggin' your pardon.

MALE ROOSTER

A big improvement in the future success of this pair when the banns are read. But it must be underlined there are no smooth paths in love or marriage for the Rooster and although the relationship of two Roosters improves with the commitment of marriage, it is still a very tough one. The Chinese say, pointedly, that two Roosters under one roof might well suit each other, but they are likely to make life extremely difficult for everyone else. So there you have it. Happy, or not, with each other, spare a thought for the rest of us. Nick Faldo is a Rooster and divorced his former Rooster wife on October 17, 1984. Points for this one are a mess.

Star Rating: One through to four. Usually one.

MALE DOG

Male dog and female Rooster have not had a particularly deep engagement; that is to say, there have not been a great many inner revelations. Marriage tends to demand that honest folk, who include both Dogs and Roosters, come clean about what they really care about. This could mean that the loyal Dog and candid Rooster might well find they do not share quite as much in common as they had previously imagined. But there is still plenty of scope for understanding and although the Chinese hand these two signs a poor mark for marriage, my experience is that it holds up rather well. Winston Churchill was a Dog and his wife, Clem, a Rooster. It was not an easy marriage.

Star Rating: Three, but drifting down a few stars in some cases; for example, an over anxious Dog.

MALE PIG

Pigs do like to enjoy themselves, and usually with no holds barred. In and out of marriage, a Pig male plays as hard as he works and his view of morality is not high. Certainly, he does not share the Rooster's somewhat morally imperious attitude towards fun and games. Roosters demand an organised world and are straightforward in their thinking, in spite of the impression they give to the contrary. Roosters can spend with the best, but a deeply conservative interior often prevents them from falling off the edge. The Pig/Rooster pair will need to martial their resources, deal carefully with their finances and invest all spare energies into home and garden if they are to stick together. Ronald Reagan was born in a Pig year and Nancy (say no to drugs) Reagan in the year of the Rooster. They seem to have got it right.

Star Rating: Two or three.

COMPATIBILITY OF MALE ROOSTERS IN FRIENDSHIP

MALE RAT

Astonishingly this is a friendship which can succeed, but there needs to be some very straight talking in order to establish what the boundaries are. Roosters, if they are the less moral type, and a Rat who has found his niche, might well find they have formed a friendship, against all odds. A business partnership is no bad idea and the chances of success improve considerably if the pair are an introverted Rooster and introverted Rat. Barry Hearne is a Rat and Steve Davis is a Rooster.

Star Rating: Three.

MALE BUFFALO

So few relationships work out for a Buffalo that it is a delight to be able to say that the Rooster and Buffalo relationship is a winner in every department. Both intensely private about their most personal feelings and conservative in their views, Buffalo and Rooster have an understanding which neither needs to openly admit. A long chat about the merits of courgette pollination is likely to be the centre of a conversation between Buffalo and Rooster. A strong and solid friendship without frills. Bobby Robson is a Rooster and Peter Shilton a Buffalo. Robson's loyalty to Shilton has bordered, some have said, on the side of foolishness, playing him in an England side when the once great keeper was past his international prime.

Star Rating: Five almost always.

MALE TIGER

Here's a pair of mates without a future. No matter that the Rooster is a saver, or high spender or thrifty, and no matter how generous or overt the Tiger, these two have nothing in common. All Roosters are private at heart, and the Tiger is the most outgoing of all signs. When there's no hope, it's better to face up to it. That way, no one is left feeling bad about the consequences of a broken friendship. Try to imagine Jimmy White and Steve Davis having a night out together.

Star Rating: Zero.

MALE CAT

The male Cat has an easy way with even the most tricky people, and he is an expert at concealing his true feelings. That's why the Chinese consider the Cat to be such a fine diplomat. And the Cat will need all his qualities of diplomacy and human understanding to deal with the male Rooster, especially if he is the extrovert. Never one for hiding from others what he thinks, the Rooster speaks his mind and does so often. But he is honest and usually incorruptible, something the Cat applauds. Not the greatest of pairings, but better than would at first appear. Richard Briers, a Rooster, has long been one of the favourite leads of playwright and Cat Alan Ayckbourn.

Star Rating: Two, and that's good here.

MALE DRAGON

Another great partnership. The Dragon is not always helped by everyone telling him he is a great guy – a little criticism does him no harm at all and our old friend the candid Rooster is quick to pull the Dragon up short. In turn, the Dragon is quick to spot the Rooster's habit of building castles in the air, which he re-creates into something more attainable. Whereas the Monkey will let the Dragon carry the can when things go wrong, the Rooster will share all kinds of responsibility – personal and business. A clean relationship this, with much honest talk and the most positive side of both signs given a first rate chance of developing. The two geniuses behind the Spaghetti Western style of film making were a Dragon and Rooster. Director and writer Sergio Leone, a Rooster, dreamed up the plots and Dragon Ennio Mariccone created the music.

Star Rating: Five.

MALE SNAKE

The candid and outspoken Rooster, if he is also the spendthrift type of bird, has almost nothing at all in common with the subtle and thrifty Snake. It is really difficult to discover where a Rooster and Snake friendship could go. Snakes can be very funny, in an original and very personal way, and most male Roosters love to be the centre of attention. There's mileage in a comedy partnership, perhaps. Michael Caine had a very up and down, publicity-rich relationship with his sometime friend and restaurant partner, the late Peter

Langhan. Caine is a Rooster, Langhan was a Snake. But these two signs are not meant to be. Sorry.

Star Rating: One at the very most.

MALE HORSE

If a Horse born, say, in 1954 found life tough with someone born in 1956, a Monkey, then take the Chinese Horoscope's advice and move on a year. The next year's sign, the Rooster, is tailored to do business with the wit- and personality-rich Horse. Both signs are gifted in different skills; the Rooster has method and the Horse a strong work capacity. Combined, these qualities lead to the Horse and Rooster creating one of the all time great friendships. The brilliant pianist Daniel Barenboim is a Horse, and his recordings of Beethoven's five piano concertos under the great German conductor Otto Klemperer are considered by many experts to be the finest ever made. Otto was a Rooster, born in 1885.

Star Rating: Five.

MALE GOAT

Non sexual friendship is perhaps the only really possible partnership between a Goat and a Rooster. The males of both signs are capable of demanding more than their fair share of the limelight and it follows that if the friendship involves any kind of show business or public performance, there is a better than average chance that this pair of farm-yard chums will get through the difficult early stages of understanding – or misunderstanding. Big spenders and a little full of themselves as a couple, Goat and Rooster males have a good platform for a successful relationship. Chas and Dave are a Goat and Rooster respectively, and a splendid example of the possibilities open to both signs.

Star Rating: Three at the most.

MALE MONKEY

The Rooster male is something of an enigma, being both thrifty and spendthrift, boastful and private. None of the

Rooster's strengths or weaknesses fits into any of the Monkey's. The Monkey *can* adapt to suit another's personality, but all in all the Rooster's demands do not appeal. Having said that, one of the great tennis doubles partnerships, that of John Newcombe and Tony Roche, was a Monkey and Rooster. A sporting outlook seems to be the solution.

Star Rating: Love all. Maybe one at a pinch.

MALE ROOSTER

As in all relationships involving two Roosters, it is often better for the birds than those around them. For two male Roosters there is one sure way for friendship to grow – through their influencing sign's tendency to build castles in the air. Pipe dreams *can* be useful; it depends on how difficult they are to make a reality. And even the most far-fetched dreams can come true. A business selling dreams might be just the answer; it certainly was for two of the most successful song writers of popular music ever. 'Love Me Tender' and 'Jailhouse Rock' are just a couple of the multi-million-selling songs written by Roosters Jerry Leiber and Mike Stoller.

Star Rating: Zero or five. Impossible to judge dreamers.

MALE DOG

Not much going for this pair. The loyal Dog has set views on the world, and his ideas on how it should be changed to make it a better place to live in do not usually coincide with the Rooster's. And it must be emphasised that Dogs do not stand idly by while others suffer, no matter how great or small the suffering. The Rooster is a conservative at heart and his outspoken manner and sometimes boastful nature (especially if he is the extrovert kind) will alienate the Dog. But both are honest signs and if the Dog's loyalty can be harnessed to the Rooster's candour, this might be a friendship used for the good of others.

Star Rating: Zero usually. Two would be the tops.

MALE PIG

The relationship of daydreaming, boastful Rooster and hard-working, socially well informed Pig has the makings of one that will last longer than many. There is something in the Pig's ability to work and play with equal ability that balances the Rooster's tendency to promise more than he can deliver. Both signs are essentially honest, which means that should they form a business, there is little possibility that one will trick the other. Ex-10cc stars Lol Creme and Kevin Godley are a Pig and Rooster respectively.

Star Rating: Two through to four.

COMPATIBILITY OF FEMALE ROOSTERS IN FRIENDSHIP

FEMALE RAT

If the Rat is the type to spend her money as she earns it – the extrovert Rat – and the Rooster is the kind to empty her bank account at a stroke this pair can become good friends. Afternoons spending in the high street is the usual plan, followed by tea and a generous helping of cakes. But Roosters are moralists deep down and Rats tend not to be. There could be a few uneasy moments should the Rat let her comparative lack of moral fibre get the better of her. So it all depends on both signs being well-balanced, outgoing types.

Star Rating: Four at best. Three as a rule.

FEMALE BUFFALO

Hats off to one of the great relationships. Here, lady Rooster and lady Buffalo have no end of subjects in common. Both deeply conservative and careful not to let the other peer too deeply into their personal lives, this is a friendship born from mutual trust and affection. Hours in the rose garden, chats over coffee, trips to the museums – there is no limit to the boundaries of friendship and understanding. Need I say more? The Chinese wouldn't.

Star Rating: Five plus!

FEMALE TIGER

Here's a pair of females without a future. No matter that the Rooster is a saver or high spender or thrifty, and no matter how generous or overt the Tiger, these two have nothing in common. All Roosters are private at heart, and the Tiger is the most outgoing sign of all. When there's no hope, it's better to face up to it. That way, no one is left feeling bad about the consequences of a broken friendship. Try to imagine Princess Anne and Joan Collins forming a relationship.

Star Rating: Just about nil.

FEMALE CAT

The female Cat has an easy way with even the most tricky people, and she is an expert at concealing her true feelings. That's why the Chinese consider the Cat to be such a fine diplomat. And the Cat will need all her qualities of diplomacy and human understanding to deal with the female Rooster, especially if this bird is the extrovert. Never one for hiding from others what she thinks, the rooster speaks her mind and does so often. But she is honest and usually incorruptible, something that the Cat applauds. Not the greatest of pairings, but better than would at first appear.

Star Rating: Two, and that's good here.

FEMALE DRAGON

All the makings of a firm friendship, but there are a few problems. The Dragon female is not always helped by expecting everyone to be as perfect as she is – or thinks she is. She may not like it, but a little criticism does no harm. Our old friend the candid Rooster is quick to pull the Dragon up short. In turn, the Dragon is quick to spot the Rooster's habit of building castles in the air, which she re-creates into something more attainable. Whereas the Monkey will let the Dragon carry the can when things go wrong, the rooster will share all kinds of responsibility – personal and business. A clean relationship this, with much honest talk and the most positive side of both signs given a first-rate chance of developing. My mother is a Rooster, and enjoys a splendid relationship with a Dragon, a nurse she met while in hospital.

Star Rating: Five.

FEMALE SNAKE

The candid and outspoken Rooster, if she is also the spend-thrift type of bird, has almost nothing in common with the subtle and thrifty Snake. It is really difficult to discover where a Rooster and Snake friendship could go. Snakes can be very funny, in an original and very personal way, and most female Roosters love to be the centre of attention. There's mileage in a comedy partnership, perhaps. But these two signs are not meant to be. Sorry.

Star Rating: One at the very most.

FEMALE HORSE

If a horse born, say, in 1954 found life tough with someone born in 1956, a Monkey, then take the Chinese Horoscope's advice and move on a year. The next year's sign, the Rooster, is tailored to do business with the wit- and personality-rich Horse. Both signs are gifted in different skills; the Rooster has method and the Horse a strong work capacity. Combined, these qualities lead to the Horse and Rooster creating one of the all time great friendships. My wife is a Rooster and typically, does not make friends easily. Yet all her long term friendships have been formed with Horses. In fact, it was this single instance of how accurate the Chinese Horoscopes are in terms of relationships that led me to study them as deeply as I have.

Star Rating: Five.

FEMALE GOAT

Non sexual friendship is perhaps the only really possible partnership between a Goat and Rooster. The females of both signs are capable of demanding more than their fair share of the limelight and it follows that if the friendship involves any kind of show business or public performance, there is a better than average chance that this pair of farm-yard chums will get through the difficult early stages of understanding – or misunderstanding. Big spenders and a little full of themselves as a couple, Goat and Rooster females have only a moderate platform for a successful relationship.

Star Rating: Three at the most.

FEMALE MONKEY

The Rooster female is something of an enigma, being both thrifty and spendthrift, boastful and private. None of the Rooster's strengths or weaknesses fits into any of the Monkey's. The Monkey *can* adapt to suit another's personality, but all in all the rooster's demands do not appeal. Of the two pairings, Monkey and Rooster female are not entirely without hope and there is a slight chance of a relationship. But it will not last a lifetime.

Star Rating: One. Maybe one and a half at a pinch.

FEMALE ROOSTER

As in all relationships involving two Roosters, it is often better for the birds than those around them. For two female

Roosters there is one sure way for friendship to grow – through their influencing sign's tendency to build castles in the air. Pipedreams *can* be useful; it depends on how difficult they are to make a reality. And even the most far-fetched dreams can come true. A business selling dreams might be just the answer. Two of the three Beverly sisters, the twins, are both Roosters – Joy is a Horse. The twins once told me they were more like friends than sisters, in spite of their hit of years ago 'Sisters'.

Star Rating: Zero or five. Impossible to judge dreamers.

FEMALE DOG

Not much going for this pair. The loyal Dog has set views on the world, and her ideas on how it should be changed to make it a better place to live in do not usually coincide with the Rooster's. And it must be emphasised that Dogs do not stand idly by while others suffer, no matter how great or small the suffering. The Rooster is a conservative at heart and her outspoken manner and sometimes boastful nature (especially if she is the extrovert kind) will alienate the Dog. But both are honest signs and if the Dog's loyalty can be harnessed to the Rooster's candour, it might be a friendship used for the good of others. It might even make them laugh. French and Saunders are a Rooster and Dog duo.

Star Rating: Zero usually. Two would be tops.

FEMALE PIG

The relationship of daydreaming, boastful Rooster and hard-working, socially well informed Pig has the makings of one that will last longer than many. There is something in the Pig's ability to work and play with equal ability that balances the Rooster's tendency to promise more than she can deliver. Both signs are essentially honest, which means that should these ladies form a business, there is little possibility that one will trick the other.

Star Rating: Two through to four.

THE DOG

1910	February 10th to January 29th	1911
1922	January 28th to February 15th	1923
1934	February 14th to February 3rd	1935
1946	February 2nd to January 21st	1947
1958	February 18th to February 7th	1959
1970	February 6th to January 26th	1971
1982	January 25th to February 12th	1983
1994	February 10th to January 30th	1995

Dog, dog – I like a good dog –
Towser or Bowser or Star –
Clean sort of pleasure –
A four-footed treasure –
And faithful as few humans are!
Scott Fitzgerald & Edmund Wilson

THE YEAR OF THE DOG

Dogs are born under the sign of idealism and no matter what size or shape they come in, a Dog's honesty and loyalty are there for all to see. Whether a stray down on his luck or Cruft's champion of champions, the eternally touching expression in a Dog's eyes is invariably one of unconditional devotion. Few animal signs have such a wide range of influences as Man's Best Friend and a Dog's many faceted outlook is perfectly described by the 16th-century vicar and natural historian, the Rev. Edward Topsell. He wrote: 'There be some Dogs which bark and do not bite, Dogs which bark and bite, and some which bite bitterly before they bark.'

Champion of the underdog, the Chinese see Dogs as men and women of the Left – strong advocates for change and social reform. Indeed, most Dog people will seek out injustice and fight it with every means possible. Once a Dog has been given a task worthy of his or her trust, no other animal sign can equal their stubborn determination to see it through at all costs. Equality, freedom and justice are what Dogs fight for, and they demand that their open and sometimes blunt voice is heard.

It is always worth remembering that once you have earned a Dog's trust – something that will seldom be given lightly – you may count on them for anything. A Dog will move mountains to carry out a task, or prove their worth. But it must be stressed that for all their warmth and devotion, Dogs will not easily forget or forgive an act of cruelty. Mistreat a Dog and you will find yourself no longer the object of their devotion. In cases where Dogs have been badly abused the advice is to take great care when building up a relationship. And it may be the case that the Dog in question might never fully overcome their grievances. Dogs feel hurt very deeply and they have little or no technique for dealing with long term emotional pain.

Stubborn, watchful and often defensive, Dogs are quick to criticise our lack of concern for the world's injustices. Fear of not being thought to do their best frequently causes a Dog to become anxious A Dog will speak out of turn and appear cynical at times, often unaware that those around are doing their best. The Dog's main ambition is to please. Failure to be thought well of might swiftly lead a Dog into a state of anxiety, which they find almost impossible to escape from. This in turn leads a Dog to respond to life's setbacks with more pessimism than is normally thought to be healthy. Faced with uncertainty or lack of purpose, Dogs will never fully distinguish the wood from the trees. Although Dogs might easily make money, often huge sums, it will never bring the comforts or security it does for many others. In fact, Dogs care virtually nothing for wealth and place their only high premium on personal relationships.

The three phases of a Dog's life will all be affected by the undercurrent of anxiety. Dog children will act dutifully and stay close to home and parents. The middle period often calls for flexibility, a quality that Dogs find difficult unless there is a true purpose to it, and may be a bit uphill. Old age offers no respite, adding a sad but true reflection on the old expression it's a Dog's life. But Dogs may console themselves with the fact that of all the signs, they are noble beyond compare.

COMPATIBILITY OF MALE DOGS IN LOVE

FEMALE RAT

Rats and Dogs are not a pairing that comes easily to mind, unlike cats and mice or cats and dogs. But female Rats are attracted to the idealistic male Dog, who is loyal and caring. These qualities are enough for the warm-hearted Rat to respond with open arms. And there is something else that attracts the Rat. Dogs are forgiving, which they need to be when they fall in love with a Rat. Without intending to do so, a Rat might easily take their Dog lover for granted. This in turn will tend to place a negative perspective on the relationship and the Dog might become over anxious as a result. Turn-off time for the Rat and much pessimistic barking from the Dog.

Star Rating: Three, especially if the Dog has not been too ill-treated as a puppy.

FEMALE BUFFALO

There is something in the idealism of the gentleman Dog that the strong minded Buffalo finds both laudable and attractive. He is warm and open in his affections and the Buffalo responds to his constant attentiveness. In turn the male Dog feels to a certain degree protected by the female Buffalo's strength of character. So what's wrong? Dogs are apprehensive and tend to worry over details. They are anxious and uncertain at times whereas the Buffalo sets her path out before her and follows it come what may. There are times when lovers must by their very nature travel the same path, but Buffalo and Dog will eventually find their paths head in different directions.

Star Rating: Two, sometimes three.

FEMALE TIGER

In the early stages of romance, a Dog and Tiger discover they have more to share than just a physical relationship. There are few better partners for the Tiger and the Dog is quick to appreciate this happy state of affairs. Dogs, more the men than the women, tend to suffer from a constant niggling sense of anxiety, which the Tiger, with her warm generosity and straight talk, is more than capable of dispelling. In turn, the female Tiger is fired by the Dog's strong will and his thoughtfulness during her not infrequent periods of inner uncertainty. So good is the long term relationship, that short term, this pair merits fewer stars than expected.

Star Rating: Three, sometimes two.

FEMALE CAT

Cats and Dogs are supposed to fight, but in my experience this is not the case. The Chinese agree and explain that the loyal and idealistic Dog looks to the Cat for support. The Cat is thoughtful and a considerate lover, if at times a little too easily defeated by the inevitable emotional stress that comes from being in love. But there is plenty of warmth in a love created and shared by both Cat and Dog. The lady Cat, it must be said, does a great job calming the ever-anxious Dog, who in turn is not slow to show his gratitude.

Star Rating: Three is about right.

FEMALE DRAGON

The Dog and Dragon are a long term disaster area, more so if both signs, especially the Dragon, live up fully and honestly to their animal influences. Dog ladies do have great warmth and their openness utterly beguiles the impulsive Dragon, but the troublespot is that the Dragon has no real heart. The carnival leader is paper and paste, easily seduced and just a bit too overpowering. The male Dog will struggle with the lady Dragon's self-assurance and forgive her determination to act as she wishes, but is a genuine and loyal lover who can be easily hurt. The chances are that neither side will ever truly understand the other.

Star Rating: One at most.

FEMALE SNAKE

This is a common relationship in spite of its low rating. The loyal and idealistic Dog is easily bewitched by the female Snake, who is quick to respond to her partner's open show of affection. And let it be understood that although ever anxious, Dog fellows have devoted hearts, which they give without asking much in return. But they do ask something, and it is usually more than Snake ladies can give. Snakes have long periods when they simply hibernate, and their emotions, including their sexuality, are in flux. Dogs require stability once they fall in love and to be rejected, even temporarily, can create incurable scars.

Star Rating: Two.

FEMALE HORSE

In the farmyard, the horse and dog do different jobs, and seldom meet. But when they do, they have much in common, if only in their help to mankind. Horse and Dog signs benefit from a mutual interest outside any particular hobby or field of endeavour. Sex is a useful starting point and all that goes with it. Socially active, the Horse female provides the male Dog with masses of opportunities to free himself from the nagging need to be loved and appreciated. The Horse is great fun to be with and her free spirit acts to soothe the sometimes anxious Dog. He in return provides much genuine and, a bonus for the Horse, undemanding love.

Star Rating: Four or five.

FEMALE GOAT

Dogs are faithful, loyal and totally self deprecating in the face of a true loving relationship. Seeing themselves as the partner who must always win approval, rather than expecting it. Dog men are the reverse side of the romantic coin to the capricious and often self centred Goat. Although generous and witty, female Goats are often trend followers at heart, and they love to perform and be the centre of attention. They also change their mind more quickly than any other sign, a trait which Dog gentlemen simply find hard to keep up with. And Goats are no idealists, in bed or out.

Star Rating: One at the most. Usually zero.

FEMALE MONKEY

This is a relationship which looks good on paper but the reality is often different. The Monkey is something of a trickster in every respect of her life. She loves intrigue and games. She might even play off one friend against another, and one lover against the next. Dog males are warm if anxious about their love life and once committed will not enjoy being taken for granted, no matter how much the Dog's influence of loyalty and devotion is exercised. Too many tricks and not enough respect mark the Monkey's love affair with the Dog as a non starter, or a quick finisher.

Star Rating: Zero. Maybe a half point at best.

FEMALE ROOSTER

Once again, there is a problem confronting both these animal signs. Neither really enjoys casual relationships and a commitment to long term loving definitely broadens the possibilities. Rooster females are often very demanding in the sense they are not very flexible, especially in terms of personal feelings. The same, but for different reasons, is also true of the Dog. Rooster ladies are conservative in outlook; Dog chaps are anxiously liberal. The chances of true understanding are therefore extremely remote. But it is possible. Male Dog/female Rooster couples have the best chance of the two pairs.

Star Rating: One or two.

FEMALE DOG

It is almost impossible to be precise about two Dogs, of either sex, making the most from a love relationship – or any other! Just like the domestic canine, a pair of Dogs will either hit it off at once or get into a Top Dog syndrome, which by its very nature is not one of give and take. But for those Dogs who discover the strength and good companionship that lies within their influence, there is every chance of an affair becoming a long-lasting partnership. Love is a powerful factor in a Dog's life and it is seldom given lightly. In my researches, however, I have not found a pair of loving Dogs to be a common feature on the Chinese Horoscope list of compatibility ratings.

Star Rating: Three is about right.

FEMALE PIG

Pigs and dogs hit the jackpot in the love stakes. The warm-hearted and generous, sexually giving lady Pig is perfectly matched with the sometimes anxious, eager to please male Dog. The Dog, who has a tendency to worry over emotional details, finds he is enjoying a rare inner freedom when exposed to the bundles of good humour and easy-going temperament of his loving Pig companion. In love a Dog and Pig, who are genetically quite close in the animal kingdom, rate extremely highly.

Star Rating: Five most times.

COMPATIBILITY OF FEMALE DOGS IN LOVE

MALE RAT

Rats and Dogs are not a pairing that is found very often in the Chinese Horoscope, as indeed, they are not found often in nature. Cats and Dogs, yes. Dogs and Rats? Er . . . not really. But Rats are attracted to the idealistic female Dog, who is frequently blessed with beautiful hair and eyes. And there is something else that attracts the Rat. Dog ladies are warm and forgiving, which they need to be when they fall in love with a Rat. Without intending to do so, a Rat might easily take his loyal Dog lover for granted. This in turn will tend to place a negative perspective on the relationship and lady Dog might become over anxious as a result. Turn off time for the Rat.

Star Rating: Three, especially if the Rat is the introverted planner and stickler for detail.

MALE BUFFALO

There is something in the idealism of the lady Dog that the strong minded Buffalo finds both laudable and attractive. She is warm and open in her affection and the Buffalo responds to her attentiveness. In turn the female Dog feels herself protected by the male Buffalo's strength of character. So what's wrong? Dogs are apprehensive and tend to worry over details. They are anxious and uncertain at times whereas the Buffalo sets his path out before him and follows it come what may. There are times when lovers must by their very nature travel the same path, but Buffalo and Dog will eventually find their paths head in different directions.

Star Rating: Two, sometimes three.

MALE TIGER

In the early stages of romance, a Dog and Tiger discover they have more to share than just a physical relationship. There are few better partners for the Tiger and the Dog is quick to appreciate this happy state of affairs. Dogs tend to suffer from a constant niggling sense of anxiety, which the Tiger, with his warm generosity and straight talk, is more than capable of dispelling. In turn, the Tiger is fired by the Dog's strong will and care during his not infrequent periods of inner uncertainty. So good is the long term relationship that short term it merits fewer stars than expected.

Star Rating: Three, sometimes two.

MALE CAT

Cats and Dogs are supposed to fight, but in my experience this is not the case. The Chinese agree and explain that the loyal and idealistic Dog looks to the Cat for support. Dog ladies generally are not so shy as their male counterparts and less prone to the anxiety which dogs all Dog people. The Cat is thoughtful and a considerate lover, if at times a little too easily defeated by the inevitable emotional stress that comes from being in love. But there is plenty of warmth in a love created and shared by both Cat and Dog, the male Cat/ female Dog pair having the slightest of edges.

Star Rating: Three is about right.

MALE DRAGON

The Dog and Dragon are a long term disaster area, more so if both signs, especially the Dragon, live up fully and honestly to their animal influences. Dog ladies do have great warmth and their openness utterly beguiles the impulsive Dragon, but the troublespot is that the Dragon has no real heart. The carnival leader is paper and paste, easily seduced and just a bit too fond of himself. The lady Dog will forgive his indiscretions, but she is a genuine and loyal lover who can be hurt. The chances are neither side will ever truly understand the other, and although the lady Dog/male Dragon is by far the better of the two combinations, it is still a difficult affair.

Star Rating: One at most.

MALE SNAKE

This is a common relationship in spite of its low rating. The loyal and idealistic Dog lady is easily bewitched by the male Snake, who is quick to respond to his partner's open show of affection. And let it be understood that Dog ladies have devoted hearts which they give without asking much in return. But they do ask something, and it is usually more than Snake men can give. Snakes have long periods when they simply hibernate, and their emotions, including their sexuality, are in flux. Dogs require stability once they fall in love and to be rejected, even temporarily, can create incurable scars.

Star Rating: Two.

MALE HORSE

In the farmyard, the horse and dog do different jobs, and seldom meet. But when they do they have much in common, if only in their help to mankind. Horse and Dog signs benefit from a mutual interest outside any particular hobby or field of endeavour. Sex is a useful starting point and all that goes with it. Socially active, the Horse male provides the lady Dog with masses of opportunities to free herself from the nagging need to be loved and appreciated. The Horse is great fun to be with and his free spirit acts to soothe the sometimes anxious Dog lady. She in return provides much genuine and, a bonus for the Horse, undemanding love. Paul McCartney, a Horse, was *very* much in love with Dog lady Jane Asher and desperately wanted to marry her.

Star Rating: Four or five.

MALE GOAT

Dogs are faithful, loyal and totally self deprecating in the face of a true loving relationship, seeing themselves as the partner who must always win approval, rather than expecting it. Dog ladies are the reverse side of the romantic coin to the capricious and often self centred Goat. Although generous and witty, male Goats are trendsetters at heart, and they love to perform and be the centre of attention. They also change their mind more quickly than any other sign, a trait which Dog ladies simply find hard to keep up with. And Goats are no idealists, in bed or out. Sara Keays was born in a Dog year and Cecil Parkinson in the Year of the Goat.

Star Rating: One at the most. Usually zero.

MALE MONKEY

This is a relationship which looks good on paper but the reality often takes a different view. The Monkey is a bit of a trickster in every aspect of his life. He loves intrigue and games. He might even play off one friend against another, and one lover against the next. Dog ladies are warm if anxious about their love life and once committed will not enjoy being taken for granted, no matter how much the Dog's influence of loyalty and devotion is exercised. Too many tricks and not enough respect mark the Monkey's love affair with the lady Dog as a non starter, or a quick finisher.

Star Rating: Zero. Maybe a half point at best.

MALE ROOSTER

Once again, there is a problem confronting both these animal signs. Neither really enjoys casual relationships and a commitment to long term loving definitely broadens the possibilities. Rooster males are often very demanding in the sense that they are not very flexible, especially in terms of personal feelings. The same, but for different reasons, is also true of the Dog lady. Rooster men are conservative in outlook; Dog ladies are anxiously liberal. The chances of true understanding are therefore extremely remote. But it is possible. The worst scenario is that one's negativity will corrupt the other, as it did in the case of Bonny (Dog) and Clyde (Rooster).

Star Rating: One or two.

MALE DOG

It is almost impossible to be precise about two Dogs, of either sex, making the most of a love relationship – or any other! Just like the domestic canine, a pair of Dogs will either hit it off at once or get into a Top Dog syndrome, which by its very nature is not one of give and take. But for those Dogs who discover the strength and good companionship that lies within their influence, there is every chance of an affair becoming a long lasting partnership. Love is a powerful factor in a Dog's life and it is seldom given lightly. In my researches, however, I have not found a pair of loving Dogs to be a common feature on the Chinese Horoscope list of compatibility ratings.

Star Rating: Three is about right.

MALE PIG

Pigs and Dogs hit the jackpot in the love stakes. The warm hearted and generous, sexually giving Pig male is perfectly matched with the sometimes slightly over anxious, eager to please lady Dog. The Dog, with her tendency to worry over emotional details, finds herself enjoying a rare inner freedom when exposed to the bundles of good humour and easy-going temperament of her loving Pig companion. In love a Dog and Pig, who are genetically quite close in the animal kingdom, rate extremely high.

Star Rating: Five most times.

COMPATIBILITY OF MALE DOGS IN MARRIAGE

FEMALE RAT

There is a marked decrease of understanding when a Rat and Dog get hitched. In a purely sexual/romantic relationship, the more negative aspects of each of these two animal signs are less obvious. But there is only a little of the Dog's strong sense of idealism in even the most idealistic lady Rat and setting the world to rights is not normally her priority. Dogs become more set in their ways the older they get and the openness and changeability which may often dominate the Rat's personality only succeeds in driving a wedge between them. This in turn causes the Dog to become increasingly anxious and critical. Should the Rat be introverted and keen on the minutiae of life, the marriage stands a marginally better chance.

Star Rating: One

FEMALE BUFFALO

Alas, a more than reasonable love affair does not improve with marriage. The Dog is an idealist and worries about the underprivileged at every level. Male Dogs care strongly about injustices and are anxious to make this a better world. Buffalo females are not so caring. They are born leaders of any group or relationship and often lack the kind of intimate sensitivity that the Dog frequently seeks in a long term companion. A family might make a difference, offering some mutual interest outside their lack of shared ideals. But on the whole it is a marriage to avoid unless it is understood that ideals are not important.

Star Rating: Zero rising to two at most.

FEMALE TIGER

A short romance and a long and usually wonderfully productive marriage. From a few stars to the maximum for the Tiger and Dog, neither of whom find long term relationships easy. Both signs demand a great deal from their partners and in this case they get everything and more. The idealist Dog has the perfect foil in the explosive and rebellious Tiger and few family units are better served or protected by these strong-willed and often stubborn signs. The Tiger is the more inspiring parent, but the Dog is ever on hand to add his own kind of devotional care without asking for any reward. A top-notch partnership in every single department and one helped by a large family.

Star Rating: Five plus.

FEMALE CAT

A good middle of the road marriage for the Cat and Dog – although the male Cat/female Dog is the better of the two pairings. There is much understanding from the Cat for her Dog husband's more trivial anxieties, a common problem facing all Dogs, and plenty of Dog devotion in return. Dog men look to homes that provide both elegance and safety – a bit like a well-appointed kennel, I suppose – and female Cats are not slow to introduce their own highly accomplished sense of refinement and decorative skills. A lovely home with gentle people and varied friendships is the result of a Dog and Cat going down the aisle. Not a great place for untidy kids perhaps, or too much stress.

Star Rating: Three.

FEMALE DRAGON

Not recommended. The Chinese Horoscopes go to great lengths to point out that Dogs and Dragons have little or no understanding. In my experience I have found this to be mainly the case, but I must say that I have met a number of very successful Dog and Dragon marriages – if not love affairs. The act of marriage does give the Dog the security he craves at heart, and in turn the female Dragon's often self-centred existence is given broader horizons by being in constant contact with the Dog's sense of idealism. But it must be remembered that the Dog's anxiety to do the right thing may be misunderstood as mere fretting over details, and that the Dragon might, as a result of her own self-esteem, over-look the Dog's efforts to please. Dog males/female Dragons are the best of the two pairs.

Star Rating: Zero, but there might be two or even three in the right circumstances.

FEMALE SNAKE

This is a very common relationship and a large number of this particular pairing would vouch for it being better than the low rating the Chinese give it. Loyal and idealistic, the male Dog certainly benefits from the female Snake's positive qualities; they are wise, extremely thoughtful and give their time freely without asking for anything in return. But there is always the Dog's more negative streak to contend with – his anxiety. Dogs worry over details and can be very stubborn, sometimes for no apparent reason. This causes tension, and in turn will lead to much misunderstanding. Dog male/Snake female is the best pairing.

Star Rating: Two, but there are a few extra points when the Dog partner is less fretful.

FEMALE HORSE

The Dog's patience and understanding are seldom called on when the Horse is his married partner. The female Horse has bags of energy, wit and enthusiasm, plus a wonderful sense of style. This usually means a comfortable and elegant home. The male Dog offers warmth and true friendship, qualities on which every lasting marriage are founded. The male Dog's constant anxieties are diminished in number by the female Horse's clear-headed view of life. In return, the Horse's tendency to become suddenly bored and change direction, an act which can have quite serious repercussions, is often avoided by the Dog's demand for an honest simplicity in terms of family hopes and ideals.

Star Rating: Four.

FEMALE GOAT

Goats and Dogs of both the male and female variety do not have much in common. When you look at the archetypal farmyard, where the origins of Chinese Horoscopes were first considered, goats do not normally bump into dogs – they have different functions, which are not usually linked. However, the male Dog husband is extremely devoted, even though his female Goat wife might not exactly return such blind devotion. But the male Dog's anxiety level might be stretched by the fickle female Goat's heart.

Star Rating: One at the most.

FEMALE MONKEY

From a no-no love affair, the element of promising a long term commitment from the Monkey adds an important dimension to the relationship. Put simply, over a period of time the Dog's high idealism and loyal outlook will transform his Monkey wife's general attitude to one of relatively honest endeavour. As a result the Monkey wife will frequently adopt an uncharacteristic single mindedness, thus providing this curious couple with more than an even chance of making the marriage a success. Kids would be a good idea.

Star Rating: Three, surprisingly.

FEMALE ROOSTER

Male Dog and female Rooster have not had a particularly deep engagement; that is to say, there have not been a great many inner revelations. Marriage tends to demand that honest folk, which include both Dogs and Roosters, come clean about what they really care about. This could mean that the loyal Dog and candid Rooster might well find they do not share quite as much in common as they had previously imagined. But there is still plenty of scope for understanding and although the Chinese give these two signs a poor mark for marriage, my experience is that it holds up rather well. Winston Churchill was a Dog and his wife, Clem, a Rooster. It was not an easy marriage.

Star Rating: Three, but drifting down a few stars in some cases; for example, an over-anxious Dog.

FEMALE DOG

The transition from an affair to marriage creates very little change in terms of two Dogs. The same loyalties exist, as do the same basically honest tenets of straight dealing and mutual trust. Provided both Dogs build a secure home and establish their territory, there is plenty of hope. And if there is a challenge for the couple to get their teeth into, even better. But everything depends on the Dog being internally secure for the marriage to work. One of Judy Garland's husbands was also a Dog – Vincent Minelli. It was thought to be one of the great Dog performer's better choices.

Star Rating: Three. No change.

FEMALE PIG

The Pig may have the most of the marriage, but if the Dog is one who has not enjoyed a happy childhood he might begin to take his Pig wife a little too much for granted. Dog husbands who are unhappy tend to talk too much and fret like mad. Where there was once a happy, jovial and outgoing home, the mood becomes bleak and nervy. In the end the Pig, as big hearted as she may be, runs out of patience. However, this pairing usually produces a model marriage, which, nine times out of ten, lasts the course. Film producer Blake Edwards is a Dog and married to a Pig, Julie Andrews – happily I'm told.

Star Rating: Five.

COMPATIBILITY OF FEMALE DOGS IN MARRIAGE

MALE RAT

There is a marked decrease of understanding when a Rat and Dog get hitched. In a purely sexual/romantic relationship, the more negative aspects of each of these two animal signs are less obvious. But there is little of the Dog's strong sense of idealism in the Rat and setting the world to rights is not his priority. Dogs become more idealistic the older they get and the opportunism and aggressive streak which may dominate the male Rat only succeeds in driving a wedge between them. This in turn causes the Dog to become increasingly anxious and critical. Should the Rat be introverted and keen on the minutiae of life, the marriage stands a marginally better chance. Actress Jane Asher is a Dog and her husband is a Rat, self-promoting cartoonist Gerald Scarfe. Another Rat/Dog pair are pop wizard Jean-Michel Jarre and his wife, Charlotte Rampling.

Star Rating: One.

MALE BUFFALO

Alas, a more than reasonable love affair does not improve with marriage. The Dog is an idealist and worries about the underprivileged at every level. Lady Dogs in particular care very strongly about injustices and are anxious to make this a better world. Buffalo males are not so caring. They are born to be leaders of men and often lack the kind of intimate sensitivity that the Dog seeks in a long term companion. A family might make a difference, offering some mutual interest outside their lack of shared ideals. But on the whole it is a marriage to avoid unless it is understood that ideals are not important. Wealth would help strengthen the bonds. Perhaps that's why Carlo Ponti, a Buffalo, and his beautiful Dog wife, Sophia Loren, have survived; not much idealism in Hollywood.

Star Rating: Zero rising to two at most.

MALE TIGER

A short romance and a long and usually wonderfully productive marriage. From a few stars to the maximum for the Tiger and Dog, neither of whom find long term relationships easy. Both signs demand a great deal from their partners and in this case they get everything and more. The idealist Dog has the perfect foil in the explosive and rebellious Tiger and few family units are better served or protected by these strong-willed and often stubborn signs. The Tiger is the more inspir-

369

ing parent, but the Dog is ever on hand to nurse, heal and love without reward. A top notch partnership in every single department and one helped by a large family.

Star Rating: Five plus.

MALE CAT

A good middle of the road marriage for the Cat and Dog – the male Cat/female Dog being the best of the two pairings. There is much understanding from the Cat for his Dog wife's more trivial anxieties, a common problem facing all Dogs, and plenty of Dog devotion in return. Dog ladies, more than Dog men, do create the most wonderful homes and male Cats are not slow to introduce their own highly accomplished sense of refinement and decorative skills. A lovely home with gentle people and varied friendships is the result of a Dog and Cat going down the aisle. Not a great place for untidy kids perhaps.

Star Rating: Three.

MALE DRAGON

Not recommended. The CHinese Horoscopes go to great lengths to point out that Dogs and Dragons have little or no understanding. In my experience I have found this to be mainly the case, but I must say that I have met a number of very successful Dog and Dragon marriages – if not love affairs. The act of marriage does give the Dog the security she craves at heart, and in turn the male Dragon's often self important existence is given a broader horizon by being in constant contact with the Dog lady's sense of idealism. But it must be remembered that the Dog's anxiety to do the right thing may be misunderstood as mere fretting over details, and that the Dragon might, as a result of his own self importance, overlook the Dog's efforts to please. Ringo Starr is a Dragon and his second wife, Barbara Bach, is a Dog, which might just have something to do with his drinking habits. Watch this space for an update!

Star Rating: Zero, but there might be two or even three in the right circumstances.

MALE SNAKE

This is a very common relationship and a large number of this particular pairing would vouch for it being better than the low rating the Chinese give it. Loyal and idealistic, the female Dog certainly benefits from the male Snake's positive qualities; they are wise, extremely thoughtful and give their time freely without asking anything in return. But there is always the Dog's more negative streak to contend with – their anxiety. Dogs worry over details and can be very stubborn, sometimes for no apparent reason. This causes tension, and in turn will lead to much misunderstanding.

Star Rating: Two, but there are a few extra points when the Dog partner is less fretful.

MALE HORSE

The Dog's patience and understanding are seldom called on when the Horse is her married partner. His occasional rages are really few and far between and his love of hard work usually means a comfortable and somewhat fashionable lifestyle. The lady Dog offers warmth and true friendship, qualities on which every lasting marriage are founded. The Dog's anxieties are diminished in number by the Horse's clear-headed view of life. In return, the Horse's tendency to become suddenly bored and change direction, an act which can have quite serious repercussions, is often avoided by the Dog's demand for an honest simplicity in terms of family hopes and ideals. TV's 'Most Beautiful Bottom' winner and small-screen presenter, Anneka Rice, is a Dog who has married a Horse, Nick Allot.

Star Rating: Four.

MALE GOAT

Goats and Dogs of both the male and female variety do not have much in common. When you look at the archetypal farmyard, where the origins of Chinese Horoscopes were first considered, goats do not normally bump into dogs – they have different functions, which are not usually linked.

371

However, the female Dog wife is extremely devoted, even though her male Goat husband might not exactly return such blind devotion. But there is a strong element of the peacemaker in both signs and a marriage which included a religious or spiritual aspect would help. Drama man Jack Rosenthal is a Goat, married to actress Dog Maureen Lipman.

Star Rating: One at the most.

MALE MONKEY

From a no-no love affair, the element of promising a long term commitment from the Monkey adds an important dimension to the relationship. Put simply, over a period of time the Dog's high idealism and loyal outlook will transform her Monkey husband's general attitude to one of relatively honest endeavour. As a result the Monkey husband will frequently adopt an uncharacteristic single-mindedness, thus providing this curious couple with more than an even chance of making the marriage work. Kids would be a good idea. Ray Davis, leader of one of the only original sixties pop groups still performing, The Kinks, is a Monkey. He enjoyed a long marriage to his Dog wife Rasa before divorcing her. Long by pop standards, that is.

Star Rating: Three, surprisingly.

MALE ROOSTER

Male Rooster and female Dog have not had a particularly deep engagement; that is to say, there have not been a great many inner revelations. Marriage tends to demand that honest folk, which include both Dogs and Roosters, come clean about what they really care about. This could mean that the loyal Dog and candid Rooster might well find they do not share quite as much in common as they had previously imagined. But there is still plenty of scope for understanding and although the Chinese give these two signs a poor mark for marriage, my experience is that it holds up rather well.

Star Rating: Three, but drifting down a few stars in some cases; for example, an over-anxious Dog.

MALE DOG

The transition from an affair to marriage creates very little change in terms of two Dogs. The same loyalties exist, as do the same basically honest tenets of straight dealing and mutual trust. Provided both Dogs build a secure home and establish their territory, there is plenty of hope. And if there is a challenge for the couple to get their teeth into, even better. But everything depends on the Dogs being internally secure for the marriage to work. One of Judy Garland's husbands was also a Dog – Vincent Minelli. It was thought to be one of the great Dog performer's better choices.

Star Rating: Three. No change.

MALE PIG

The Pig may have the most of the marriage, but if the Dog is one who has not enjoyed a happy childhood she might begin to take her Pig husband a little too much for granted. Dog wives who are unhappy tend to lack direction and fret like mad. Where there was once a happy, jovial and outgoing home, the mood becomes bleak and nervy. In the end the Pig, as big-hearted as he may be, runs out of patience. However, this pairing usually produces a model marriage, which, nine times out of ten, lasts the course. Sixties hit makers Sonny and Cher ('I Got You Babe') were a Dog lady and male Pig marriage. Cher's Doggy neurosis – expressed in her need to remake her body under the surgeon's knife – could well have started the rot.

Star Rating: Five (usually).

COMPATIBILITY OF MALE DOGS IN FRIENDSHIP

MALE RAT

A Rat might easily benefit from a friendship with a Dog, who brings a powerful sense of loyalty to any relationship. In turn, the Rat can offer his sharp wits and humour to help calm the Dog's more anxious moments. But there is no great understanding between them and it is not a common pairing. Perhaps that's why.

Star Rating: One, sometimes a point extra.

MALE BUFFALO

Faithful and idealistic the loyal Dog demands little but affection and appreciation. Buffaloes in turn demand loyalty and lots of it. So why does this friendship rate so poorly? The truth is that in their hearts Buffaloes are reactionaries, no matter what their political status, and Dogs are left wing, determined radicals who will risk everything for what they believe. A clash of principles is inevitable. Martin Amis, the author and son of Kingsley, is a Buffalo. Mr Amis senior is a Dog. They have so little understanding that the two writers even refused to sit together to have their joint portrait painted for the National Portrait Gallery.

Star Rating: One, maybe two at most. Most times zero.

MALE TIGER

This is the odd couple out. In marriage and as lovers Dogs and Tigers rate among the highest of all couples. The commitment, especially that made in a marriage, is central to a Dog and Tiger making the most of their respective influences. The less the commitment, the less a Dog and Tiger will find they have to offer each other. There's little doubt that as chums at the pub, or anywhere else, they will find more obstacles than bridges. On no account should they go into business.

Star Rating: Not easy to be accurate. Zero through to two.

MALE CAT

It is said that Cats and Dogs fight, but that is not true of the animal signs of the Chinese Horoscope. Here the relationship is reasonably strong, one in which the thoughtful and considerate Cat does much to quell the Dog's frequently anxious nature. The Dog pays back the Cat's concern with large helpings of loyal protection, especially in those periods when the Cat, under pressure, tends to find life too much.

Star Rating: Three.

MALE DRAGON

The Chinese say Dog and Dragon have no understanding, and this is thought to be the least auspicious of all the Dragon's relationships. Dogs have a pessimistic streak; they worry over details and are genuinely concerned over the welfare of others less fortunate than themselves. Dragons are not so inclined. But Dragons admire the Dog's devotion, and once shown how, he will readily return it. Any friendship involves good and bad times, and all friends have to work at putting the bad times right. This the Dog does instinctively, provided that he has not been treated poorly as a child; a kicked Dog may easily turn nasty. Dragons find forgiveness harder. This pair has more than a fair chance, but with reservations.

Star Rating: Three, and points up and down.

MALE SNAKE

Snakes and Dogs do have a habit of forming strong friendships in all departments but only truly succeed where there is deep love and affection. Two chums having a pint in the pub will not be enough to bring this pair of signs close enough to form a lasting relationship. The Dog will be constantly anxious in the face of the Snake's long periods of inner silence and neither can help themselves break the tension.

Star Rating: Two at most.

MALE HORSE

There's plenty of room for these two signs to move in and at the same time form a close understanding. The Dog's idealism is admired and taken up by the Horse and he is less anxious in the face of life's more troublesome moments, helped by the Horse's good sense and logical judgement. Neither Dog nor Horse is hypocritical, which means a relationship founded on honest endeavour and offered as a tool for others in less fortunate circumstances. It has been suggested that Horse Paul McCartney had the closest understanding of the Beatles' manager, Brian Epstien, a Dog who sadly took his own life when personal anxieties got on top of him.

Star Rating: Three or even four.

MALE GOAT

Dog men are always a touch anxious. Wanting the best for everyone, they are idealists and loyal – sometimes to a fault. Goat men tend to please themselves as to how they behave. Kind, artistic and open minded they may be, but all Goat males are not over blessed with large doses of reciprocal loyalty. Dog chums will put up with a lot but when the lake of dependability eventually runs dry, the Dog will finally turn and bite, so to speak. Frank Muir and Dennis Norden, one of post-war Britain's most successful script writers, are a Goat and Dog. They don't do too much together these days, except sit on opposing sides of panel games. An OK friendship over a short distance.

Star Rating: One through to three. Two average.

MALE MONKEY

A no go area if there ever was one. Dog blokes are straight-forward in their dealings and care about those who are less well off. They don't like the cunning outwitting the stupid, however much it might be deserved. Given that the Monkey has no such scruples he always, no matter what he might say to the contrary, suits himself in life. Not much to add, apart from the warning not to go into business either.

Star Rating: None.

MALE ROOSTER

Not much going for this pair. The loyal Dog has set views on the world, and his ideas on how it should be changed to make it a better place to live in do not usually coincide with the Rooster's. And it must be emphasised that Dogs do not stand idly by while others suffer, no matter how great or small the suffering. The Rooster is a conservative at heart and his outspoken manner and sometimes boastful nature, (especially if he is the extrovert kind) will alienate the Dog. But both are honest signs and if the Dog's loyalty can be harnessed to the Rooster's candour, it might be a friendship used for the good of others.

Star Rating: Zero usually. Two would be the tops.

MALE DOG

Not always a clear-cut relationship, with the problem of the Dog's need to establish a pecking order. But if, and it is a big if, both Dogs can decide on an equal share of the responsibilities that all relationships demand there is every chance of a long and fruitful friendship. It follows that should the loyal and idealistic Dogs find a role to exercise their great strengths, perhaps in the field of support for the under-privileged, so much the better. In spite of the concept of two Dogs getting on well, it is a less than common pairing. Blood relatives who are Dogs tend to create the strongest links.

Star Rating: Two, sometimes three. Seldom more.

MALE PIG

This is a very good pairing, one which usually finds Pig and Dog forming a strong partnership. There is a great deal of mutual support, and the honest Pig, coupled with the Dog's idealism, invariably leads to two mates who have a wide variety of social and professional skills. Good in company and happy to help others, the Dog and Pig rate highly on the Chinese Horoscope compatibility charts. The only point to remember is that a badly treated puppy turns into an unhappy adult dog. Dog people with a history of child neglect tend to become unstable and the Pig will find he has his hands full repairing the damage. This was exactly what happened to Pig snooker player Cliff Thorburn when he took his fellow Canadian Kirk Stevens, a Dog, under his wing following the discovery of the younger star's drug problem.

Star Rating: Five in most cases.

COMPATIBILITY OF FEMALE DOGS IN FRIENDSHIP

FEMALE RAT

Of the two signs, lady Dogs tend to be the most loyal and forgiving. They are not cynical as a rule and tend to look for the best in a friend. Rats, on the other hand, flow with the tide and, deep as their affections are, they can shift them from one to another with ease. Of all the pairings, Dogs and Rats are one of the least common.

Star Rating: Two as an average. But anything goes.

FEMALE BUFFALO

Dog ladies have fewer anxious moments than their male counterparts, or should I say that they allow anxiety to hold less sway. This may lead them to enjoy a relationship free of self doubt and constant analysis: 'Have I done the right thing?' etc., etc. Friendships are the centre of a Dog's life and they often treat a relationship as carefully as a fragile flower. Buffaloes are not so friendship-orientated. They ask loyalty and don't bother giving it in return. They make demands that the Dog is happy to go along with, at least in the early stages. For a picture of these two signs just bring to mind the attitude of Mrs Edwina Curry, a Dog, to that dear Buffalo, Mrs T.

Star Rating: One or two. Three is the very top.

FEMALE TIGER

This is the odd couple out. In marriage and as lovers Dogs and Tigers rate among the highest of all couples. The commitment, especially that made in a marriage, is central to a Dog and Tiger making the most of their respective influences. The less the commitment, the less will a Dog and Tiger find they have to offer each other. There's little doubt that as companions they will find more obstacles than bridges. On no account should they go into business. As in a number of cases, ladies have a better chance of a friendship working out than males.

Star Rating: Not easy to be accurate. One, two or three.

FEMALE CAT

It is said that Cats and Dogs fight, but that is not true of the animal signs of the Chinese Horoscope. Here the relationship is reasonably strong, one in which the thoughtful and considerate Cat does much to quell the Dog's frequently anxious nature. The Dog pays back the Cat's concern with large helpings of loyal protection, especially in those periods when the Cat, under pressure, tends to find life too much.

Star Rating: Three

FEMALE DRAGON

The Chinese say Dog and Dragon have no understanding, and this is thought to be the least auspicious of all the Dragon's relationships. Dogs have a pessimistic streak; they worry over details and are genuinely concerned over the welfare of others less fortunate than themselves. Dragons are not so inclined. But Dragons admire the Dog's devotion, and once shown how, she will readily return it. Any friendship involves good and bad times, and all friends have to work at putting the bad times right. This the Dog does instinctively, provided that she has not been treated poorly as a child; a kicked Dog may easily turn nasty. Dragons find forgiveness harder. This pair has more than a fair chance, but with reservations. Female Dragon/female Dog are the best.

Star Rating: Three, and points up and down.

FEMALE SNAKE

Snakes and Dogs do have a habit of forming strong friendships in all departments but only truly succeed where there is deep love and affection. Two girls sipping hock in the wine bar will not be enough to bring this pair of signs close enough to form a lasting relationship. The Dog will be constantly anxious in the face of the Snake's long periods of inner silence and neither can help themselves break the tension.

Star Rating: Two at most.

FEMALE HORSE

There's plenty of room for these two signs to move in and at the same time form a close understanding. The Dog's idealism is admired and taken up by the Horse and she becomes less anxious in the face of life's more troublesome moments, helped by the Horse's good sense and logical judgement. Neither Dog nor Horse is hypocritical, which means a relationship founded on honest endeavour and offered as a tool for others in less fortunate circumstances.

Star Rating: Three or even four.

FEMALE GOAT

Dog ladies are always a touch anxious. Wanting the best for everyone, they are idealists and loyal – sometimes to a fault. Goat ladies tend to please themselves as to how they behave. Kind, artistic and open-minded they may be, but all goat females are not over-blessed with large doses of reciprocal loyalty. Dogs will put up with a lot but when the lake of dependability eventually runs dry, the Dog will finally turn and bite, so to speak. An OK friendship over a short distance.

Star Rating: One through to three. Two average.

FEMALE MONKEY

A no go area if ever there was one. Dog lasses (or should it be Lassies?) are straightforward in their dealings and care about those who are less well off. They don't like the cunning outwitting the stupid, how ever much it might be deserved. Given that the Monkey has no such scruples she always, no matter what she might say to the contrary, suits herself in life. Not much to add, apart from the warning not to go into business either.

Star Rating: None.

FEMALE ROOSTER

Not much going for this pair. The loyal Dog has set views on the world, and her ideas on how it should be changed to make it a better place to love in do not usually coincide with the Rooster's. And it must be emphasised that Dogs do not stand idly by while others suffer, no matter how great or small the suffering. The Rooster is a conservative at heart and her outspoken manner and sometimes boastful nature (especially if she is the extrovert kind) will alienate the Dog. But both are honest signs and if the Dog's loyalty can be harnessed to the Rooster's candour, it might be a friendship used for the good of others. It might even make them laugh. French and Saunders are a Rooster and Dog duo.

Star Rating: Zero usually. Two would be the tops.

FEMALE DOG

Not always a clear cut relationship, with the problem of the Dog's need to establish a pecking order. But if, and it is a big if, both Dogs can decide on an equal share of the responsibilities that all relationships demand there is every chance for a long and fruitful friendship. It follows that should the loyal and idealistic Dogs find a role to exercise their great strengths, perhaps in the field of support for the underprivileged, so much the better. In spite of the concept of two Dogs getting on well, it is a less than common pairing. Blood relatives who are Dogs tend to create the strongest links.

Star Rating: Two, sometimes three. Seldom more.

FEMALE PIG

This is a very good pairing, one which usually finds Pig and Dog forming a strong partnership. There is a great deal of mutual support, and the honest Pig, coupled with the Dog's idealism, invariably leads to two mates who have a wide variety of social and professional skills. Good in company and happy to help others, the Dog and Pig rate highly on the Chinese Horoscope compatibility charts. The only point to remember is that a badly treated puppy turns into an unhappy adult dog. Dog people with a history of child neglect tend to become unstable and the Pig will find she has her hands full repairing the damage.

Star Rating: Five in most cases.

THE PIG

猪

1911	January 30th to February 17th	1912
1923	February 16th to February 4th	1924
1935	February 4th to January 23rd	1936
1947	January 22nd to February 9th	1948
1959	February 8th to January 27th	1960
1971	January 27th to February 14th	1972
1983	February 13th to February 1st	1984
1995	January 31st to February 18th	1996

Pigs grow fat where lambs starve.

German Proverb

THE YEAR OF THE PIG

Pigs are born under the sign of honesty and whereas the West tends to downgrade the Pig's status, the East is far more enlightened. They consider it a compliment to be called a Pig, knowing the great value that comes from having a Pig in the family. One often-quoted Chinese proverb says, 'A teacher should never abandon his books, or the poor man his Pig.' And no wonder. No other animal works harder or plays harder. Well informed and gregarious, the robust and hearty Pig loves company and shines in a happy throng.

Although the Pig is essentially a masculine sign, both male and female Pigs share one characteristic – they really go to town when it comes to their wardrobe. Others may simply get dressed; Pigs dress up. Spot someone in a snazzy outfit, perhaps a little over the top, and the odds are that you're looking at a Pig. Not generally career people, Pig ladies excel in a domestic environment. On the other hand, the Chinese point out that a small number of Pigs have homes a bit like . . . well, pigsties. These Pigs care nothing for their surroundings, are not very bright upstairs and dress in anything that comes to hand. But both Pig types live just the way they want.

Pigs, male and female, tend to be big hearted and well organised people who are not given to much self-analysis or bothered by world problems. They are down to earth and durable, which is why the Chinese say that Pigs seldom go hungry. Because of this, the Pig tends to be over confident and is therefore a prime target for con men of all sorts. Pigs, it is said, are easily duped in both romance and business. But once taken for a ride, the previously credulous Pig becomes over-suspicious and rapidly constructs an emotional defensive wall which is almost impossible to break down.

Great lovers of gossip, Pigs usually get straight to the point in serious discussions, having first waited in the background to gauge their position. Although they argue forceably, Pigs are prone to get their facts wrong. Pigs hate disputes of any kind and handle them badly; first making their point too strongly and then retreating when the going gets rough. However, Pigs do not bear grudges and because they hold themselves in such high self esteem, care little of what others think. 'Take me as you find me,' is the Pig's motto.

Pigs in love pose a problem for themselves and everyone else. They fall in love far too easily and tend to wear their hearts on their sleeves. No other sign has so many stars for auspicious relationships. The Chinese emphasise the point by saying that Pigs, lacking initiative, will always perform better in partnerships.

The three phases of a Pig's life will not be greatly varied. The Piglet will enjoy a well balanced childhood, although some of their dreams might not always be realised. Love poses a problem to a Pig in mid-life, as do the ever present confidence tricksters, but the Pig's ability to work all hours will usually ensure there's enough in the bank to compensate for a broken heart. Old age holds no fears and the Pig who gets to his or her four score and ten will have a full and happy final stage, reflecting on the many busy hours.

COMPATIBILITY OF MALE PIGS IN LOVE

FEMALE RAT

The Rat in love with a Pig has many advantages, one of the most notable being that it often leads to marriage. The combination of Rat and Pig is one of the most common in the Chinese Horoscopes and improves when the banns are read. But there is nothing at all wrong with Rat and Pig who wish to remain just good friends. The point is that since so many of their mutual interests are social and centred on good living, it makes sense that they tie the knot and keep it tied. First class understanding sexually. Both sexes have an equal chance of a wonderful relationship. The relationship between Rat, Lauren Bacall and Pig Humphrey Bogart highlights how well the two signs make out.

Star Rating: Three rising to four and even five in some cases.

FEMALE BUFFALO

A big romance with all the frills for the female Buffalo and male Pig. The jovial Pig male – full of fun and easy going does wonders for the often romantically complex Buffalo. She laughs at his jokes, cooks him breakfast and makes him feel comfortable, the state most Pigs seek to obtain. In return, the Pig's honest and open brand of love making creates an uncomplicated emotional state, something that Buffaloes seek to obtain. There can be genuine understanding between a Buffalo and a Pig, but there is a warning note which should be heeded. Pig fellows do not always enjoy life at the steady pace created by the Buffalo Ms. What's more, the Chinese Horoscopes point out that Pigs care little for their reputation, which is another way of saying they are not over interested in fidelity for its own sake. So Buffalo beware: do not take the big hearted Pig for granted.

Star Rating: Four, with an occasional five.

FEMALE TIGER

Another winner for the male Porker, which suits Mistress Tiger down to the ground as a result. Like the Dog, the Pig male offers the energetic and powerful Tigress a splendidly solid emotional stage to perform on. Pig males build the Tiger's confidence. The Pig's influence is based on a mix of hard work and equally hard play, which offers the Tiger plenty of room to move around in. At no time will she feel caged – a fatal position for the Tiger, as you can doubtless imagine. Pigs get large doses of the Tiger's open heart and her generous nature for their trouble, plus a few headaches when the Tiger is down in the dumps! But the honest Pig is not one to shirk from a personal crisis and will be on hand to lift his wonderful Tiger's spirits.

Star Rating: Four

FEMALE CAT

Another middle of the road relationship which can easily catch fire. Honesty is a strong feature of Pigs, as is their love of a good time. A Cat lady responds quickly to the Pig chap's fun loving antics and approves of their single minded attitude to romance. But in spite of their honesty, some Piggy people are easily duped, or, in the case of romance, seduced. This is not what the female Cat is looking for and unless she has an easy going temperament with plenty of understanding, this affair will not last.

Star Rating: Three is average, but it can go higher or lower depending on the level of fidelity.

FEMALE DRAGON

This is a jolly good tumble in the hay. The robust and easy-going Pig (how difficult it is not to call him a bit of a push-over) is a perfect foil for the positive and self assured Dragon. But the Chinese Horoscopes do not rate this love match very high, suggesting that the over amorous Pig male does not 'read' the Dragon's moods and that he has a tendency to be demanding at the wrong moments. But my experience is that most Western Dragons are pleased for the attention and uncomplicated attentions a Pig gentleman might easily make. He will certainly not spare himself in trying to please – a bit unsubtle, but a real raver.

Star Rating: The Chinese say two. I say four.

FEMALE SNAKE

Pigs adore Snakes, both female and male alike. Big hearted and affectionate in the extreme, Pig chaps find the wise and sexually attractive Snake a real catch. My experience is that this is a very common pairing, with the honest and easy going Pig creating a near perfect partner for the subtle and charismatic charms of the Snake. Marriage makes it an even better bet, which is why in love the couple only rate a relatively mediocre score. Female Snake/male Pig is the best. Jackie Kennedy's open and heady relationship with Aristotle Onassis gives you some idea of the power these two signs generate in love.

Star Rating: Four.

FEMALE HORSE

Curious how poor this relationship promises to be. Pigs get on with just about everyone, except the Horse. Try as I might, I cannot work it out and rely on the fact the Chinese have been doing their horoscopes for three thousand years and I have only been studying them for fifteen. Perhaps the Horse's vanity conflicts with the Pig's sometimes high self-esteem. Maybe the kind of Pig male who leaves the home like a sty meets more Horses who expect their stable to be beautifully swept and clean. Maybe there isn't one reason but lots of little niggling factors that leave the Horse and Pig in a position where their most positive attributes conflict. I don't know. Just accept the Chinese verdict.

Star Rating: Zero. Perhaps just one.

FEMALE GOAT

Male Pigs are great fun, as a rule, and the female Goat is quick to cash in on the Pig's good nature and warm, open heart. Like so many affairs, though, the best is at the beginning. In this case, the reason is to be found in the Goat and Pig sharing too much in common. There is no real drama outside the clash between the decision about where to eat and what club to go to after. Sexual relationships need a degree of tension, and there is not enough in the love affair of a Goat and Pig to keep it bubbling.

Star Rating: Two, three or even four (for a very short affair).

FEMALE MONKEY

Here's a fine romance. Monkeys and Pigs positively revel in each other's highly social and fun-loving company. Pig fellas love getting dressed up for a night out and Ms Monkey will spare no effort in finding the right time and place to make everything go with a bang. Neither animal sign cares much about what others say about them, so expect an open and high-stepping affair. Go for it.

Star Rating: Five of the best.

FEMALE ROOSTER

Roosters and Pigs are not a common mix, which is curious because their star rating is quite high. Perhaps it is because the relationship succeeds through praising the absence of negative qualities in the union rather than acknowledging the fewer positive points. The truth is that the robust Pig poses no threats to the female Rooster, who nevertheless might be quick to take offence at his sometimes blunt advances. Once up and running, this pair might have fun; they might not. Depends on what each see as the long term outcome. Woody Allen is a Pig and Diane Keaton is a Rooster. Their affair didn't work out. And then there's the much-publicised affair between Pig Michael Winner and the beautiful Rooster Jenny Seagrove. Marriage is not advised.

Star Rating: One or three

FEMALE DOG

Pigs and Dogs hit the jackpot in the love stakes. The warm hearted and generous, sexually giving Pig male is perfectly matched with the sometimes slightly over anxious, eager to please lady Dog. The Dog, with her tendency to worry over emotional details, finds herself enjoying a rare inner freedom when exposed to the bundles of good humour and easy going temperament of her loving Pig companion. In love a Dog and Pig, who are genetically quite close in the animal kingdom, rate extremely high.

Star Rating: Five most times.

FEMALE PIG

Bonus time. Two Pigs are pretty non-stoppable in love and let it all hang out – no one will fail to see love's bloom in all its glory. But having said that it's a milk and honey number, I know surprisingly few examples of this relationship in action. The point is, perhaps, that Pigs can be just a little too alike, and that a lasting partnership requires a more variable mix of personalities. Even so, the Pigs that are happy in the poke will be truly so. Mutual lovers of the dance (and weren't they great?) Fred Astaire and Ginger Rogers were both born in a Pig year. So were Maria Callas and Aristotle Onassis.

Star Rating: Five when it happens.

COMPATIBILITY OF FEMALE PIGS IN LOVE

MALE RAT

The Rat in love with a Pig has many advantages, one of the most notable being that it often leads to marriage. The combination of Rats and Pigs is one of the most common in the Chinese Horoscopes and improves with marriage. But there is nothing at all wrong with Rats and Pigs who wish to remain just good friends. The point is that since so many of their mutual interests are social and centred on good living, it makes sense that they tie the knot and keep it tied. First class understanding sexually.

Star Rating: Three rising to four and even five in some cases.

MALE BUFFALO

A big romance with all the frills for the male Buffalo and female Pig. The jovial Pig lady – full of fun and easy going – does wonders for the often romantically complex Buffalo. She laughs at his jokes, cooks him breakfast and makes him feel comfortable, the state most Pigs seek to obtain. There can be genuine understanding between a Buffalo and Pig, but there is a warning note which should be heeded. Pig ladies do not always enjoy life at the steady pace created by Buffalo males. What's more, the Chinese Horoscopes point out that Pigs care little for their reputation, which is another way of saying they are not over interested in fidelity for its own sake. So Buffalo beware: do not take Miss Piggy for granted.

Star Rating: Four, with an occasional five.

MALE TIGER

Another winner for the Pig and good news for the Tiger as a result. Like the Dog, the Pig lady offers the energetic and powerful Tiger a splendidly solid emotional stage to perform on. Pig ladies build the Tiger's confidence. The Pig's influence is based on a mix of hard work and equally hard play, which offers the Tiger plenty of room to move around in. At no time will he feel caged – a fatal position for the Tiger, as you can doubtless imagine. Pigs get large doses of the Tiger's open heart and generous spirit for their trouble, plus all the headaches when the Tiger is down in the dumps! But the honest Pigette is not one to shirk from a personal crisis and will be on hand to lift her Tiger's spirits.

Star Rating: Three minimum but often rising to five for the male Tiger/female Pig combination.

MALE CAT

Another middle of the road relationship which can easily catch fire. Honesty is a strong feature of Pigs, as is their love of a good time. A Cat chap responds quickly to the Pig lady's fun loving antics and approves of their single minded attitude to romance. But in spite of their honesty, some Piggy people are easily duped, or, in the case of romance, seduced. This is not what the male Cat is looking for and unless he has an easy going temperament with plenty of understanding, this affair will not last.

Star Rating: Three is average, but it can go higher or lower depending on the level of fidelity.

MALE DRAGON

This is a jolly good tumble in the hay. The robust and easy-going Pig (how difficult it is not to call her a bit of a push-over) is a perfect foil for the positive and self assured Dragon. But the Chinese Horoscopes do not rate this love match very high, suggesting that the over amorous Pig lady does not 'read' the Dragon's moods and that she has a tendency to be demanding at the wrong moments. But my experience is that most Western Dragons are pleased for the attention, and uncomplicated attention, a Pig lady might easily give. She will certainly not spare herself in trying to please – a bit unsubtle at times, but a real raver. Male Dragon and female Pig are the hottest of the two pairs.

Star Rating: The Chinese say two. I say four.

MALE SNAKE

Pigs adore Snakes, both female and male alike. Big hearted and affectionate in the extreme, Pig ladies find the wise and sexually attractive Snake a real catch. My experience is that this is a very common pairing, with the honest and easy going Pig creating a near perfect partner for the subtle and charismatic charms of the Snake. Marriage makes it an even better bet, which is why in love the couple only rate a relatively mediocre score.

Star Rating: Three.

MALE HORSE

Curious how poor this relationship promises to be. Pigs get on with just about everyone except the Horse. Try as I might, I cannot work it out and rely on the fact that the Chinese have been doing their horoscopes for three thousand years and I have only been studying them for fifteen. Perhaps the Horse's vanity conflicts with the Pig's sometimes high self-esteem. Maybe the kind of Pig lady who leaves the home like a sty meets more Horses who expect their stable to be beautifully swept and clean. Maybe there isn't one reason but lots of little niggling factors that leave the Horse and Pig in a position where their most positive attributes conflict. I don't know. Just accept the Chinese verdict.

Star Rating: Zero. Perhaps just one.

MALE GOAT

Female Pigs are great fun, as a rule and the male Goat is quick to cash in the Pigette's good nature and warm, open love. Like so many affairs, though, the best is at the beginning. In this case, the reason is to be found in the Goat and Pig sharing too much in common. There is no real drama outside the clash between the decision about where to eat and what club to go to after. Sexual relationships need a degree of tension, and there is not enough in the love affair of a Goat and Pig to keep it bubbling.

Star Rating: Two, three or even four (for a very short affair).

MALE MONKEY

Here's a fine romance. Monkey's and Pigs positively revel in each other's highly social and fun loving company. Pig ladies love getting dressed up for a night out and Monkey men will spare no effort in finding the right time and place to make everything go with a bang. Neither animal sign cares much about what others say about them, so expect an open and high stepping affair. Go for it.

Star Rating: Five of the best.

MALE ROOSTER

Roosters and Pigs are not a common mix, which is curious because their star rating is quite high. Perhaps it is because the relationship succeeds through praising the absence of negative qualities in the union rather than acknowledging the fewer positive points. The truth is that the fun loving Pigette poses no threats to the Rooster, who nevertheless might be quick to take advantage of her easy virtue. And the male Rooster/female Pig partnership is undoubtedly the better of the two couplings. Once up and running, this pair might have fun; it might not. Depends on what each see in the long term as to the outcome. Marriage is not advised.

Star Rating: One or three.

MALE DOG

Pigs and Dogs hit the jackpot in the love stakes. The warm-hearted and generous, sexually giving lady Pig is perfectly matched with the sometimes anxious, eager to please male Dog. The Dog, who has a tendency to worry over emotional details, finds he is enjoying a rare inner freedom when exposed to the bundles of good humour and easy going temperament of his loving Pig companion. In love a Dog and Pig, who are genetically quite close in the animal kingdom, rate extremely highly.

Star Rating: Five most times.

MALE PIG

Bonus time. Two Pigs are pretty non-stoppable in love and let it all hang out – no one will fail to see love's bloom in all its glory. But having said that it's a milk and honey number, I know surprisingly few examples of this relationship in action. The point is, perhaps, that Pigs can be just a little too alike, and that a lasting partnership requires a more variable mix of personalities. Even so, the Pigs that are happy in the poke will be truly so. Mutual lovers of the dance (and weren't they great?) Fred Astaire and Ginger Rogers were both born in a Pig year. So were Maria Callas and Aristotle Onassis.

Star Rating: Five when it happens.

COMPATIBILITY OF MALE PIGS IN MARRIAGE

FEMALE RAT

There is not a great deal of point in a Rat and Pig simply living together when a fuller and more complete life is waiting for them with their marrying. That is not to say that being in love isn't without it complications, especially since the Rat always has her eye open for new experiences and the male Pig is easily seduced. But marriage frequently creates the atmosphere in which a Rat and Pig can discover their most positive characteristics. Both are social and enjoy good living. Given their mutual interests, it makes sense to put their combined energy under one roof. And since most children flourish under a Rat and Pig's collective parental warmth, marriage is a natural step.

Star Rating: Four and a bit. A female Pig/male Rat is the stronger pair.

FEMALE BUFFALO

A fine romance but if it ends in marriage there'll be a few red faces and unhappy Pigs and Buffaloes. Things swing in a love affair, with the eager to please Piggy gentleman getting the most from the deeper sexuality found in the Buffalo lady. But the Buffalo female presents difficulties in terms of long term relationships. She wants a lasting marriage, that is certain, but there is something in the male Pig that falls short of her high handed demands. Perhaps it is his easy-going nature and his ability to flirt without feeling guilt that bothers her. It may be that the Pig husband wants more to life than the domestic role the Buffalo unintentionally places him in. If the Buffalo lady lives up to the side of her influence which creates in her a home-maker, then the chances of success are greatly improved. It, however, she is a Buffalo who is only interested in domestic power struggles, forget the wedding plans. The marriage created by EastEnders, Angie and Dirty Den is not untypical of Pig male and female Buffalo. Not surprisingly, in real life Anita Dobson is a Buffalo and Leslie Grantham a Pig.

Star Rating: Two in most cases but with a point plus or minus depending on the Buffalo's ambitions.

FEMALE TIGER

As discovered early in their romantic phase, marriage looks like a splendid idea, and it is. The hard working, hard living, hard loving Pig provides an ideal partner for the get-up-and-go Tiger. Offering plenty of support during his low periods, the Pig receives big helpings of Tiger generosity for his trouble – not that a Pig would ever think of it that way! Lacking initiative, and better off when in a partnership, this a marriage full of mutual support, and there is little or nothing to prevent both partners enjoying a happy and eventful life together. Again, the female Tiger is the more stimulating parent, and a family is advisable if these two signs are to retain their high star status. Male Tiger and female Pig get top marks.

Star Rating: Four lowest, five most times.

FEMALE CAT

Another very good marriage, without going over the top on points. Pig blokes are usually great socialisers and love nothing more after a tough day at the office than to greet a bunch of fun lovers with the mutual purpose of enjoying a tough night out somewhere. Cats adore being made a fuss over and respond well to the providers of creature comforts. If there is plenty of fresh cream and quiet snoozes by the fire in winter, so much the better. Routine is essential to a Cat in marriage as it is in all things. But there's a certain type of Pig who hates being pinned down and lives only for the minute, and he is the type usually the most attractive to Cats. This Pig is rather too full of himself and it is here that the trouble might start – the Cat wanting more mental and physical support than the Pig is prepared to give, or is capable of giving. But there'll always be money in the bank for the rainy day. TV host and hostess Michael Parkinson and his wife, Mary, are Pig and Cat respectively. They seem OK; plenty of spondulicks.

Star Rating: Three.

FEMALE DRAGON

On paper, this looks like a first class marriage, and it might well turn out that way. But the problem is that the Pig males have a somewhat high opinion of their considerable homemaking talents, which the Dragon lady admires but prefers not to have too openly displayed – she's the boss, or thinks she is! Pig chaps are honest souls at heart and are easily duped as a result, something the Dragon is constantly irritated by. And it must be said that some male Pigs treat their home a little too casually – mess everywhere and friends staying till the early hours. Marriages frequently fail because one partner is a slob and can't handle the simple routines marriage creates. Billionaire Saudi businessman Adnan Khashoggi is a Pig and his former wife, socialite Saraya, a Dragon. A typical female Dragon, she demanded $1 billion as a divorce settlement. But for once the Pig was not duped and she ended up with a lot less out of court.

Star Rating: One, two or three.

FEMALE SNAKE

A high scoring marriage where we find both signs totally at one with each other. The Pig is a perfect partner to most signs, often preferring to work in conjunction with another than by themselves, and the Snake is quick to respond. Easy going and warm, the big hearted Pig fellow has practically all the qualities a female Snake looks for, and in return, the Snake offers her wise council and humour. Children should be happy in the home of a Pig and Snake. But as always, there is a side of the Snake, her inner mystery, which might upset the apple cart. Pig males must make a note to avoid confrontation during a Snake's 'quiet periods' as they are easily upset at these times and might bite. Pig chaps and lady Snakes have the highest rating. When Jackie Kennedy re-married, she did so with a Pig – Aristotle Onassis.

Star Rating: Four, or even five.

FEMALE HORSE

This is a marriage of what the two signs want it to be. The Horse and Pig have many options open as both are adaptable to internal and external changes. But the Horse lady is easily led off course and the Pig male, so the Chinese Horoscopes point out, a little too fond of fun. In marriage, who you stay out late with is not usually a matter for breakfast discussion, and should either Horse or Pig find themselves attracted to another outside their marriage they will do best to keep it quiet. The problem is, though, that the Pig is prone to boast-ing and the Horse falls heavily. But affairs to one side, this is

a strong enough union with a warm home life and two reliable, unfussy and thoughtful parents.
  Star Rating: Three.

FEMALE GOAT

One of the better marriages for both Pig and Goat. The high
octane social activity is a pronounced feature of this couple
getting together and as long as there are plenty of friends and
enough money left for the free spending pair to entertain
them, there is every chance of a long and bump-free
marriage. Goat females are decorative home makers, and Pig
males are in the main caring, jolly home builders. Sexually
compatible, this is a marriage to be given serious thought.
The only slight hint of danger is that both signs lack initiative
and perform better in partnerships. Once in a while, even a
deeply attached married partner must act on his or her own.
  Star Rating: Four.

FEMALE MONKEY

A really fun marriage this. After a splendid romance, the Pig
male and Monkey female who decide to settle down usually
find there's still plenty in common and there's bags of laughs
for everyone else. A strong circle of friends and a big bouncing family, with plenty of mum's funny stories and dad's
warm and generous nature, suggest it is all systems go for
Monkey and Pig. And so it is. Honest Pig and sharp Monkey
combine to keep the party going, bringing the best out in
each other.
  Star Rating: Five.

FEMALE ROOSTER

Pigs do like to enjoy themselves, and usually with no holds
barred. In and out of marriage, a Pig male plays as hard as he
works and his view of morality is not high. Certainly, he does
not share the Rooster's somewhat morally imperious attitude

towards fun and games. Roosters demand an organised world and are straightforward in their thinking, in spite of the impression they give to the contrary. Roosters can spend with the best, but a deeply conservative interior often prevents them from falling off the edge. The Pig/Rooster pair will need to martial their resources, deal carefully with their finances and invest all spare energies into home and garden if they are to stick together. Ronald Reagan was born in a Pig year and Nancy (say no to drugs) Reagan in the Year of the Rooster. They seem to have got it right.

Star Rating: Two or three.

FEMALE DOG

The Pig may have the most of the marriage, but if the Dog is one who has not enjoyed a happy childhood she might begin to take her Pig husband a little too much for granted. Dog husbands who are unhappy tend to lack direction and fret like mad. Where there was once a happy, jovial and outgoing home, the mood becomes bleak and nervy. In the end the Pig, as big hearted as he may be, runs out of patience. However, this pairing usually produces a model marriage, which, nine times out of ten, lasts the course. Sixties hit makers Sonny and Cher ('I Got You Babe') were a Dog lady and male Pig marriage. Cher's Doggy neurosis – expressed in her need to remake her body under the surgeon's knife – could well have started the rot.

Star Rating: Five (usually).

FEMALE PIG

A first rate marriage between two normally really well-balanced and highly social animals. Pig people prefer fun and games to strife, and hard work to idleness. Put into the context of married life, it would seem that nothing can go wrong – and it seldom does. There is, nevertheless, a word of warning. Pigs are all a little smug about themselves, a characteristic which leaves them vulnerable. When pushed into a tight spot, especially in a domestic argument, the Pig feels threatened like no other sign and, driven over the top, he or she will turn into an unrecognisably aggressive creature capable of great harm. Pigs can be extremely cruel when hurt, and their hurt will fester long after the event. Publicity conscious and expensively dressed ex-Liverpool councillor Derek Hatton is a Pig, and so is Mrs Hatton.

Star Rating: Five, but dropping in the case of easily wounded Pigs.

COMPATIBILITY OF FEMALE PIGS IN MARRIAGE

MALE RAT

There is not a great deal of point in a Rat and Pig simply living together when a fuller and more complete life is waiting for them with their marrying. That is not to say that being in love isn't without its complications, especially since the Rat always has his eye open for new experiences and the lady Pig is easily seduced. But marriage frequently creates the atmosphere in which a Rat and Pig can discover their most positive characteristics. Both are social and enjoy good living. Given their mutual interests, it makes sense to put their combined energy under one roof. And since most children flourish under a Rat and Pig's collective parental warmth, marriage is a natural step. Prince Andrew is a Rat and Fergie is a Pig.

Star Rating: Five.

MALE BUFFALO

A fine romance but if it ends in marriage there'll be a few red faces and unhappy Pigs and Buffaloes. Things swing in a love affair, with the eager to please Piggy lady getting the most from the deeper sexuality found in the Buffalo chap. But the Buffalo male is a tough nut to crack in terms of long term relationships. He wants a lasting marriage, that is certain, but there is something in the Pig lady's character that falls short of his high handed demands. Perhaps it is her easy-going nature and her ability to flirt without feeling guilt that worries the complex Buffalo. It may be that the Pig wife wants more to life than the domestic role the Buffalo places her in. If the Pig lady lives up to her reputation as a home-maker, then the picture changes for the better. It, however, she is a Pig who is only interested in a good time, forget the wedding plans.

Star Rating: Two in most cases but with a point plus or minus depending on the Pig's ambitions.

MALE TIGER

As discovered early in their romantic phase, marriage looks like a splendid idea, and it is. The home-maker style Pig, which is the most usual variety, provides an ideal partner for the get-up-and-go Tiger. Offering plenty of support during his low periods, the Pig receives big helpings of Tiger generosity for her trouble – not that a Pig would ever think of it that way! This is a marriage full of mutual support, and there is little or nothing to prevent both partners enjoying a happy and eventful life together. Again, the Tiger is the more stimulating parent, and a family is advisable if these two signs are to retain their high star status. Male Tiger and female Pig get top marks.

Star Rating: Five.

MALE CAT

Another very good marriage, without going over the top on points. Pig women are usually great socialisers and love nothing more after a tough day at the office than to greet a bunch of fun lovers with the mutual purpose of enjoying a tough night out somewhere. Cats adore being made a fuss over and respond well to the providers of creature comforts. If there is plenty of fresh cream and quiet snoozes by the fire in winter, so much the better. Routine is essential to a Cat in marriage as it is in all things. But there's a certain type of Pig who hates being pinned down and lives only for the minute, and she is the type usually the most attractive to Cats. This Pig is rather too full of herself and it is here that the trouble might start – the Cat wanting more mental and physical support than the Pig is prepared to give, or is capable of giving. But there'll always be money in the bank for the rainy day.

Star Rating: Three.

MALE DRAGON

On paper, this looks like a first-class marriage, and it might well turn out that way. But the problem is that the Pig lady is in the main a home-maker and eager to display her domestic skills. Some Pig ladies, the Pig introverts, care nothing for their home and live in a tip. It is this particular brand of Pigette that the Dragon should avoid. Perfectionists, Dragons like tidy homes and they place a great deal of importance on rituals, in which tidiness often plays a part. It is odd, but marriages frequently fail because one partner is a slob and can't handle the simple routines marriage creates.

Star Rating: One, two or three.

MALE SNAKE

A high-scoring marriage where we find both signs totally at one with each other. Pigs are a perfect partner to most signs, often preferring to work in conjunction with another than by themselves, and the Snake is quick to respond. Easy going and warm, the Pig lady has practically all the qualities a male Snake looks for, and in return, the Snake offers his wise counsel and humour. Children should be happy in the home of a Pig and Snake. But as always, there is a side of the Snake, his inner mystery, which might upset the applecart.

Pig males must make a note to avoid confrontation during a Snake's 'quiet periods' as they are easily upset at these times and might bite.

Star Rating: Four.

MALE HORSE

This is a marriage of what the two signs want it to be. The Horse and Pig have many options open as both are adaptable to internal and external changes. But the Horse is easily led off course and the Pig lady, so the Chinese Horoscopes point out, a little too fond of her fun. In marriage, who you stay out late with is not usually a matter for breakfast discussion, and should either Horse or Pig find themselves attracted to another outside their marriage they will do best to keep it quiet. The problem is, though, that the Pig is prone to boasting and the Horse falls heavily. But affairs to one side, this is a strong enough union with a warm home life and two reliable, unfussy and thoughtful parents.

Star Rating: Three.

MALE GOAT

One of the better marriages for both Pig and Goat. The high octane social activity is a pronounced feature of this couple getting together and as long as there are plenty of friends, and enough money left for the free spending pair to entertain them, there is every chance of a long and bump-free marriage. Goat men are useful home builders, and Pig ladies are in the main caring, jolly home makers. Sexually compatible, this is a marriage to be given serious thought. The only very slight hint of danger is that both signs lack initiative and perform better in partnerships. Once in a while, even a deeply attached married partner must act on his or her own.

Star Rating: Four.

MALE MONKEY

A really fun marriage this. After a splendid romance, the Pig lady and Monkey male who decide to settle down usually find there's still plenty in common and there's bags of laughs for everyone else. A strong circle of friends and a big bouncing family, with plenty of mum's cream cakes and dad's witty and talkative nature, suggest it is all systems go for Monkey and Pig. And so it is. Honest Pig and sharp Monkey combine to keep the party going, bringing the best out in each other.

Star Rating: Five

MALE ROOSTER

Lady Pigs do like to enjoy themselves, and usually with no holds barred. In and out of marriage, a Pig lady plays as hard as she works and her view of morality is not high. Certainly, she does not share the Rooster's somewhat morally imperious attitude towards fun and games. Roosters demand an organised world and are straightforward in their thinking, in spite of the impression they give to the contrary. Roosters can spend with the best, but a deeply conservative interior often prevents them from falling off the edge. The Pig/Rooster pair will need to martial their resources, deal carefully with their finances and invest all spare energies into home and garden if they are to stick together.

Star Rating: Two or three.

MALE DOG

The Pig may have the most of the marriage, but if the Dog is one who has not enjoyed a happy childhood he might begin to take his Pig wife a little too much for granted. Dog husbands who are unhappy tend to talk too much and fret like mad. Where there was once a happy, jovial and outgoing home, the mood becomes bleak and nervy. In the end the Pig, as big hearted as she may be, runs out of patience. However, this pairing usually produces a model marriage, which, nine times out of ten, lasts the course. Film producer Blake Edwards is a Dog, and married to a Pig, Julie Andrews – happily, I'm told.

Star Rating: Five.

MALE PIG

A first rate marriage between two normally really well balanced and highly social animals. Pig people prefer fun and games to strife and hard work to idleness. Put into the context of married life, it would seem that nothing can go wrong – and it seldom does. There is, nevertheless, a word of warning. Pigs are all a little smug about themselves, a characteristic which leaves them vulnerable. When pushed into a tight spot, especially in a domestic argument, the Pig feels threatened like no other sign and, driven over the top, he or she will turn into an unrecognisably aggressive creature capable of great harm. Pigs can be extremely cruel when hurt, and their hurt will fester long after the event. Publicity conscious and expensively dressed ex-Liverpool councillor Hatton is a Pig and so is Mrs Hatton.

Star Rating: Five, but dropping in the case of easily wounded Pigs.

COMPATIBILITY OF MALE PIGS IN FRIENDSHIP

MALE RAT

One of the Rat's better choices in friends. Plenty of late nights on the tiles will ensure that this couple of mates enjoy a long and good-humoured friendship. And should they have enough in common to start a business venture, they should go for it. The Pig's honesty and knack of making money will appeal greatly to the Rat. But the Pig will have to keep his eye on friend Rat's natural sense of opportunism. And he might keep the safe key on his keyring. The way Pig sign Ronnie Reagan trusted and promoted Rat sign George Bush is typical of this animal relationship.

Star Rating: Four.

MALE BUFFALO

A high number of Pigs and Buffaloes get on extremely well together and it is one of the better relationships. The Pig lacks a degree of initiative and the broad imagination of the Buffalo and his solid and dependable nature are all a bonus in forming the partnership and building confidence. Hard working and honest, the Pig's influence is a highly compatible feature in the creation of a friendship. But the social life, which Pigs adore, is not something the Buffalo always places high on their list of priorities, so a business partnership is recommended. But even the most serious Buffalo is warmed by the open hearted Pig. Charles Rolls was a Buffalo and his partner in building the world's finest automobile, Henry Royce, was a Pig.

Star Rating: Four tops, two bottom.

MALE TIGER

Nice one! Tigers and Pigs, especially the male variety, have a clear and precise understanding of each other and come to terms easily with their respective differences. Easy going Pigs go along with the Tiger's extremes and are not phased by the Tiger's hot-headed response to authority. In fact, the Pig enjoys most of what the Tiger offers. But Pigs are not rebels and do not share the Tiger's constant need to change things – the only serious difference. Even so, with all the robust fun and bubbling energy these two create, there's plenty to keep them together. Elton John is a Pig. His influential lyricist, Bernie Taupin, is a Tiger and between them they enjoyed a highly successful, if on/off, relationship.

Star Rating: Three or four.

MALE CAT

A very strong bond can exist between a male Cat and Pig. The good natured and honest Pig has almost as many choices as the Cat when choosing a chum, and making a life long friend is no problem. Since both animal signs look for the best in others and tend, on the whole, not to be over zealous in their criticism of each other's weaker points, these two signs are a splendid match. But the Cat has not got the robust energy of a Pig, who must remember to live at the Cat's more even pace. The greatest jazz composer partnership of all time was a Pig and Cat, Duke Ellington and Billy Strayhorn.

Star Rating: Four and five.

MALE DRAGON

Dragons are usually fine on their own. If they have to face life in their damp and dark caves, so be it. But Pigs are social creatures and adore to be in with the crowd. This means that a friendship between Pig and Dragon requires a centre, or a purpose of some kind, in order to make the most of it. Great in relationships, Pigs are willing and extremely honest in their dealings with those they like – which is practically everyone. A business partnership is a natural conclusion to a Pig and Dragon's friendship. Jeffrey Archer, a Dragon, had his major best-selling books edited by a Pig, Richard Cohen. Some have suggested it was the Pig who did most of the work, but I know for a fact it was shared evenly – the Dragon thinking up the plot and the Pig polishing up the prose.

Star Rating: Five

MALE SNAKE

A solid sort of friendship for two signs who, on the surface, would not appear to have a great deal in common. But the Pig is a good and open-hearted fellow who genuinely admires the Snake's wisdom and sensitivity. Lacking initiative, or, to put it another way, better in partnership, the Pig enjoys his role as the Snake's ally. In turn the Snake is not slow to appreciate the Pig's gift for keeping the party going, and, if there is a business to consider, his talent for making money. The snag in business may be that Pigs are easily duped, and the Snake, it is said, has a tight fist. Dean Martin and Jerry Lewis, the great Hollywood comic film duo of the fifties, were a Snake and Pig respectively.

Star Rating: Three.

MALE HORSE

This is not a totally bad idea. The Horse needs to express his independence, even in the firmest relationship, and it is said that a Pig only truly arrives at his full potential when in partnership. Perhaps it is this sense of being fettered by a relationship that hangs over the Horse and eventually disrupts it. The Chinese say that this pair should steer well clear of a business relationship although one of the most successful men's Wimbledon doubles teams in recent times consists of a Horse and Pig. Respectively they are Peter Fleming and John McEnroe.

Star Rating: One usually. Three is the limit.

MALE GOAT

Pigs get on with just about every sign and make no exception in the case of the Goat. Here we have two good friends, if a little too vain for their own good, who enjoy a night out and, spend plenty of time discussing trends and getting into just about as many as there are on offer. Business relationships are strong in the multiple hoofs of these signs. As long as the Goat pulls his weight and the Pig isn't too easily duped, any endeavour inspired by the peace loving, artistic Goat and hard working, honest Pig is likely to last. Ronald Reagan is a Pig and Mikhail Gorbachev is a Goat.

Star Rating: Four.

MALE MONKEY

Plenty of opportunities here for Pig and Monkey to create something really useful in terms of a lasting friendship. The Monkey is full of schemes and the hard working Pig, a little slower when left to work outside of a relationship, finds extra zest in this one. Monkeys and Pigs look for a good time and their friendship promises one of good humour and genuine understanding.

Star Rating: Five.

MALE ROOSTER

The relationship of daydreaming, boastful Rooster and hard working, socially well informed Pig has the makings of one that will last longer than many. There is something in the Pig's ability to work and play with equal ability that balances the Rooster's tendency to promise more than they can deliver. Both signs are essentially honest, which means that should they form a business, there is little possibility that one will trick the other. Ex-10cc stars Lol Creme and Kevin Godley are a Pig and Rooster respectively.

Star Rating: Two through to four.

MALE DOG

This is a very good pairing, one which usually finds Pig and Dog forming a strong partnership. There is a great deal of mutual support, and the honest Pig, coupled with the Dog's idealism, invariably leads to two mates who have a wide variety of social and professional skills. Good in company and happy to help others, the Dog and Pig rate highly on the Chinese Horoscope compatibility charts. The only point to remember is that a badly treated puppy turns into an unhappy adult dog. Dog people with a history of child neglect tend to become unstable and the Pig will find he has his hands full repairing the damage. This was exactly what happened to Pig snooker player Cliff Thorburn when he took his fellow Canadian Kirk Stevens, a Dog, under his wing following the discovery of the younger star's drug problem.

Star Rating: Five in most cases.

MALE PIG

Two male Pigs are good news, both for themselves and for those around them. They bring a feeling of promise and their good humour and ease with even quite difficult types is ever present. In business, they can do nothing but succeed. But there is always the nagging problem that one might be easily duped, leaving the other to pick up the pieces. Yet even here, there is every chance of good natured forgiveness. Fun and work in equal proportions provide this pairing with high marks. Ben Elton and Rick Mayall enjoyed a hugely profitable partnership, both born in the same Pig year.

Star Rating: Five, sometimes four, depending on the effects of their possible collective gullibility.

COMPATIBILITY OF FEMALE PIGS IN FRIENDSHIP

FEMALE RAT

A right on friendship if ever there was one. Fast living, plenty of nights out and four hands grabbing all that's going is the way this team expresses their mutual affection. Obviously, as in all friendships, there will be moments of misunderstanding. These usually arise from the Pig's ability to get herself duped at the drop of a hat, landing the Rat in it with her. But there'll be no hard feelings and they'll soon be back in the swing.

Star Rating: Five.

FEMALE BUFFALO

A very good understanding exists between the Pig lady and her Buffalo friend. Pigs generally make pals with everyone, are extremely sociable and are capable of enjoying themselves without going over the top. With the Pig lady as a companion, the Buffalo is able to let herself go. Lacking a little initiative, Pigs are attracted to the Buffalo's sense of conviction. In turn, the Buffalo has a partner who does not attempt to try and direct the way the relationship should develop. Plenty for both to do and plenty to keep them together.

Star Rating: Four.

FEMALE TIGER

Nice one! Tigers and Pigs usually have a clear and precise understanding of each other and come to terms easily with their respective differences. The easy going Pig goes along with the Tiger's extremes and is not phased by the Tiger's hot-headed response to authority. In fact, the Pig enjoys most of what the Tiger offers. But Pigs are not rebels, and do not share the Tiger's constant need to change things – the only serious difference. Even so, with all the robust fun and bubbling energy these two create, there's plenty to keep them together.

Star Rating: Three or four.

FEMALE CAT

A very strong bond can exist between a female Cat and Pig. The good-natured and honest Pig has almost as many choices as the Cat when choosing a chum, and making a life-long friend is no problem. Since both animal signs look for the best in others and tend, on the whole, not to be over-zealous in their criticism of each other's weaker points, these two signs are a splendid match. But the Cat has not got the robust energy of a Pig, who must remember to live at the Cat's more even pace.

Star Rating: Four and five.

FEMALE DRAGON

Dragons are usually fine on their own. If they have to face life in their damp and dark caves, so be it. But Pigs are social creatures and adore to be in with the crowd. This means that a friendship between Pig and Dragon ladies requires a centre, or a purpose of some kind, in order to make the most of it. Great in relationships, Pigs are willing and extremely honest in their dealings with those they like – which is practically everyone. A business partnership is a natural conclusion to a Pig and Dragon's friendship.

Star Rating: Five.

FEMALE SNAKE

A solid sort of friendship for two signs who, on the surface, would not appear to have a great deal in common. But the Pig is a generous soul who genuinely admires the Snake's wisdom and sensitivity. Lacking initiative, or, to put it another way, better in partnership, the Pig enjoys her role as the Snake's ally. In turn the Snake is not slow to appreciate the Pig's gift for keeping the party going, and, if there is a business to consider, her surprising talent for making money. The snag in business may be that Pigs are easily duped, and the Snake, it is said, has a tight fist.

Star Rating: Three.

FEMALE HORSE

This is not a totally bad idea. The Horse needs to express her independence, even in the firmest relationship, and it is said that a Pig only truly arrives at her full potential when in partnership. Perhaps it is this sense of being fettered by a relationship that hangs over the Horse and eventually disrupts it. The Chinese Horoscope says that female Pig and female Horse have the least chance of lasting friendship and they should not form a business partnership under any circumstances. I still am not convinced so just take the Chinese Horoscope's word for it.

Star Rating: One at most.

FEMALE GOAT

Pigs get on with just about every sign and make no exception in the case of the Goat. Here we have two good friends, if a little too vain for their own good, who enjoy a night out, and spend plenty of time discussing fashion trends and getting into just about as many as there are on offer. Business relationships are strong in the multiple and well-manicured hoofs of these two signs. As long as the goat pulls her weight and the Pig isn't too easily duped, any endeavour inspired by the peace-loving, artistic Goat and hard working, honest Pig likely to last.

Star Rating: Four.

FEMALE MONKEY

Plenty of opportunities here for Pig and Monkey to create something really useful in terms of a lasting friendship. The Monkey is full of schemes and the hard working Pig, a little slower when left to work outside a relationship, finds extra zest in this one. Monkeys and Pigs look for a good time and their friendship promises one of good humour and genuine understanding.

Star Rating: Five.

FEMALE ROOSTER

The relationship of daydreaming, boastful Rooster and hard-working, socially well-informed Pig has the makings of one that will last longer than many. There is something in the Pig's ability to work and play with equal ability that balances the Rooster's tendency to promise more than they can deliver. Both signs are essentially honest, which means that should they form a business, there is little possibility that one will trick the other.

Star Rating: Two through to four.

FEMALE DOG

This is a very good pairing, one which usually finds Pig and Dog forming a strong partnership. There is a great deal of mutual support, and the honest Pig, coupled with the Dog's idealism, invariably leads to two mates who have a wide variety of social and professional skills. Good in company and happy to help others, the Dog and Pig rate highly on the Chinese Horoscope compatibility charts. The only point to remember is that a badly treated puppy turns into an unhappy adult dog. Dog people with a history of child neglect tend to become unstable and the Pig will find she has her hands full repairing the damage.

Star Rating: Five in most cases.

FEMALE PIG

Two female Pigs are good news, both for themselves and for those around. They bring a feeling of promise and their good humour and ease with even quite difficult types is ever present. In business, they can do nothing but succeed. But there is always the nagging problem that one might be easily duped, leaving the other to pick up the pieces. Yet even here, there is every chance of good natured forgiveness. Fun and work in equal proportions provide this pairing with high marks.

Star Rating: Five, sometimes four, depending on the effect of their possible collective gullibility.

The author is grateful to the following reference sources for additional material:

Chinese Horoscopes, Paula Delsol. Pan
The Way to Chinese Astrology: The Four Pillars of Wisdom, Jean-Michel Huon de Kermadec, Unwin
The Handbook of Chinese Horoscopes, Theodora Lau, Arrow.

All Sphere Books are available at your bookshop or newsagent, or can be ordered from the following address: Sphere Books, Cash Sales Department, P.O. Box 11, Falmouth, Cornwall TR10 9EN.

Please send cheque or postal order (no currency), and allow 60p for postage and packing for the first book plus 25p for the second book and 15p for each additional book ordered up to a maximum charge of £1.90 in U.K.

B.F.P.O. customers please allow 60p for the first book, 25p for the second book plus 15p per copy for the next 7 books, thereafter 9p per book.

Overseas customers, including Eire, please allow £1.25 for postage and packing for the first book, 75p for the second book and 28p for each subsequent title ordered.